Cognition and the Creative Machine

Ana-Maria Oltețeanu

Cognition and the Creative Machine

Cognitive AI for Creative Problem Solving

 Springer

Ana-Maria Olteţeanu
Department of Mathematics and Computer Science
Freie Universität Berlin
Berlin, Germany

ISBN 978-3-030-30324-2   ISBN 978-3-030-30322-8   (eBook)
https://doi.org/10.1007/978-3-030-30322-8

This Springer imprint is published by the registered company Springer Nature Switzerland AG
The registered company address is: Gewerbestrasse 11, 6330 Cham, Switzerland

"Insight is suddenly seeing the problem in a new way, connecting the problem to another relevant problem/solution pair, releasing past experiences that are blocking the solution, or seeing the problem in a larger, coherent context."

– Sternberg and Davidson

In memory of Aglaia Leonte, my extraordinary Nana, and for Ştefan Smărăndoiu, my maths teacher. Your set of values combined with your belief in me made seeing myself through your eyes both the highest motivation and the biggest self-indulgence. My work is dedicated to you, as I am part of your work.

Preface

You would think that a scientist researching creativity would have an easier task than others to trace the origins of her ideas, through professionally trained awareness of the topic. Despite this, I am not quite sure how the idea to direct my second doctoral thesis towards creative problem solving came about. I believe the topic sneaked up on me, and when I realized it, it had already blossomed.

With my first doctorate thesis being on aesthetics and classical music, I often had colleagues and friends asking me whether I was planning to produce some mix of my previous and current field of interest, and make for example music performing AI agents. But, in reality, I saw my interests in music on one hand, and AI & cognitive systems on the other, as having their root in a different place; in a curiosity about how minds work, and how they make sense of the world. My first thesis was, in essence, about how a listener could make different types of sense of the same piece of music, how the interpreter could direct this sense making as an aesthetic and emotional experience for the listener, and how the form of the piece of music supported these processes.

The second thesis became about how one can give new and creative meaning to objects, when needing to solve a problem one has never encountered before, or did not have the resources to solve. And how one can change the meaning and form of the entire problem, when that is the only way to solve it. About what kind of mind it takes to do that, and how it is or can be done.

In retrospect, perhaps it is all about how form supports process: how the form of the music piece, which one can see in the music sheet, supports cognitive processes of meaning making; how knowledge organization in a natural or artificial mind could be designed to support varied types of creative processes.

The effects of conducting the research on these topics, which continues in my lab today, were multiple and long lasting. One of them is a renewed understanding of just how great some of the cognitive capacities we take for granted are.

We tend to believe that problems have predefined solutions, that we must or can find. I now believe this is an illusion. Many problems do not have solutions. We define these solutions, and we also define the initial thing as being a problem. It is all part of the way we organize and sort through our world. And sometimes, about how we sort things in your cognitive worlds. The reason we sometimes lose respect for this is that we don't catch our creative problem solving process in action, and we often rely on solutions (and problem definitions) we have already memorized in order to act and understand things. But most of these solutions and problem definitions were invented at some point. And we can invent other solutions, and other definitions. We are problem definers and creative problem solvers, and these capacities are a marvellous thing. This is how we change our world, both externally, through innovation and action, and internally, through seeing things in different ways and integrating new meanings.

During the process of exploring these topics I had a lot of fun. I also learned a lot about tolerating ambiguity; and about creatively building tools myself, when I needed them for this research and they weren't anywhere to be found. If there is something I wish to you, reader, is that you share a little bit of the fun; also that you share in that sense of amazement at how great our capacity of making sense of the world and creating solutions is. I hope you go back to your life looking at this beautiful instrument you possess with a renewed sense of play. And always remember, especially in dark moments, that this capacity is always within you. And when you are stuck, you may be closer to insight than you think. You are a creator of worlds.

Now start reading so that I can thank my colleagues and collaborators.

When working on a thesis, one is supposed to accumulate knowledge, skills and abilities. If lucky, one also accumulates a debt of gratitude to the many people who have served to shape, challenge and encourage one's ideas to turn into science. It is my belief that this debt of gratitude cannot be expressed in words, and can only be paid forward, by honouring what one has learned in these years through what one becomes. However, a warm thank you goes to the following:

Christian Freksa for being a wonderful thesis advisor and head of group, from whose vision and character one cannot ever learn enough. We have had many insightful and interesting conversations, and I am sure many more are still to come.

Zoe Falomir for being a great colleague, artificial intelligence scientist and female role-model. For being enthusiasthic about new ideas and nudging me gently to bring them to life.

Holger Schultheis, who kept an open door and, due to spatial proximity at the time, served as bouncing board for many creative ideas. For providing good criticism and advice on general empirical psychology practice.

Thomas Barkowsky, who served as a thorough and supportive reviewer at my graduate seminars, where some of these ideas were first explored. Also, his invaluable work as a scientific manager of the SFB kept everything running smoothly, so that we could all do our work in peace.

Aaron Sloman, for interesting discussions and his inspiring ideas on analogical representation. The proofreaders of this work and the peer-reviewers of scientific articles I published which cover some of this content. Your comments have all helped improve this.

My partner Anton Mykell Sykes for making endless amounts of coffee, for understanding so many moments of random quietness or unexplainable bouts of excitement when I was caught by a new set of ideas, and for getting more knowledgeable on cognitive science and artificial intelligence every day by listening to me talk about my interests, work and process.

Finally, to the German Research Foundation (DFG) for the SFB/TR 8 that I was so lucky to be part of. This provided generous funding and support for summer schools, conferences, and a lovely place to work, think and disseminate ideas in.

Berlin,
October 2018

Dr. Dr. Ana-Maria
Olteţeanu

Contents

1

Introduction

The story goes that Kekulé day-dreamt of an Ouroboros symbol (a snake eating its own tail) or a Tibetan knot, when trying to find the structure of the benzene molecule (Fig. 1.1a). An equally mesmerizing tale tells of Watson dreaming of spiral staircases before doing his part in coming up with the double helix structure of DNA (Fig. 1.1b).

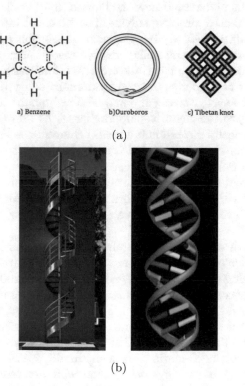

(a)

(b)

Fig. 1.1: Dreams and day-dreams: (a) Kekulé's, (b) Watson's.

© Springer Nature Switzerland AG 2020
A.-M. Olteţeanu, *Cognition and the Creative Machine*,
https://doi.org/10.1007/978-3-030-30322-8_1

One can easily see the visual similarity between the (day)dreamt object and the discovered "object". Unfortunately we cannot take such stories at face value, no matter how beautiful. Nor can we engineer for people to discover new molecules every day and in controlled conditions in the experimental lab, in order to study how they do it. The questions such stories trigger, though, are very alluring ones:
- how do humans solve such problems creatively? And much simpler problems for that matter too, as creativity is a thing often encountered in daily life, and
- will we ever be able to create artificial cognitive systems that do the same, or that have such insight into cognitive processes, that they can help humans creatively problem solve more often and with more ease?

This book is an investigation of these questions and offers the beginning of a possible answer.

The subjects of creative problem solving and productive cognition addressed in tandem are topics of great interest to both Artificial Intelligence and Cognitive Science. For Cognitive Science, designing systems that can perform various levels of creative problem solving and testing hypotheses on such systems can contribute to the proposal of further cognitive models of creativity, thus helping us understand how the human mind works when performing various types of creative problem solving. For Artificial Intelligence, the topic can set the foundations to enable the next generation of creative assistive systems — systems which can make creative associations and propose novel solutions or new lines of enquiry; these creative inferences should be expressed in ways which are easy to comprehend by humans and integrate in a normal workflow; the more such systems understand how human creativity works, the more they could provide cognitive support for it. AI and CogSci working together have historically yielded many great achievements and ways of looking at the core questions of what a mind is and what does it take to make one.

For Computer Science, the topic can set to explain how new (valid) information can be created out of old information, other than by pure logical inference. Finally, for Philosophy of Information (Floridi, 2011), the topic might help us define the limits of generative systems, and new ways of measuring informativity.

It is thus worth endeavouring to rebraid together the topics of creativity and problem solving on one hand, and those of computational and human cognitive processing on the other. Creativity (Boden, 2003) has been studied lately in more computational terms, with many computational creativity (Colton & Wiggins, 2012) systems being created. Initially, most such systems aimed to implement artistic endeavours — like poetry writing (Colton, Goodwin, & Veale, 2012) and painting (Colton, 2012b), with only a few tackling creative problem solving (Fleuriot, Maclean, Smaill, & Winterstein, 2014; Bou et al., 2015). Though a move against systems which merely generate artifacts has been made (Ventura, 2016), and the field is deeply preoccupied with the issue of evaluation, most such endeavours aim to enable computational creativity systems, to ask to ask what it is to be computationally creative, and how can it be evaluated.

That is to say, most of these systems do not set out to account for the cognitive mechanisms producing these creative results, and are merely inspired by the results of the creative mind rather than trying to elucidate its processes. Thus, the differences between various creative processes are not accounted for, the special status of some such processes — like insight (Batchelder & Alexander, 2012) — are not investigated in the computational creativity community (with the exception of concept blending (Fauconnier & Turner, 1998) and metaphor (Veale & Keane, 1992)), but mostly in the cognitive psychology literature. Psychological hypotheses on the stages of such processes are not taken into consideration, thus no further elaboration and investigation of these stages comes as a result of designing such systems. Nor are such systems able to be tested with the same tests which we give to humans (Duncker, 1945; Maier, 1931; Mednick & Mednick, 1971). On the other hand, theories of creative cognition are not implemented as often as they could be (with some exceptions like analogy (Falkenhainer, Forbus, & Gentner, 1989; Hofstadter, Mitchell, et al., 1994) and incubation (Hélie & Sun, 2010)), nor are they implemented in a unified manner — with one implementation or small set of principles acting as one architecture through which multiple creativity processes can be modeled and explained. However, new tools from computational creativity might allow the implementation of many more such theories, if only such tools would endeavour to take cognitive processing, cognitive knowledge acquisition (the kind of knowledge humans have) and knowledge organization into account.

To fill this gap between cognitive psychology, AI methods and the new field of computational creativity, this work aims to design hypotheses and implement systems which are:

a) in line with existing work in the cognitive science literature;

b) at levels of description which are adequate for cognitive science (discussing possible representation and processes) and

c) on which further cognitive models can be developed, and empirical hypotheses of how such creative processes work can be explored and tested.

Furthermore, some of these systems and the hypotheses on which they are constructed are evaluated using tests given to humans and products of human creativity as a comparison. Some others, as a result of this work, are put in a form which allows such evaluation in future work.

A main hypothesis of the following work is that knowledge organization is a key factor when approaching creative problem solving. We posit thus that knowledge organization approaches which can naturally and with ease support creative processes in computational systems need to be designed and refined. Throughout this work, knowledge organization is approached and implemented in ways which enable creative search, re-representation of previous knowledge, combinatorial creativity, associativity with similar terms and convergence upon solutions.

This is an issue of knowledge organization, not knowledge representation. The forms of representation chosen in the framework and implemented in the various systems here can be changed while maintaining similar results. However, the organization of said representations is a core principle, enabling the creative process to happen without high computational costs, in the same way in which various data structures are better at dealing with and representing various processes.

1.1 Book Structure

We will start this journey into discovering what it takes to be or build a creative problem solving cognitive system by rebraiding the strands of creativity and problem solving, in the realms of human and computational skills. We will thus look at various research threads: first at creativity and problem solving from the perspective of human creative cognition; then at problem solving from the perspective of artificial intelligence.

It is the thesis of this book that particular types of knowledge organization will have higher chances of enabling (the implementation of) creative processes. Because of this, the types of processes which have been proposed to enable creativity or problem solving and the types of knowledge which could support such processes will be briefly reviewed.

Various computational creativity systems have been implemented in the last decades. A short tour of a selection of such systems will give a taster of what creative machines the community is building in domains as varied as mathematics and magic trick making. We will then return to integrating the human and the computational, by exploring how the forms of evaluation of computational creativity systems compare to those used to assess creativity when dealing with human cognition.

It is all well and good to aim towards an integrated view of how natural and artificial cognitive systems can problem solve creatively. However, how diverse would the requirements for such a creative problem solving system be? And do we have any chance of ever addressing such a diversity of tasks with a small set of processes? In Part II we have a look at a subset of diverse requirements and put together a framework; this theoretical framework proposes a type of knowledge organization and a small set of processes aimed at solving a diverse number of creativity tasks. These processes and the framework are then explored and partially formalized.

To put some of these principles to the test and have some hands-on fun, in Part III we proceed to empirically and computationally explore them, in experiments involving both human participants and programs, with the help of our previously defined framework. First, we explore what Swiss, Cake and Cottage have in common — that is how humans solve the Remote Associates creativity test (RAT). A computational system which can solve the same task is implemented and experimented with, to test the associative principles of our framework, explore one of the earlier proposed mechanisms and to understand more about how humans solve such problems. Helped by this system, and the new understanding of the task, we ask what does it take to be a RAT — thus what are the principles the Remote Associates test is based on. We then construct a visual version of this creativity test, based on the same principles of Remote Associates, and give it to humans to solve.

Us, humans, generally ask computational systems to solve problems we have created or stumbled upon. To reverse the roles for a bit, we proceed on making our computational RAT solver create queries, rather than solve them. More than a fun pursuit, this will help us give cognitive psychologists sets of RAT queries in which they can control many more of the variables, thus allowing them to study the processes involved in solving such queries with a higher degree of precision.

We further ask what you could use a cup for. This seemingly inconspicuous question hides a wonderful skill: the ability of using objects creatively, which most humans and some animals seem to have. We build a prototype system that recommends to use dental floss if you are missing a clothesline. The system (OROC) tests some other principles of the theoretical framework proposed above, by doing creative object replacement (OR), and also a bit of object composition (OC). We pair this prototype with the Alternative Uses test, used to test creativity in humans. Will OROC be able to give sensible answers? We let humans judge its skill, evaluating it with the same metrics as humans solving the Alternative Uses test would be evaluated with. Amongst others, we investigate what kind of answers such a system gives, compared to humans, if its process is in any way similar to that of humans and what kind of properties make humans think the answer is a particularly good one.

Towards the end we finally touch upon the higher level issue of insight. Insight capable computational solvers would require a large amount of knowledge to be built in, to even begin to test quirky creative processes. We prepare for this by using the previous experiments as a gateway, and approaching insight problems in a domain in which we will be soon prepared to implement solvers.

Have you ever wondered how an insight problem is created? Insight moments might seem like aloof and legendary moments of discovery; however, empirical insight is studied in the lab, and insight problems for these settings need to be created (by not so aloof or legendary humans, though see (Duncker, 1945), at least on the legendary). We put together a strategy for creating such insight problems, based on our reverse-engineering of some of the processes we understand to be implicated in insight. We then give these and classical insight problems to people to solve, in a think aloud protocol — with people speaking as they solve each problem. We come up with a set of codes to classify and compare their answers to our theoretical framework. This is to help us explore whether the same framework principles posited before could indeed or could not be applied at the insight level.

An intriguing and at times quirky journey awaits us, which needs an open mind. Creative problem solving answers might not be perfect answers, but they reinvent our way of seeing the world, or our way of understanding a set of matters which was previously ambiguous. Before reaching insight, though, let us start at the beginning. A lot of inspired research has gone into creativity and problem solving, from different angles of interest: sometimes on both creativity and problem solving, sometimes on each separately; at times from the computational perspective, and at others from the human cognition perspective; finally, sometimes (though a bit rarer than we would like), such investigations have happened in the interdisciplinary spirit of cognitive science. Though we cannot hope to honour all the work that happened before us, in the following pages we will get a taste of it, and hope to leave it slightly better off at the end.

Part I

Rebraiding the Strands: Creativity and
Problem Solving, Human and Computational

Problem solving and creativity are often addressed together (Sternberg & Grigorenko, 2003) as higher level cognitive abilities. Both have been held in high esteem and long considered to be human-only abilities, and then proven to exist to a smaller yet still impressive extent in animals: other animals are capable of some creative tool use (Köhler, 1976) and analogy-making (Gillan, Premack, & Woodruff, 1981), and frameworks for the study of animal creativity have been proposed (Kaufman & Kaufman, 2004; Bailey, McDaniel, & Thomas, 2007). However, creativity and creative problem solving are at their pinnacle in human cognition.

Extraordinary leaps of thought have been an integral part of human history: one only needs to leaf through Haven's or Philbin's lists of greatest inventions of all time (Haven, 2006; Philbin, 2005), or through Watson's history of thought and invention (Watson, 2005, 2011) to reinstate in one's self a sense of awe regarding the human ability for creative thought. From the windmill to inventing impressionism, such inventions, brought forth by individuals or groups, seem to be leaps of thought. Nonetheless, creativity is encountered in the everyday life of most people: it happens in the kitchen, when you are producing a creative variation of a recipe, when you are repairing items around the house with improbable tools and when you are adaptively problem solving an unexpected event, creating new plans for the day.

Despite the universality and the diversity of levels creativity takes, various difficulties relating to knowledge representation, common sense knowledge and the amount of cognitive functions involved in higher level cognitive abilities stand in the way of directly modeling such processes.

Both creativity and problem solving have been addressed in psychology, AI and cognitive science, and can be conceived of as interdisciplinary fields of research. Different kinds of matters pertaining to these subjects have been studied, depending on the field doing the inquiry. Here is an example of how the field of inquiry affects the question. A question formulated by *cognitive psychology* would be: *"How does a certain creative process function in humans? How can we model it?"*. An *Artificial Intelligence* type of question: *"How can we define problem solving so that it is computable by machines and that computation can be optimized?"*. Questions relating to *cognitive science*: *"What kinds of representations and processes are necessary and sufficient to have creativity in a cognitive system?"*. An important question asked by the newly emerging field of *computational creativity* is *"What are the required criteria to call a system creative, and how can one evaluate such creativity?"*. This question seems to come loaded with the a bias shown by recent research: as soon as humans *know* by which process the system is generating its creative products, they become much more reluctant to call it creative, as if removing some of the mystery about the process might make it less valuable to some people. As the history of thought regarding human creativity comes pre-laden with such mysterious concepts as muses, daemons and inspiration, it is no wonder that peeking into the process might make some people feel that an essential aspect of creativity has vanished.

However, for the rest of us, for whom the state of wonder remains unaffected or grows in the advent of peeking behind the curtain of cognitive processes, a systematic synthesis is needed to understand the interrelations of the various fields, and the work that has gone before. To this purpose, a large amount of literature from these various domains is approached systematically in the following chapters, by grouping these subjects along these lines:

- **Chapter 2 – Creativity, Problem Solving and Insight** – describes relevant theories of creativity, problem solving (in its well-structured and ill-structured forms) and insight, as an empirically studied creative problem-solving process. Do sight and insight bear a relation? The chapter concludes by exploring which aspects of visuospatial intelligence one needs to keep an eye on or understand the structure of when talking about creative problem solving.

- **Chapter 3 – Knowledge Organization for Creative Problem Solving** – addresses the question of what kinds of representation and processes are of specific use when attempting to implement and model creative problem solving. Various representations and processes previously considered relevant to creative problem solving are reviewed. The interplay between representation and process is presented as a motivator for searching for and engineering types of knowledge organization which can support the creative process in its most relevant forms.

- **Chapter 4 – Computational Creativity Systems** – reviews formal and applied work on creative systems, presenting a selection of models and computational creativity achievements. From computational painters to computational magicians, this review can only offer a selective taster of the field, and many other interesting systems have been realized in the last years.

- **Chapter 5 – Evaluation of Human and Computational Creativity** In this section, modern work and thought on the topic of evaluation for computational creativity systems is reviewed side by side with psychology work on the assessment of creativity in human participants. This juxtaposition is meant to enable a fruitful comparison between the ways in which evaluating humans and evaluating artificial systems has been done so far.

2

Creativity, Problem Solving and Insight

What are creativity, problem solving, and insight? This section sets to present the conceptual work various researchers have put into defining these terms.

2.1 Creativity

Various theories of creativity exist, addressing various aspects of creativity. For example, a distinction is drawn between inventing the bicycle, and coming up with the creative thought that you could use a shoe to put a nail in the wall. The first is called **historical creativity** (h-creativity) by (Boden, 2003), representing creative acts which are original on the scale of human history. The second, though personally quite satisfying, is called **psychological creativity** (p-creativity) in her taxonomy, and refers to contributions which are creative from the perspective of the individual.

Boden further differentiates between **combinatorial**, **exploratory** and **transformational** creativity. Combinatorial creativity is a form of producing new, unusual combinations or associations out of known ideas. Boden's example is that of a physicist comparing an atom to the solar system. Exploratory creativity is a process of exploration of variations within a certain conceptual space. In Boden's words, *"Within a given conceptual space, many thoughts are possible, only some of which may actually have been thought.[...] someone who comes up with a new idea within that thinking style is being creative in the second, exploratory sense."* Transformational creativity is about changes to/restructuring of the conceptual space altogether. Boden exemplifies it as *"someone thinking something which, with respect to the conceptual spaces in their minds, they couldn't have thought before. [...] (the preexisting style) must be tweaked, or even radically transformed, so that thoughts are now possible which previously (within the untransformed space) were literally inconceivable"*. The term of *conceptual space* here is, according to some (Ritchie, 2001; Wiggins, 2001), vaguely defined. It is then hard to compare it to similar terms in the literature, for example the conceptual spaces used by Gärdenfors (Gärdenfors, 2004).

Margaret Boden is the author of some of the most well cited recent thought on creativity, however thought on creativity is by no means new. Take another term relevant for the study of creativity, that of **divergent thought**. Currently, divergent thinking implies a method of generating creative ideas by exploring many possible solutions. Guilford came up with the term *divergent production* in the Structure of Intellect (Guilford, 1967), referring to a form of broad search for many and varied solutions; such a search would happen mostly spontaneously and in a free flowing manner. Convergent thinking, coined as its opposite, complementary cognitive capacity, stood in his theory for a process of coming up with a solution by following a set of logical steps. The solution generated convergently would bear many restrictions and be rigorously structured. Convergent and divergent productions, the differences of which can be observed in Table 2.1, are considered by him as complementary parts of the cognitive *productive* capacity. Guilford's model for convergent and divergent productions is a common model, arguing that problem solving and creative production are the same.

Table 2.1: Difference between divergent and convergent productions, according to Guilford

Divergent productions	Convergent productions
Loose and broad problem, or incomplete grasp of it at the agent level	Answer can be rigorously structured and forthcoming
Few restrictions	Many restrictions
Broad search	Narrow search
Vague and lax criteria for success (stress variety and quantity)	Sharper, rigorous, demanding criteria

The **generative-exploratory** model or Geneplore by (Finke, Ward, & Smith, 1992) differentiates between two phases of creative thought: generation and exploration. In the generative phase, preinventive structures (which are mental representations) are constructed by the individual. In the exploratory phase, these structures are used to generate new ideas. This model, like many others, has been criticised as being too vague to implement in a program.

Gabora has proposed creativity to be a **honing** process (Gabora, 2005; Aerts & Gabora, 2005). In her view, the concept of an individual worldview takes center stage: creativity is then a process by which an individual hones, at multiple stages, their world view. This honing of a worldview is a self-organization process which aims to solve inconsistencies between ideas, attitudes and knowledge.

Other models of creativity center on the difference between implicit and explicit knowledge. **Explicit** knowledge is knowledge which can be articulated, communicated, recorded and distributed (words, numbers, mathematical and scientific formulae). **Implicit** knowledge is the opposite: knowledge which is not easy to communicate, or knowledge which the knowledge holder might even be unaware they possess. Trying to explain to someone how you ride a bicycle might give you flavour of a type of implicit knowledge: such knowledge is hard to express because it is sensorimotor in origin, rather than verbal (for some, such knowledge is called procedural).

Implicit knowledge can also refer to knowledge that you do not know you have acquired, nor can you consciously recall or recollect. If you cannot recollect it, how is such knowledge shown to exist? The presence of such knowledge has been shown in experiments on priming and skill learning (Schacter, Chiu, & Ochsner, 1993). Examples of priming involve being given word fragments with multiple possible completions (e.g. a–a–in to be turned into assassin) and completing them with previously studied items, which are however not remembered; or being given sets of lexical terms like "flig" and asked to decide whether they are words or non-words, and making the decision faster for previously studied items, though these items are not remembered. Such priming experiments use linguistic stimuli, auditory word stimuli and visual stimuli (pictures). In terms of skill learning, classic studies (Milner, Corkin, & Teuber, 1968; Glisky & Schacter, 1988) have shown that amnesic patients can acquire new perceptual and motor skills.

Creativity has historically harboured an aura of mystery, and sometimes deals with ideas and solutions which appear fully formed through a flash of insight. It is easy to see how implicit processing – that is processing which would happen without the awareness of the participant – would be an interesting topic from the studying creativity perspective. Some scholarship on creativity thus focuses on or at least integrates implicit processes. For example the **Explicit-Implicit interaction** model (EII) (Hélie & Sun, 2010) proposes a unified framework for understanding creativity in problem solving, based on the relationship between implicit and explicit processes. The EII theory has been implemented in the CLARION cognitive architecture and relies on a set of principles which include the coexistence and simultaneous involvement of implicit and explicit processes in most tasks.

Other models of creativity have also been proposed (Schmidhuber, 1991; Thaler, 2013); such models can be big picture views, and may or may not be linked to specific creative processes, like analogy, metaphor and concept blending. We will explore such types of specific processes in Chap. 3.2. However, first it is important to realize that creativity and problem solving are not often discussed in conjunction.

2.2 Problem Solving

Part of the difference between creativity and creative problem solving comes from what the results of each are, and how those results are evaluated. Thus, when speaking of creativity without the context of problem solving, one tends to generally consider the processes of creating works of art – music, poetry, paintings – which are original (the field of computational creativity is not devoid of this bias). Such works can then be evaluated in terms of their aesthetic qualities, their novelty compared to other works in the similar genre, compared to other works of the author, or their novelty in terms of process. Creative problem solving on the other hand has to satisfy problem constraints: whether the new solution has a chance at satisfying the problem matters. The usefulness of the solution can thus be as much a factor in evaluation as novelty. The field of creativity usually gets closer to the fields of problem solving and reasoning when it deals with innovation, scientific discovery and scientific reasoning (Langley, 2000; Klahr & Dunbar, 1988; Nersessian, 2008).

In order to understand creative problem solving, one must thus revisit classical problem solving definitions in Artificial Intelligence (AI), and aim to refine as to allow for the creativity component.

In AI, and later in computer science, problem solving in its classical form is defined (Newell & Simon, 1972) in certain specific terms. We will enumerate these terms, showcasing them in a classical example: the tower of Hanoi problem. As shown in Fig. 2.1, three rods and a set of disks which can slide onto the rods. The solver is supposed to move the entire stack to another rod, with the constraints that only one disk can be moved at a time, only the uppermost disk of a stack can be moved on top of another stack, and only smaller disks can be placed on other disks. Problem solving has been defined in terms of:

- An initial state of the problem. For example, the depiction in Fig. 2.1 is the initial state of the tower of Hanoi problem.
- Operators or successor functions which define reachable states of the problem $f(x)$, from any state x. A move of a disk on a larger disk or on an empty rod would constitute an operator. Thus reachable states from the initial state shown in Fig. 2.1, through one move operators, are having the red disk on either the A or the C rods.
- A state space, constituted of all the reachable states, based on applying the operators to initial states in whatever sequence. In the context of the tower of Hanoi problem, this would include all the possible states of disks in various decreasing orders on various rods that can be obtained applying the operators allowed above on the initial state of the Hanoi problem. The state space will thus include having disks 1 and 2 on rod C, as this can be achieved while respecting the available operators.
- Paths – sequences through the state space. In the tower of Hanoi, this would mean a certain set of disk moves, which will allow the navigation through different possible states of disk configurations. To achieve the

state of disks 1 and 2 on rod C, for example, the following path can be taken: 1 can be moved to A, 2 can be moved to C and then 1 can be moved on top of C.

- Path cost – a function used to evaluate the best heuristics. In tower of Hanoi, this could be the number of moves on a different move sequences (path) to reach the goal configuration.
- Goal state or goal tests (to determine if the goal state has been reached). In our example, the goal state is having all the disks on a specific other rod.
- Heuristics, which can be defined based on their success and cost (optimality). For the tower of Hanoi, a heuristic is to keep moving the smallest piece from the initial rod on a different rod, move a larger piece on a different rod, then put the smaller piece(s) on the larger piece.

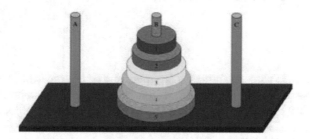

Fig. 2.1: The tower of Hanoi problem

However, a difference can be drawn between well structured and ill-structured problems (Newell, 1969). Well-structured problems can easily be described in terms of the classical problem solving definition, while ill-structured problems have ambiguous initial states, operators or goal states. Take the problem of the benzene molecule – what is the goal and what are the exact operators? Ill-structured problems are more often encountered in real environments (Simon, 1974) than well-structured problems: designing a house, increasing the water supply for a growing community, making a budget or designing a cognitive systems are all ill-structured problems.

One way to address ill-structured problems might be by using **productive**, rather then **reproductive** thinking. The distinction between the two was made by the Gestalt psychologist Wertheimer (Wertheimer, 1945). He considers reproductive thinking to be a function of repetition, conditionings, habit and familiar ways of thought. This means that applying the same known routines to solve a problem could be understood as a function of reproductive thinking. For example, calculating the length of the hypotenuse in a right triangle by applying the known pythagorean theorem, or baking a recipe which you already know can be seen as an example of reproductive problem solving. Meanwhile, productive thinking is considered to produce new ideas and be insight-based. For example, coming up with ways to calculate the length of the hypotenuse in a right triangle when not knowing the theorem, or coming up with a recipe that you can make from the ingredients at hand are examples of productive thinking. In general, coming up with new ideas and new ways of doing things which solve the problem (or, if imperfect, might solve another problem), can be seen as a function of productive thinking. Applying this definition to problem solving, productive problem solving can be defined as a process which brings about new heuristics and new ways of looking at the problem, while reproductive problem solving would mean applying the same known heuristics to the same types of problems. Productive problem solving is thus what we call creative problem solving.

In order to understand why certain ill structured problems are hard to solve and require productive problem solving, the case of insight problem solving can be taken as as an example.

2.3 Insight

The legend has it that Archimedes jumped out of his bathtub shouting *"Eureka"* because of having an insight on how to measure the volume of a crown while observing himself immersed in the water (Vitruvius Pollio, 1914). Various other anecdotes about moments of insight in scientific discovery, exist, like the ones mentioned before of Watson and Kekulé. Some such anecdotes are introspective accounts, declared (some time after the actual insightful event has happened) by the solver, thus standing chances of being distorted by reporting later (due to imperfect memory of the event) or for the sake of a good narrative.

To delve deeper into the empirical study of insight (Chu & MacGregor, 2011), one cannot rely on the introspective or anecdotal account of such insight moments regarding h-creativity discoveries. For the empirical study of insight, empirical tasks do exist. Some of them are problems, like the matchstick problem shown in Fig. 2.2. In this problem you are supposed to make the equation with roman numerals true, by moving only one matchstick, without removing it from the equation. Many people attempt to solve this problem by manipulating the various quantities, for example by moving the matchstick before the first numeral (IV) after the third numeral (I), thus turning the first numeral to V and the third to II. This problem approach is assumed to happen because of functional fixedness — that is being stuck in a perspective that certain objects can be manipulated (or are functional) only in a certain way. In the problem below, such functional fixedness could derive from having learned that, in equations, it is quantities that are being manipulated. The problem is, however, solved by manipulating not the quantities, but the signs – thus removing a matchstick from the initial equal sign, and adding it to the substraction sign. This turns the first operator into a minus sign, and the second into an equal sign, changing the equation into a correct one.

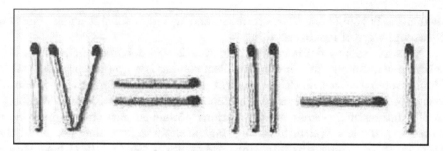

Fig. 2.2: A matchstick problem.

Such insight problems can be of various types, as we will further see when talking in more detail about the evaluation of human creativity, in Sect. 5.1. Implicit processing – that is processing which happens under the level of awareness – is assumed to have an important role in the insight process, in both modern (Hélie & Sun, 2010) and earlier accounts of insight. An early such theoretical model of the insight process belongs to Helmholtz (Helmholtz, 1896) and Wallas (Wallas, 1926), and is the so-called *four step process model* of insight. This model involves the stages of preparation, incubation, illumination (or insight) and verification (or evaluation); in some taxonomies, this is followed by elaboration. The core four steps are described as follows:

1. **Preparation** The participant gets acquainted with the problem. Various attempts are made at solving it, but they are unsuccessful.
2. **Incubation** The participant stops trying to (consciously) solve the problem, directing her attention to something else. This stage varies in length, and reflects some form of implicit processing.
3. **Illumination or Insight** The participant has a sudden idea of how to solve the problem, with all elements appearing at the same time as if *"fully formed"* in consciousness.
4. **Verification or Evaluation** At this stage, the participant tries to apply the insight in the real world or on the problem, to check if it provides the desired solution.

Thus, let us say you have been struggling with a problem like the matchstick problem, or the structure of benzene problem, and despite your best efforts, you have not come up with a way to solve it. According to the four step model, this is your preparation stage – you got acquainted with the problem, and attempt various solutions. Frustrated with your lack of success, you might go for a bit of gardening, and then decide to have a shower. Your gardening represents the incubation stage, in which you let your attention focus on other topics. While thinking of where to put the petunias, under the shower, you might realize all of a sudden that you have been approaching the problem from the wrong angle, and come up with a new way of tackling it. This is the illumination or insight stage. For example, you might realize that you can move the signs as well in the matchstick problem. The verification or evaluation is going back to the problem and trying to solve it using your new ideas and ways of looking at things.

Whether this model is entirely accurate is still debated in the literature, with some assuming that insight problem solving is a gradual process, rather than involving an actual flash of insight, and some considering that it can be both (Seifert, Meyer, Davidson, Patalano, & Yaniv, 1995; Fleck & Weisberg, 2013). Interestingly, while solving various problems, participants have been asked to provide a "warmth" rating, indicating how close they perceived the solution to be. Using this procedure, (Metcalfe & Wiebe, 1987) have shown that when the problems solved were insight problems, participants were unable to predict their closeness to solution, unlike for normal problem solving. This inability to predict one's level of progress within the problem, is generally taken as supporting evidence for the four step model of insight problem solving, with no progress being apparently achieved for a while, followed by a flash of insight in which many pieces of the puzzle fall into place. From now on, whenever we mention "Aha!" effects, we will refer to the flash of insight moment.

Batchelder and Alexander (Batchelder & Alexander, 2012) summarize the set of characteristics for insight as follows:

1. They (insight problems) are posed in such a way as to admit several possible problem representations, each with an associated solution search space.
2. Likely initial representations are inadequate in that they fail to allow the possibility of discovering a problem solution.
3. In order to overcome such a failure, it is necessary to find an alternative productive representation of the problem.
4. Finding a productive problem representation may be facilitated by a period of non-solving activity called incubation, and also it may be potentiated by well-chosen hints.
5. Once obtained, a productive problem representation leads quite directly and quickly to a solution.
6. The solution involves the use of knowledge that is well known to the solver. (For example in the matchstick problem, the solver knows both minus and equal signs, and how they operate.)
7. Once the solution is obtained, it is accompanied by a so-called "aha!" experience.
8. When a solution is revealed to a non-solver, it is grasped quickly, often with a feeling of surprise at its simplicity, akin to an "aha!" experience.

Research in insight problem solving shows the role of the problem representation to be essential: some representations are productive, that is they lead to the solution (sometimes directly), while others get the solver stuck in unproductive cycles. Thus arriving at a productive representation can be seen as an important component of the insight problem solving process, and a valuable exercise in productive thinking (Wertheimer, 1945). Restructuring (Ohlsson, 1983, 1984; MacGregor & Cunningham, 2009) and re-representation or representational change (Knoblich, Ohlsson, & Raney, 2001; Jones, 2003) are assumed to play an important role in arriving at such a productive representation. Performance in solving insight problems has been shown to sometimes improve when given enough practice (Jacobs & Dominowski, 1981).

With the role of the representation baring such importance for insight, we will need to focus our attention on knowledge representation and organization. A possible clue on tackling this might lay in the difference between ill-structured and well-structured problems. A hypothesis which we could make is that **perhaps the process of re-representation can help transgress the boundaries between the two problem categories, by turning ill-structured problems into well-structured problems**. To better understand whether this is possible, we need to first understand what the role of knowledge representation and organization is in creative problem solving, which we will endeavour to do in the next chapter.

However, first let us have a look under the hood, at a few studies overviewing the neural correlates of insight, in order to check whether the same issues of association and re-representation are relevant.

2.4 Neural Correlates of Insight

The right hippocampus and a wide area of cerebral cortex (frontal, temporal, parietal and occipital) have been shown to be involved in insight events (Luo & Niki, 2003). 45 most interesting Japanese riddles were rated out of a set of 300. These riddles were then given to participants solve (Luo & Niki, 2003) in an fMRI event-related experiment (Luo & Niki, 2003). The 16 riddles which each participant found the most interesting but could not solve where collected in a scanning session. The answer to this most interesting riddles was shown to the participants which could not solve them, eliciting "Aha!" effects. The authors posited that the formation of novel associations between already existing conceptual "nodes" was what activated the hippocampus. The hippocampus has been previously shown to have a role in the formation of associations (Wallenstein, Hasselmo, & Eichenbaum, 1998), pattern completion and conjunctive representations (Rudy & O'Reilly, 1999).

Another event-related fMRI study (Luo, Niki, & Phillips, 2004b) presented participants with incomprehensible sentences. These sentences were followed by solution cues which triggered alternative interpretations of the concepts in the sentences, thus triggering an "Aha!" reaction. Activation in the anterior cingulate cortex (ACC) and left lateral prefrontal cortical areas has been observed, areas supposed to mediate cognitive conflict. Thus a mental impasse was assumed to be broken with the presentation of the solution cues, redirecting the interpretation of the participants in a productive manner.

120 Chinese riddles of two degrees of difficulty were presented to participants in a high-density event-related potential (ERP) study (Mai, Luo, Wu, & Luo, 2004). After each riddle, the participants were given a cue which was

consistent with the assumed initial direction of thought of the participant, or which required changing the initial mental set (thus manifesting "Aha!" effects). Results concluded the ACC was involved in the breaking of the mental set, with a peak latency of 380 msec (N380). The ACC was also observed to be more involved in the condition in which the puzzles where hard to predict, than when puzzles were constructed on similar structural principles (Luo, Niki, & Phillips, 2004a).

In active solving of Chinese logogriphs (Qiu et al., 2008), event related potentials have been observed thought to be involved in initial association formation (a P200–600 in the left superior temporal gyrus and parietotemporo-occipital cortex areas), in the breaking of the mental set (a N1500–2000 in the ACC) and posited to be related to the emotional "Aha!" effect (N2000–2500 generator in the posterior cingulate cortex (PCC)).

These studies support the importance of making new associations, pattern completion and re-representation (with cues of cognitive conflict between multiple interpretations) in creative and insightful problem solving. The word insight however contains strong etymological relations to the word *"sight"*. Traced back to circa 1200, *innsihht* seems to have originally meant "sight with the 'eyes' of the mind, mental vision" and to have shifted around 1580 to having "sight into" something else, that is an understanding into some form of hidden nature[1]. Is this relation to sight just a coincidence, or are there any links between visual and perhaps spatial forms of intelligence, and insight?

2.5 Visuospatial Intelligence

Arguments have been made for visualization being essential for reasoning. (Johnson-Laird, 1998) provides a nice overview of this, including the role many scientists have emphasized imagery to play in their thought processes. For example, here is an excerpt from Einstein's letter to Hadamard (Hadamard, 1945):

> *The words of the language, as they are written or spoken, do not seem to play any role in my mechanism of thought. The psychical entities which seem to serve as elements in thought are certain signs and more or less clear images which can be "voluntarily" reproduced and combined.*

Whether imagery plays an actual role in reasoning or just occurs alongside reasoning (as an epiphenomenon), it is easy to understand why visual imagery has been regarded as a potentially interesting medium for creative problem solving: many anecdotes about flashes of insight bring to the fore the arrival of a fully formed vision of how to solve a particular problem. However, a medium which might not seem as saliently connected to flashes of insight as

---

[1] http://www.etymonline.com/index.php?term=insight

visual imagery, might play a role. This medium is that of spatial reasoning, which some authors consider of tremendous importance for problem solving[2]. For example, Freksa considers spatial reasoning to be a form of interface for abstract reasoning (Freksa, 1991):

> *"We may interpret non-spatial concepts by mentally transforming them into spatial concepts (i.e., understanding them in terms of spatial concepts), carrying out mental operations in this visualizable and graspable domain and transforming the result into the original domain. In this way, spatial inference engines may have a much more general function than the term suggests: rather than generalizing by forming a common abstraction for various domains we generalize by forming suitable analogies to a well-understood concrete domain."*

The notion that spatial relations can play an important role in abstract and creative reasoning is supported by the theory of image schemas. Image schemas are recurring structures formed from bodily interactions which are then used to understand the world and reason with. Image schemas are supposed to also play a structuring role in metaphors (Lakoff & Johnson, 1999); for example, take the by now so famous that it does not appear creative metaphor: *"Life is a journey"*. The image schema of a spatiotemporal construct, that of a *journey*, is used here for the construction of a metaphor, to give a possible interpretation or casting to the more ambiguous concept of *life*. Similarly, take the sentence *"I don't want to leave any relevant data out of my argument."* A spatial containment schema (reflected by the words *"out of"*) is here metaphorically projected onto a non spatial object – an *argument*.

For the first 5 to 6 months, infants are not effective in their control of objects. Mandler (Mandler, 2010) proposes that their own actions for this time period do not inform their conceptual system reliably, however, as infants pay attention to the world around them, motion through space, which they observe, provides such an influence. Mandler further extrapolates from empirical developmental data that spatial image-schemas are the functional base for developing abstract concepts. Image schemas, according to Mandler, are salient (perceptual) information redescribed in a simpler, schematic form, which leads to concept formation. She proposes that a small set of spatial primitives is sufficient for the conceptualizations used by preverbal infants for interpreting objects and events. Some of the spatial concepts which she proposes as primitive are: PATH, START PATH, END PATH, PATH TO, LINK, CONTAINER, (IN)TO, (OUT) OF, THING, ±MOTION, CONTACT, etc. (Mandler, 2012). For example, spatial primitives like START PATH and CONTACT can be used to differentiate between animals and inanimate things: animals start paths themselves, while inanimate things can start to move only as a consequence of previous contact with other moving things.

---

[2] Spatial reasoning could perhaps have something to do with the fully formed part of the insight or "vision".

In fact spatial concepts which are themselves abstract, like cardinal directions, might be further grounded in body-referenced axes (Tower-Richardi, Brunye, Gagnon, Mahoney, & Taylor, 2012). Priming participants with abstract spatial terms (like north, south, east, west) influences the participants' further hand trajectories when giving answers to a spatial target task which is body-referenced (about terms like up, down, left, right). This is an example of top-down influence from abstract spatial concepts, back onto an affordance of bodily motion, and implies a strong connectivity between the two.

If abstract concepts in general are indeed grounded in spatial concepts, then such spatial concepts should play an important role in knowledge representation and categorization. Such a role will make them highly relevant for the creation of new concepts, which will be influenced by existing concept categorization and representation. This kind of an influence would of course trickle straight back into the more general level of creative problem solving.

A piece of support to this spatial potential influence is that children who encounter an object they do not know the name of, tend to extend to it the name of a previously known object of a similar shape. This is called the shape bias (Landau, Smith, & Jones, 1988; Imai, Gentner, & Uchida, 1994; Markson, Diesendruck, & Bloom, 2008) and it has shown that, in the object domain, shape is an important feature in the categorization of objects (more so than color, size or material). Would a feature important in categorizing objects also be important in their knowledge grounding, representation and organization? What would the effect of such cognitive properties of knowledge organization be on creative problem solving? Would shape also be important when generating new objects rather than just organizing them? We will get a chance to test such hypotheses later.

However, before proceeding to knowledge organization topics, an interesting point about the link between perception, visuospatial intelligence and re-representation can be made via the example of ambiguous figures. Ambiguous figures, like the ones showcased in Fig. 2.3, are figures in which two different objects can be seen, albeit not at the same time. In Fig. 2.3 a), both a girl's face and a saxophonist can be seen. In Fig. 2.3, the same stand for a duck and a rabbit.

This perception-based process certainly brings to mind a certain conceptual similarity with the notion of re-representation. Thus, if in ambiguous figures, visuospatial features can be grouped in two different objects, in creative problem solving, objects of the problem might be grouped or paid attention to in different ways, invoking different known heuristics, as to bring about a productive problem representation.

We might have yet to hear the final word on the influence of visuospatial processes on creative problem solving. As things stand, we should consider this set of findings as being representative of the fact that we should not think of knowledge only as verbal or propositional when considering types of knowledge representation and processes which could implement creative processes.

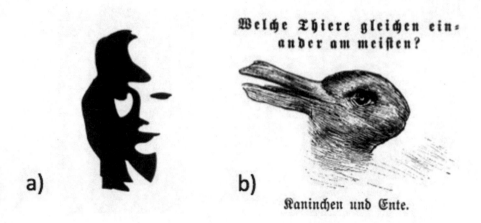

Fig. 2.3: Ambiguous figures: a) girl/saxophonist; b) duck/rabbit

3

Knowledge Organization for Creative Problem Solving

How does creative problem solving work in natural cognitive systems? How could it be implemented in artificial cognitive systems? To answer these questions, one has to start by taking a stance on a question which is more foundational in nature. That question is how is knowledge in such systems represented (or how can it be represented), and how that type of representation influences the creative problem solving processes.

The relationship between knowledge representation and processes can be, from a computational point of view, quite tight. To exemplify this, let us say that you are practicing a foreign language by reading a newspaper in that language and you have just encountered a new word. Let us say the language is Spanish and the new word is *"avestruz"*. It is not enough for you to pick up a dictionary which contains this knowledge. The dictionary has to be a linguistic dictionary (as supposed to a visual one), if you have encountered the word in a linguistic form. This will enable you to match the word you encountered to the word in the dictionary. Let us say you will pick up a big hard copy dictionary tome from your library. If this dictionary is both English to Spanish and Spanish to English, you might need to use your knowledge about how such double mapping dictionaries are organized — which might require for you to turn the dictionary around on the other side.

Furthermore, you will use the knowledge organization in the dictionary to proceed on your search — thus you will first switch to words beginning with the letter *a*, discounting other 26 word chapters beginning with the other letters of the Spanish alphabet. You will then use your knowledge about alphabetical order (*v* is towards the end) to find towards the end of the chapter the words beginning with letters *av*. Applying this technique, you will soon enough find out that the word which you were looking for means *"ostrich"*.

The knowledge in the dictionary would not have been very useful for you to solve the problem if the type of knowledge representation and knowledge organization did not support this kind of search. For example, if the dictionary harboured exactly the same knowledge about animals but with a mapping between a picture and the word *"ostrich"* in English, the information would

© Springer Nature Switzerland AG 2020
A.-M. Olteţeanu, *Cognition and the Creative Machine*,
https://doi.org/10.1007/978-3-030-30322-8_3

be pointless if you wouldn't hold the second part of the key — the mapping between *"avestruz"* and the image of the ostrich. And if you would only hold this second part mapping between the *"avestruz"* and the image of an ostrich, that would be pointless too unless you knew for sure how the animal was called in English, and that mapping existed in your mind. Though very helpful with your word to word search between these languages, the same dictionary would prove much less supportive of a different task, for example that of writing a poem in either of these languages, or a bilingual poem in both. Though you would have all the word knowledge required contained in this dictionary, a rhyme dictionary would be much more useful for that task, assuming you care for poetry that rhymes. Similarly, a thematic dictionary might be much more useful if you care to just learn words directly from a dictionary and use them to compose little essays, as it is more likely your essays will involve some form of theme coherence, and the flow of your little literary composition might be hindered if you had to search for each word in a particular theme alphabetically, with the previously mentioned dictionary.

Furthermore, if you were bilingual or trilingual you might be accessing your existing knowledge about other languages to make some prediction about what the word could mean. For example, I am Romanian, my native language is a Romance language, like Spanish, and I matched the second part of the word "avestruz" to the Romanian *"struț"* which luckily does mean *"ostrich"*. Not all such matches will hold, and some will be hindering, rather than helpful.

In all the cases above though, some form of knowledge representation and organization supports a process – the organization of the dictionary supports the process of searching for the translation of a particular word. This holds whether the knowledge is external or part of a system — certain data structures are more productive for the implementations of certain algorithms. Thus similarly, certain types of internal knowledge representation and organization can support with more ease the deployment of certain processes. Cognitive function, be it natural or artificial, may thus be supported by the organization of the knowledge within the cognitive system.

Well structured problems and ill-structured problems have been defined as easier and respectively harder to solve (requiring creativity) in natural and artificial cognitive systems. Considering the difference between them might be based on a difference of problem structure, the following section will focus on structure and process topics: (i) structured representations proposed in AI; (ii) types of processes proposed in creativity and (iii) restructuring as a process of creative problem solving, together with the need for implementing creative systems in which knowledge organization is supportive of restructuring and re-representation.

3.1 Representations and Structure

One of the themes which emerges when looking at some of the constructs proposed to be used for representing knowledge in cognitive science and AI is the theme of structured representation. Here are some constructs of knowledge representation which have in common an interest for structure:

Frames are knowledge representation schemes initially proposed by Minsky (Minsky, 1975) which were meant to capture and express essential properties of concepts and often encountered situations, like going out for dinner, going to a birthday party or being in the living room. In Minsky's words: *"When one encounters a new situation [...] one selects from memory a structure called a frame. This is a remembered framework to be adapted to fit reality by changing details as necessary. A frame is a data-structure for representing a stereotyped situation [...] Attached to each frame are several kinds of information. Some of this information is about how to use the frame. Some is about what one can expect to happen next. Some is about what to do if these expectations are not confirmed."*

Minsky carries on to explain that one can think of a frame as a network of nodes and relations, containing top levels which are fixed, representing things that are always true about the supposed situation, and lower levels which have many terminal slots which must be filled by specific instances or data. For example, Minsky describes the simplest sort of room-frame candidate to be like the inside of a box. Fig. 3.1 shows the top level structure of the room frame. According to Minsky, one has to assign the frame's terminals the things that are seen, and if the room is familiar, some of these are already assigned.

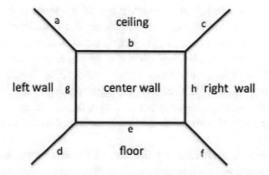

Fig. 3.1: A room frame image proposed by Minsky. The image has been reconstructed after the one presented in his 1975 paper.

Frames offer a short and poignant system of expressing knowledge in an object-oriented manner (Fikes & Kehler, 1985) and are useful for the semantic web (Lassila & McGuinness, 2001). The concept of frames later led to the development of frame-based systems, which generally share the following properties (Fikes & Kehler, 1985): a) frames are organized in tangled hierarchies; b) they are composed out of slots (attributes) for which fillers (scalar values, references to other frames or procedures) need to be specified or computed) and c) properties are inherited hierarchically from superframes to subframes in accord to some inheritance strategy.

Minsky used frames to describe representation schemes for both psychological description and artificial intelligence. **Schemata** are psychological constructs (Rumelhart, 1984; Brewer & Treyens, 1981) which aim to account for atomic parts of human generic knowledge. The somewhat similar construct of **scripts** (Schank & Abelson, 1977) refers to schemata which represent stereotyped sequences of action — i.e. the sequence of actions required for the scenario of a person ordering something in a restaurant. For example, think of the script required for the scenario of a person ordering something in a restaurant. It will involve entering the restaurant, waiting to be seated, ordering the food, eating, paying the bill and leaving. Scripts can be subdivided into scenes. For example, the eating the meal scene can further be decomposed into picking up the knife and fork, using them to partition and grab food, chewing, etc.

The term of **image schemas** has widely been used with various meanings, and has been approached in the context of metaphors in the work of Lakoff and Johnson (Lakoff & Johnson, 1980, 1999). In this work, image schemas are recurring structures which establish patterns of understanding. Some are dynamic embodied patterns, which are later used for abstract reasoning and in metaphors. For example, take the image schema of containment, and the English word *"out"*. This is used do describe physical spatial occurrences in which a trajector leaves a bounded landmark, like *"Mary went out of the room"*. In this case, Mary is the trajector, and the room the bounded landmark. However, such image schemas can be projected onto non spatial situations, like *"I don't want to leave any relevant data out of my argument."*, *"Tell me your story again, and don't leave out any details."* and *"She finally came out of her depression."* (Johnson, 2013). The use of image schemas further supports compositionality, and some conceptualization of spatial schemas (Gattis, 2001). Some evidence points at the existence of image schemas in the human brain (Rohrer, 2005).

Analogical representations (Sloman, 1971) are representations in which some of the properties and relations between parts represent corresponding properties and relations in the world (or in some hypothesised/imagined world). Sloman makes the point that this correspondence can however be complex. He illustrates this with a two dimension picture of a three dimension scene (Sloman, 1971), mentioning that "distances in the picture represent distances in the scene in a complex context-sensitive way." The structure of analogical representation however does give information about the structure of what is represented. Sloman contrasts such analogical representations to

Fregean representations: he mentions maps, images and scaled models as analogical representations, with predicate calculus, programming languages and natural languages (mostly, but not exclusively) Fregean.

The concept of **mental models** was first proposed by Kenneth Craik (Craik, 1943). Mental models were meant to be molecular models of reality built by the human cognitive system in order to reason, anticipate events and provide explanations. Models have been further supposed to be constructed in the working memory (Marr, 1982; Johnson-Laird, 1983). One of the defining characteristics of mental models, which makes them very similar to Sloman's concept of analogical representation (Sloman, 1971), is that the structure of the mental models is in a relation of correspondence with the structure of the world that is being represented.

The argument for **structured representation** goes further, when connected with the topic of creativity and creative problem solving. However, a look at creative processes is first warranted.

3.2 Creative Processes

Various processes have been proposed to account for mechanisms of creativity.

Bisociation is a concept developed by Arthur Koestler (Koestler, 1964), which discusses it in "The Act of Creation". Bisociation is the process of blending elements drawn from two previously unrelated matrices or frames of thought into a new matrix of meaning. For example, in humour, a certain outcome is expected by the audience because of a particular story line, however a punch line replaces this original matrix. The process allowing such a blending can involve comparison, abstraction and categorisation, and Koestler regarded many processes involving comparison – like analogy and metaphor — to be a form of bisociation.

Koestler believed that the discovered needed to be prepared. This preparation, perhaps compatible to the preparation phase in insight theories, he called *"ripeness"*. Koestler also refers to the need for something similar to an incubation phase by talking about the unconscious mind as the generator of discoveries. He also alludes to different modes of ideation, in which verbal language does not play a central part: *"The creative process of discovery depends on the unconscious resources and presupposes a regression to modes of ideation which are indifferent to the rules of verbal logic"*. Koestler differentiated between creativity as being the "production of a new recipe", compared to "the skilled routine of providing variations for it".

The study of human category making and concept formation has yielded a variety of theories, including prototype theory (Rosch, 1975), exemplar theory (Medin & Shoben, 1988), theory theory (Murphy & Medin, 1985). Some members of conceptual categories are more central than others – for example, when asked to iterate through concepts of the category *furniture*, people would mention *chair* more often than *stool*; *robins* and *sparrows* will be seen as better examples of the *bird* category than *chicken* and *penguins*. Prototype theory argues that a form of statistical average of category members forms a prototype of the category. Exemplar theory argues instead that a new stimulus is compared to multiple known exemplars in a category. Theory theory proposes that concepts are organized within and around theories, which means concept acquisition involves theory learning, and concepts exist in theoretical contexts. An issue connected to concept formation, less tackled by of major importance to creativity, is that of the process of **concept creation**. Assuming concepts and categories are not just the result of experience of interacting with the world, but can also be at the productive end of a creative process, theories of creativity need to find a way to answer the issue of concept creation. Amongst others (Aerts & Gabora, 2005), the process of **conceptual blending**, a descendent of bisociation has been proposed as a form of creating new concepts (Fauconnier & Turner, 1998). Concept blending is defined by Fauconnier as a basic mental operation of constructing a partial match between two inputs, projecting selectively from those inputs into a "blended space" which has as a result the emergence of a new structure and of new meaning.

Associativity is also relevant process for creativity. According to Csikszentmihalyi (Csikszentmihalyi, 1996) *"Cognitive theorists believe that ideas, when deprived of conscious direction, follow simple laws of association. They combine more or less randomly, although seemingly irrelevant associations between ideas may occur as a result of a prior connection"*. This supports an associationist view of creativity. Mednick (Mednick, 1962) also embraced the view that association, especially remote association, was what laid at the foundation of the creative process. In *"The Associative Basis of the Creative Process"* he states that the ability to *"bring mutually remote ideas into contiguity facilitates creative problem solving"*, and further that *"the organization of an individual's associations will influence the probability and speed of attainment of a creative solution"*. Associative principles are reflected at various levels of granularity in cognitive science and artificial intelligence concepts. For example, the principle of hebbian learning (Hebb, 1949), currently applied for artificial neural networks, but initially formulated for neurons, presupposes that neurons which *"fire together, wire together"*. Semantic networks (Sowa, 1992), which are graphs consisting of concepts (vertices) and the relations between them (edges) can be used for implementing forms of associativity.

Analogy (Gentner, 1983; Holyoak & Thagard, 1996), an important mechanism in creativity and scientific discovery (Dunbar, 1995), is the process of understanding a concept, process or situation via another. For example *"An electric battery is like a reservoir"* is an analogy. Thus a concept, process or situation that is familiar, called the *source* analog (in this case the reservoir), might be used to understand another less familiar concept, process or situation, called the *target* (in this case the electric battery). It is currently assumed that various stages are part of the analogy-making process. A mapping or aligning of the representational structures (Gentner, 1983; Falkenhainer et al., 1989; Gentner, 2010) allows projections of inferences. For example, the inference that the electric battery stores potential energy can be projected on the basis of knowledge about the reservoir. An evaluation of analogy and the inferences produced by it follows. After this, one or both initial representation might change, being adapted or re-represented. Analogy making is a process which has been amply studied in the literature, with various computational approaches (Evans, 1964; Halford ct al., 1994; Hofstadter et al., 1994; Forbus, Gentner, & Law, 1995; Falkenhainer et al., 1989).

It is worth noting that Gabora's honing theory is also supportive of associative, structure-relevant processes, as she thinks the process of analogy is "constrained by content-addressable structure of associative memory to naturally retrieve items that are [...] structurally similar" (Gabora, 2005, 2015).

Metaphor is the process of using one concept, process or situation to designate another. For example, the phrase *"The wheels of justice turn slowly"* is based on a metaphor. Metaphors make implicit comparison between two concepts, processes and situations (in the example here, between the concepts "justice" and "machine"). Metaphors differ from similes by not using language (e.g. words such as "like", "as", etc.) to make such a comparison overt. Lakoff and Johnson (Lakoff & Johnson, 1980) discuss the role of structural metaphors as allowing people to use the structure of a concept in order to structure another. They further posit the existence of structure in the metaphorical system as a whole, as "neural connectivity of the brain makes it natural for complex metaphorical mappings to be built out of preexisting mappings"(Lakoff & Johnson, 1999). Various formal approaches to modeling metaphors exist (Indurkhya, 1999; Gust, Kühnberger, & Schmid, 2006).

3.3 Restructuring or Re-Representation and the Link between Knowledge Representation and Process

Support for a structured creativity approach comes not only from structured approaches in artificial intelligence, but from empirical psychology as well (T. B. Ward, 1994; Brédart, Ward, & Marczewski, 1998; T. B. Ward, Patterson, Sifonis, Dodds, & Saunders, 2002). Some work shows that category structure has an important role to play in creative generation.

For example, in one of Ward's studies (T. B. Ward, 1994), the participants were given the task of creating imaginary animals that could live on a different planet in the galaxy. The participants created drawings and descriptions of such animals, of members of these animals' species and of members of other species. The responses generated for this task were structured by properties of known earthly animals. Furthermore, when asking the participants for animals with a particular attribute (e.g. feathers), categorical knowledge was shown to be called upon and influence the imagined animal, which also held other attributes correlated with that particular feature (e.g. beaks and wings). Ward has shown that similar knowledge base categorical constraints apply to creative writers, for examples science fiction authors, and proposed the concept of *structured imagination*.

A further set of experiments was performed using categories of *animals, tools and fruit* (T. B. Ward et al., 2002). First, lists of exemplars were gathered for these categories from some participants, as to determine accessibility of different category exemplars. Then, other participants were asked to draw and describe novel categories of those exemplars, which might live on an imaginary planet. Items rated as highly accessible in the lists provided by the first participants had a higher influence in imaginary production of new exemplars.

These experiments show the importance and influence of the structure existing in the knowledge base of the cognitive agent when approaching a creative task. This is noteworthy, considering that *restructuring* or re-representation are considered to play an important role in insight and creative problem solving (Duncker, 1945; Davidson & Sternberg, 1984; Kaplan & Simon, 1990).

Thus a link between the process of (structured) knowledge representation and the creative process, as a process of restructuring, can be drawn. Let us return for a moment to the well-structured – ill-structured problems divide. What are the implications of structured knowledge representation, and processes of restructuring, on this divide? Could it be, for example, that **the answer to dealing with ill-structured problems, is to bring structure from already existing knowledge representations or from well structured problems, in order to improvise, define, extrapolate or create the structure such ill-structured problems lack?** This intriguing hypothesis will become a central point of our pursuit, and we will follow it further in Chapters 6 and 7, when defining the desiderata for an integrated approach to creative problem solving, and proposing knowledge organization and mechanisms capable of such feats.

For now it is worth remembering that many signs of the previous literature point in the direction of the following: a type of knowledge organization which allows restructuring and re-representation seems essential for the implementation of creative processes.

4

Computational Creativity and Systems

Computational creativity is, according to some of its major figures (Colton & Wiggins, 2012): *The philosophy, science and engineering of computational systems which, by taking on particular responsibilities, exhibit behaviours that unbiased observers would deem to be creative.* Though engineering systems which are or appear to be creative is by no means all that computational creativity aims to do, and a move has recently been made against mere generation of artefacts (Ventura, 2016), the computational creativity community has been very productive for quite a while on building such systems and thinking of ways to evaluate them.

Computational creativity systems have been implemented in domains as varied as:

- **mathematics** (Lenat, 1976; Colton, Bundy, & Walsh, 2000; Colton, 2012a);
- **music** (Pearce & Wiggins, 2004; Pachet, 2012; B. D. Smith & Garnett, 2012; Eppe et al., 2015);
- **art** (Cohen, 1995; Colton, 2012b);
- **poetry** and **text composition** (Carpenter, 2004; Gervás, 2010; Greene, Bodrumlu, & Knight, 2010; Colton et al., 2012);
- **architecture and design** (Schneider, Fischer, & König, 2011);
- **discovery of physical laws** (Langley, 1978, 1981; Langley, Bradshaw, & Simon, 1981);
- **magic trick making** (Williams & McOwan, 2014);
- **video games** (Cook & Colton, 2014), etc.

With more and more systems being implemented each year, it is hard to keep full track of all of them. This chapter will give a taster of some of the work in the field, by shortly examining a few such systems from different domains. The selection of these systems is aimed to be diverse, not exhaustive, and many interesting systems will not be mentioned here.

© Springer Nature Switzerland AG 2020
A.-M. Olteţeanu, *Cognition and the Creative Machine*,
https://doi.org/10.1007/978-3-030-30322-8_4

4.1 AM

The AM system (Lenat, 1976) acts in the domains of elementary set and number theory, and paved the way in concept formation and conjecture making. AM had a database of 115 elementary mathematical concepts, like the concept of equality, and a set of heuristics. These concepts were represented as pieces of Lisp code. AM reinvented concepts from set and number theory and some known conjectures, by choosing which heuristics were to be applied to a specific task and applying those heuristics. As such heuristics had multiple tasks, and subtasks, part of the computational work of AM was to choose which tasks to apply first. This decision making process was guided by adding values to concepts, their facets and actions which could be taken on the concepts, which were then used to calculate a task value.

A second part of the decision making process was to assess interestingness using other heuristics, based on interesting properties, related conjectures to a concept, whether examples of a concept have been found or not, etc. Later, Lenat was criticised for over-interpreting the output of AM, which basically generated and manipulated short Lisp programs. He tackles the issue of whether the discoveries reside in the output of AM or are an interpretation of the observer in his paper, *Why AM and Eurisko appear to work* (Lenat & Brown, 1984).

4.2 HR

The HR system (Colton, 2012a), named after the mathematicians Hardy and Ramanujan, is meant to produce theories in pure mathematics domains, taking as input simple concepts and axioms. HR produces new mathematical concepts and forms new theories by using a pre-defined set of production rules. Such production rules act as structure and constraints propagators within the new formed concepts. Third party automated reasoning software is used by HR in order to attempt to prove the new conjectures.

The search for new concepts and mathematical conjectures is driven in HR by various measures of interestingness (Colton et al., 2000). Such measures of interestingness involve properties of complexity and surprise of both concepts and conjectures.

4.3 Aaron

Aaron (Cohen, 1995) is a drawing and painting computational creativity system on which Cohen started working in the mid seventies from the cognitive question "What is the minimum condition under which a set of marks functions as an image". Aaron started as a simple program which could distinguish between figure and ground, closed and open forms, and perform simple structure manipulations, with a feedback mode, which allowed it to consider its overall goal in relation to its current accomplished parts of the drawing. After observing the behaviour of children in scribbling, in which *"a scribble migrates outwards and becomes an enclosing form for the rest of the scribble"*, Cohen added to Aaron a simple strategy to trace a path around core figures, which greatly enhanced the complexity of the forms it generated, and their similarity to forms drawn from visual experience.

Aaron continued to be developed over time, with the addition of physical ambience around its figures, knowledge of anatomical parts (as complex connected parts) and postural rules, while still operating with knowledge of two and a half dimensional figures. Then, in order for it to turn from a drawing expert system (the drawings of which Cohen painted himself) to a painter system, a three-dimensional knowledge base was added. Many of its knowledge sets of points are derived from medical illustrations of the skeleton. In order to achieve different points of view, Aaron places its figures, after constructing them and transforming them to the appropriate pose, in a three-dimensional world, and then places its point of perspective (its *eye*) in the same world. Aaron specifies its plans at the highest level of abstraction, with the lower levels generating instances of such plans. Its drawings and paintings have been exhibited publicly from as early as 1979[1].

4.4 The Painting fool

The Painting fool (Colton, 2012b) has been initially designed as an art project, as to work in real time, adding strokes to a canvas one by one. Colton would like the Painting Fool to be taken as an artist in its own right, rather than as a creativity simulation machine, and has invested interest in what helps people perceive a work or process as more valuable and creative than others. The works of the Painting Fool have received wide media coverage, have been entered in exhibitions and competitions, and videos of the Painting Fool at work can be found online[2].

Besides its ability to simulate various styles in charcoal, acrylic, chalks and pencil, the Painting Fool has various artistic styles in its knowledge base annotated based on emotion keywords. This enabled the system to create a painting in a style corresponding to a given emotion. Such an emotion can also be read as an input by a machine vision program from the face of a person. A further mix with the HR system and an expansion based on an evolutionary approach enabled the Painting Fool to produce scenes which have been optimized for fitness functions created by HR; the choices on what to optimize are thus being made computationally as well.

---

[1] http://aaronshome.com/aaron/
[2] www.thepaintingfool.com

4.5 Poetry systems

Poetry systems like for example that of (Colton et al., 2012) demonstrate an interesting use of structure (as templates), word associations and similes. Templates are used to construct poems, with given constraints on sentiment, rhyme, meter, stress, word frequency and word similarity. Content is generally mined from a corpus or from a pre-established lexicon. Corpuses thus mined can be very large, like the 85 million words parsed from the British National Corpus for the Electronic Text Composition (ETC) poetry engine (Carpenter, 2004). Some such systems (Colton et al., 2012) intend to go beyond artefact generation. One way to do this is having the system construct their mood for the day (by analysing newspaper articles or online news), and then subsequently using this mood to determine both the article to base the poem on and the template for the poem. Another is to create an aesthetic based on various metrics, and then search for an instantiation of this template which aims to maximize the aesthetic. Yet another is to have the system provide a commentary to the whole process, thus framing it.

Here is an example from Colton, Goodwin and Veale of such a computationally generated framing and poem: *It was generally a bad news day. I read an article in the Guardian entitled: "Police investigate alleged race hate crime in Rochdale". Apparently, "Stringer-Prince, 17, has undergone surgery following the attack on Saturday in which his skull, eye sockets and cheekbone were fractured" and "This was a completely unprovoked and relentless attack that has left both victims shocked by their ordeal". I decided to focus on mood and lyricism, with an emphasis on syllables and matching line lengths, with very occasional rhyming. I like how words like attack and snake sound together. I wrote this poem.*

Relentless attack

a glacier-relentless attack
the wild unprovoked attack of a snake

the wild relentless attack of a snake
a relentless attack, like a glacier
the high-level function of eye sockets

a relentless attack, like a machine
the low-level role of eye sockets
a relentless attack, like the tick of a machine

the high-level role of eye sockets
a relentless attack, like a blood hound

At a smaller scale than poetry systems, but still dealing with linguistic creativity, some systems produce evocative image builders in the form of *similes* from readymades (Veale & Hao, 2011) like *as cold as a robot fish, as dark and sophisticated as chocolate martini* and *as cold as a wet haddock*; others produce and validate *neologisms* (Veale, 2006). The corpus used by the former (Veale & Hao, 2011) is also used for poetry generation in (Colton et al., 2012) — demonstrating re-use of resources in computational creativity.

4.6 BACON

BACON.3 (Langley, 1981) is a production system[3] aimed at data-driven discovery of physical laws. Named after the philosopher of science Sir Francis Bacon (1561-1626), the system applies principles in the spirit of his beliefs. Bacon thought that when one has gathered enough data, its regularities will *leap out* at the observer (Langley, 1981). In a similar manner, BACON.3 aims to see regularities in its data, and develop its observations based on these regularities. According to his author, BACON.3 has rediscovered Kepler's law of planetary motion, the ideal gas law, Ohm and Coulomb's laws, the pendulum and constant acceleration laws of Galileo. It is important to observe that there is quantitative data which can be given to the system as input data for these regularities to be observed, until a law it is deduced.

Unlike its predecessor BACON.1 (Langley, 1978) and allegedly more successful because of it, BACON.3 doesn't make a sharp distinction between data and hypotheses. BACON.3 allows hypotheses which aim at explaining data to be used as data themselves, thus allowing for different levels of description. Thus regularities observed in description at one level (which are equivalent to hypotheses) become descriptive clusters at a higher level.

BACON.5 on the other hand (Langley et al., 1981) also implements a simple form of reasoning by analogy, in order to make the discovery of laws containing symmetric forms easier. With BACON.5 the following laws were rediscovered: conservation of momentum, Snail's law of refraction, Joule's formulation of conservation of energy and Black's specific heat law.

4.7 Magic trick making

Williams and McOwan (Williams & McOwan, 2014) provide computational tools for magic trick making, or assistance with magic trick making. Magic tricks generally rely on perceptual errors and illusions, thus Williams and McOwan use in their systems experimentally derived perceptual and cognitive data, together with mathematical principles, in order to create and optimize magic tricks.

---

[3] Production systems generally consist of a set of facts, a collection of productions (rules) and an algorithm for producing new facts from the old. Rules generally fire when their preconditions are fulfilled by a subset of the elements in working memory.

Genetic algorithms[4] are used to evolve solutions which satisfy psychophysical constraints known from empirical literature, thus optimizing the trick in order to make it more compelling for human perception. Two case studies are approached in order to exemplify their methodology — a magical jigsaw and a mind reading card effect.

For example, in the magic jigsaw shown in Fig. 4.1, printed graphic elements (*"spells"* between the hands) appear and disappear depending on how the given jigsaw is constructed and reconstructed. Thus if on the left side we can see twelve such *"spells"* between the twelve pairs of hands, the rearrangement on the right side only shows ten such spells, whereas the spells between two pairs of hands have disappeared.

The jigsaw is based on The Principle of Concealed Distribution (Gardner, 2014): segments of one shape (part of the original elements) are redistributed amongst the other elements (which are part of the remaining elements in the jigsaw reconstruction).

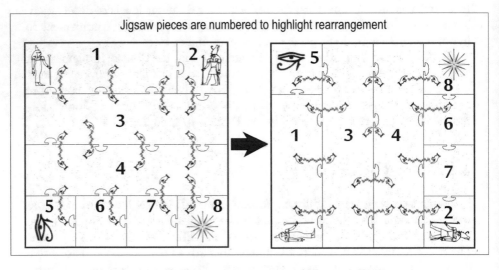

Fig. 4.1: Magic jigsaw — courtesy of Howard Williams

The computational optimization of this magic trick takes into account psychological observations, like the threshold of length increase detection available to humans for rectangles, the number of jigsaw pieces that can be prac-

---

[4] Genetic algorithms mimic processes observed in natural evolution. Generally, a group of individuals are created randomly from a population. Then, an evaluation function provided by the programmer is used to evaluate each individual's fitness. Individuals with high scores on such fitness functions are allowed to reproduce. In each generation the offspring might be made to experience various mutations. Thus processes of selection, mutation, inheritance and recombination are used with the goal of solving a problem.

tically assembled, and the number of easily countable rectangles. The mind reading card effect[5] is similarly created, using psychological observation on likeable cards, and cognitive visibility of mobile phone gimmick prop.

The tricks so created are then evaluated in empirical settings, in qualitative studies (by asking the participants to describe how the trick worked, or asking the participants viewing the trick to select words to describe their reaction), and via public performances.

As can be seen from the above short descriptions, computational creativity systems have been engineered in a wide variety of domains, and employ multiple approaches. How are such systems evaluated, and how is human creativity is evaluated? This question is the topic of the next chapter.

---

[5] This mind reading card trick is available as an app called Phoney in the Google Play Store.

5

Two Types of Evaluation: Human Creativity, Computational Creativity

One cannot talk about creativity without discussing the way creativity can be evaluated. In the following, two views on evaluation of creativity will be explored. One deals with the evaluation of creativity in humans via empirical means, mainly through the use of creativity tests. The other describes recent work on constructing forms of evaluation for computational creativity systems.

5.1 Creativity Testing for Human Participants

Creativity is an inherently hard thing to measure in humans, as we have no complete definitions of it. However, empirical tests for measuring creativity do exist. In the following chapter, some of the most important such tests are presented, and what they measure is discussed. These tests are:
- The Alternative Uses Test
- The Torrance Tests of Creative Thinking (TTCT)
- Riddles
- The Remote Associates Test and
- Empirical Insight Tests

The Alternative Uses Test

Set a countdown timer at 2 minutes, and get a pen and a piece of paper. Ready? What kind of uses can you think of for a *string*? Start the timer, and start talking, or writing the uses you come up with.

This is the Alternative Uses Test (Guilford, 1967), developed by J.P. Guilford, and it involves the procedure mentioned above: participants are given an everyday object (for example *a Brick*), and a certain amount of time (generally between 1 and 3 minutes) to think of as many possible uses for that object as they can come up with.

For example, for *Brick*, one could come up with some of the following uses:

© Springer Nature Switzerland AG 2020

A.-M. Olteţeanu, *Cognition and the Creative Machine*,

https://doi.org/10.1007/978-3-030-30322-8_5

1) *to build houses with*;
2) *to draw on the pavement*;
3) *as a paperweight*;
4) *to stop a car from rolling downwards*;
5) *to stop a door from closing*;
6) *to build a toy tower with*;
7) *to smash in martial arts*;
8) *to climb on and become taller*;
9) *around a fire*;
10) *to hit a nail with*;
11) *to press a newspaper with, etc.*

After the allocated time to give uses for an object has expired, the procedure is repeated with another object.

This test is assumed to measure divergent thinking (the ability to diverge from subjectively familiar uses and think of other uses), and is normally graded across four different dimensions:

- **Fluency** – the number of uses the participant can come up with. For example, the Fluency score of the example above is 11;
- **Flexibility** – the number of conceptual domains the answers relate to (e.g. tools, accessories, musical instruments are different domains) or the number of distinctly conceptually different uses that the answers relate to. In the example above, to the stimulus *Brick*, the answers *"as a paperweight"* and *"to press a newspaper with"* would together receive the Fluency score 2, as they are different answers, but the Flexibility score 1, as they represent more or less the same use;
- **Originality** or **Novelty**. **Originality** is a measure of how uncommon the uses are, as compared to the uses other participants came up with. For example if only 5% of participants come up with the use *A brick can be used around a fire*, that use can be considered original; if only 1% of participants come up with a use, that can be considered highly original. **Novelty** an the other hand is measured through the assessment of human judges - that is human judges will rate on a scale, let us say from 1 to 7, how Novel they consider a particular use to be;
- **Elaboration** – a measure of how detailed these answers are (though one can see how there is a trade-off between Fluency – coming up with many different uses – and Elaboration – coming up with them fully formed).

This is a task no classical AI classical system has previously attempted to model. One way of thinking of it is that it asks participants to come up with new affordances for objects, besides the traditional affordances they would normally think of.

The term *affordance* was coined by James J. Gibson (J. J. Gibson, 1977) to represent *"action possibilities available in the environment to an individual, independent of the individual's ability to perceive this possibility"* (McGrenere & Ho, 2000), and later developed and further studied in James J. Gibson and

Eleanor J. Gibson's books (J. J. Gibson, 1979; E. J. Gibson & Pick, 2000). For example, for James J. Gibson, a horizontal, flat, extended and rigid surface may afford support for a particular actor, but not for another, because of different weight and size. More recently, an affordance has been defined in the human computer interaction community as *"a relationship between the properties of an object and the capabilities of the agent that determine just how the object could possibly be used"* (Norman, 2013). Norman's use of the term refers thus centers around *perceived affordances*, referring to how objects suggest they may be interacted with, and thus to practical design problems. For example, the size and shape of a door handle make it great for pressing or turning by humans, and it matches their past experience with similar objects.

The Alternative Uses Test starts from the assumption that being able to use an object in more than just its traditional setting is a function of creative cognition. The creative skill emphasized by the Alternative Uses Test is thus the ability to creatively infer new affordances about known objects.

The Torrance Tests of Creative Thinking (TTCT)

Let us say that you were given the drawing in Fig. 5.1a and asked to complete it. How would you go about performing this task, and what would that say about your creative ability?

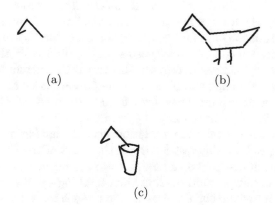

(a)   (b)

(c)

Fig. 5.1: Incomplete figure in the style of TTCT figures with two possible answers.

Figs. 5.1b and 5.1c show two possible answers. This type of task is part of the battery of Torrance Tests of Creative Thinking (TTCT), developed by Ellis Paul Torrance. TTCT has two main components: TTCT-Verbal and

TTCT-Figural (Torrance, 1998a, 1998b; Torrance & Ball, 1998; Torrance, 1998c, 1998d; Kim, 2006).

The stimuli for TTCT-Verbal are pictures to which people answer in writing in five different types of tasks:

- **ask-and-guess** – the participant is supposed to ask questions based on the drawings on a page. Meant to reveal the participant's ability to notice what is indiscernible by looking at the picture, and ask questions to fill in gaps of knowledge;
- **guessing causes and consequences** – the participant is required to make guesses on causes and consequences of things in the drawing. Meant to reveal ability for causal reasoning.
- **product improvement** – the participant things of ways to improve a product – for example if the participant is a child, they are asked to think of ways in which they could change a toy in order to make it more fun to play with;
- **unusual uses** – similar to Guildford's Alternative Uses test – the participant is asked to come up with as many uses as possible for various objects;
- **just suppose** – the participant is asked to suppose that an improbable situation is happening, and predict possible outcomes and consequences.

TTCT-Figural consists of three different types of tasks:

- **picture construction** – participants are given a shape (looking like a pear or jellybean) as a stimulus and asked to construct a picture which includes the shape;
- **picture completion** – a set of 10 incomplete figures is given to the participants, which must make of it an object or a picture;
- **repeated figures** (lines and circles) – the participants are given pages of lines or circles which they must use as part of objects or their picture.

One of the most interesting parts of this test is the incomplete figure test. This is not a test of image completion in the Gestaltist sense, as the picture presented is never only a few lines away from pattern completion, but rather requires quite a lot of elaboration to be "completed".

It is also not clear what the correlation between having a higher drawing skill and scoring well at this test is, or whether part of the deployed creative intelligence does not also rely on a mix of motor intelligence and drawing skill - like drawing something around the line, then checking again what object could be constructed out of the current drawing, in a much more interactive process than simply "seeing" with immediacy what bigger picture the part could belong to. Obviously, the solution set is rather unconstrained in this test, unlike in some creative or insight problems, where one has to navigate constraints to find a very unlikely but only possible solution, given the resources or objects at hand.

The Verbal TTCT is scored on Fluency, Flexibility and Originality. The Figural TTCT is scored on five subscales:

- **Fluency**, representing the number of ideas produced;

- **Originality**, a statistical measure of infrequent or unique ideas;
- **Elaboration**, showing ability to develop or detail ideas;
- **Abstractness of titles**, scale relying on the premise that creativity and abstractness go hand in hand and
- **Resistance to premature closure**. This relies on the premise that creativity is linked to personality traits of open-mindedness, and to cognitive abilities to consider large and various amounts and types of information before closing in on the solution.

Riddles

Though no comprehensive set of riddles test exists, performance on riddles has been used to study or enhance creative problem-solving skills (Whitt & Prentice, 1977; Qiu et al., 2008). Answering riddles correctly and even being informed of the answer to a riddle the solution of which eluded the solver can trigger flash of insight effects.

Different types of riddles exist, depending on the process and resources required to solve them. One categorisation system splits them into two types – enigmas and conundra. Enigmas are the riddles which are phrased in metaphorical or allegorical language, thus requiring a form of what we could call metaphorical reverse-engineering from the part of the solver. The conundra type of riddles involve punning, for example word play in which the words can have double meaning.

Example of conundra, that is language based riddles, are the following:

- *What gets wetter as it dries?*[1];
- *What is greater than God, more evil than the devil, poor people have it, rich people need it, and if you eat it, you will die?*[2]

Some examples of enigmas, which require metaphorical reverse engineering, are the following:

- *Which creature has one voice and yet becomes four-footed and two-footed and three-footed?*[3]
- *There are two sisters: one gives birth to the other and she, in turn, gives birth to the first. Who are the two sisters?*[4]
- *A box without hinges, key or lid, yet golden treasure inside is hid. What is it?*[5]

Other types of riddle categorisation exist, however following the categorisation system mentioned above, the riddles which we find the most interesting and characteristic of the riddle genre are the ones from the enigma category.

---

[1] Answer: *A towel.*

[2] Answer: *nothing.*

[3] The first riddle of the Sphinx to Oedipus. The answer is *a human*, who crawls on all fours as a baby, then walks on two feet as an adult, then has three "feet" when using a walking stick as an elder.

[4] The second riddle of the Sphinx to Oedipus. The answer is *day and night.*

[5] From Tolkein - The Hobbit; Answer: *egg.*

The Remote Associates Test

The Remote Associates Test (Mednick & Mednick, 1971) is a creativity test aimed to measure ability to use associates to come up with an answer. The Remote Associates Test is administered as follows: the participant receives three words, like MANNERS, ROUND AND TENNIS, and is required to come up with a forth word that connects with each of them. In this example, a correct answer is TABLE, with the three connections being TABLE MANNERS, ROUND TABLE and TABLE TENNIS.

Here are other RAT questions examples:
- FISH MINE RUSH[6]
- DEW COMB BEE[7]
- SENSE COURTESY PLACE[8]

You might find this test hard to answer if English is not your native language. The Remote Associates Test cannot be translated directly into other languages, as it depends on existing structures within the language. Some items might be translatable, but most need adaptation, or need to be generated from scratch. For example, a RAT query in Italian, like ERBA, SPINATO, DIRETTO (GRASS, BARBED, DIRECT), has the answer FILO (WIRE, because in the context of grass, *filo* means the equivalent of *blade* (thus yielding *grass blade*), while in the context of *direct* it means the equivalent of *line* (thus yielding *direct line*).

The RAT starts from the premise that *association* is used in creativity, and that the ability to make associates between remote concepts across wide domains shows a higher degree of creative ability. This test measures the performance of the solvers in terms of response times and percentage of queries solved. The Remote Associates Test will be further discussed in Chap. 9.

Empirical Insight tests

Various empirical insight tests exists. However, depending on the type of knowledge they elicit, they can be split into various categories. Such categories include: mathematical insight problems, verbal insight problems, spatial insight problems and practical object insight problems. In the following, we will give examples of problems in each of the first three categories:

1. Mathematical insight problem
Which would be worth more, a pound of 10 dollar pure gold coins or half a pound of 20 dollar pure gold coins; or would they be worth the same? Explain your answer. (Dow & Mayer, 2004)

---

[6] Answer: *gold*
[7] Answer: *honey*
[8] Answer: *common*

2. Spatial insight problem

Given Fig. 5.2a, without lifting your pencil from the paper, show how you could join all 4 dots with 2 straight lines.

Given Fig. 5.2b, without lifting your pencil from the paper, show how you could join all 9 dots with 4 straight lines.

(Solutions are provided in Fig. 5.3.)

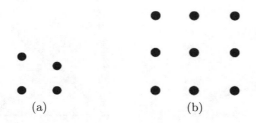

(a)   (b)

Fig. 5.2: The (a) four dots and (b) nine dots problems

3. Verbal insight problem

The legendary runner Flash Fleetfoot was so fast that his friends said he could turn off the light switch and jump into bed before the room got dark. On one occasion Flash proved he could do it. How?

The solutions for these problems are the following:

1. A pound of gold is worth more than half a pound of gold. The insight here is to use gold as the comparison unit, rather than dollars.

2. Drawing an answer to this problem requires exiting the imaginary space created by the four dots, like in Fig. 5.3a, or the nine dots, like in Fig. 5.3b. Sometimes, these problems are given with a box contour around the dots, to make the insight (of literally exiting the box) even harder. A solution for joining all the dots with 3 straight lines also exists for the 9 dots problem.

3. He went to bed during the day. This problem relies on the bias that solvers would assume *jumping into bed* refers to going to bed at night.

Some empirical insight problems can be called object problems or practical insight problems, due to their use of objects and object affordance in their formulation and solving. Some such problems are the candle problem (Duncker, 1945) and the two strings problem (Maier, 1931). These will be presented and discussed in Chap. 11.

When solving insight problems, human participants sometimes encounter functional fixedness (Adamson, 1952; Arnon & Kreitler, 1984), that is a cognitive bias which limits the solver to only seeing one way or a few ways of solving the problem, and persisting in attempting these solutions, while being unable to create new solutions. In terms of object problems for example, the participant would mostly be drawn to using an object in one particular way which might be traditional, or very familiar to the participant. This generally prevents participants from using objects (be it concrete or abstract) for atypical functions, and thus solving such insight problems. Functional fixedness has been shown to affect solvers from technologically sparse cultures as well (German & Barrett, 2005). Some authors compare fixedness in approaching the problem with getting stuck in a mental rut (S. M. Smith, 1995).

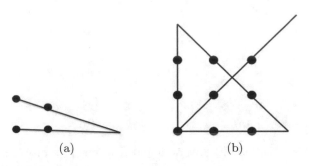

(a)   (b)

Fig. 5.3: The (a) four dots and (b) nine dots problems solved

5.2 Creativity Evaluation in Computational Creativity Systems

Now that we've seen some of the ways in which human creativity is assessed empirically, how are computational creativity systems which produce artefacts, like the ones in Chap. 4, evaluated?

Various attempts at and theories about assessing creativity in computational systems exist. In the following, an overview of four such systems of evaluation is presented:

(i) Wiggins's model of the universe of possibilities and transformational creativity;
(ii) Ritchie's typicality criteria and the inspiring set;
(iii) process, novelty and quality based evaluation in the work of Pease, Winterstein and Colton and
(iv) the FACE and IDEA descriptive models.

Wiggins's Model of the Universe of Possibilities and Transformational Creativity

As mentioned in Sect. 2.1, Boden differentiated between combinatorial, exploratory and transformational creativity (and between historical and psychological creativity), and while she exemplified, she never formalized these differences. Wiggins (Wiggins, 2006) proposes a model for the description, analysis and comparison of creative systems, starting to formalize Boden's descriptive hierarchy of creative processes. In order to proceed to such a formalization, he defines the notions of *creative system*, *creative behaviour*, *novelty* and *value* as follows:

- **Creative system** – A collection of processes, natural or automatic, which are capable of achieving or simulating behaviour which in humans would be deemed creative.
- **Creative behaviour** – One or more of the behaviours exhibited by a *creative system*.
- **Novelty** – The property of an artefact (abstract or concrete) that is the output of a *creative system* which arises from prior non-existence of like or identical artefacts in the context in which the artefact is produced.
- **Value** – The property of an artefact (abstract or concrete) that is the output of a *creative system* which renders it desirable in the context in which it is produced.

This definition of the creative system aims to circumvent the fact that humans are considered capable of creativity, while machines performing similar feats might encounter more scepticism and criticism before being deemed *"creative"*. Such scepticism may partly be supported by the fact that it is easier to understand creative processes when these have been computationally implemented. Therefore, some of the critics of computational creativity might view computationally implemented processes as less creative simply because they are easier to define than the ones performed by humans.

Wiggins's definition of Novelty can be seen as one centered on the production process. Thus the creative system which produces an artefact is supposed to produce it in a context in which no identical or "like" artefacts are produced. The "like" part is hard to assess in this context. -Similarity of what kind and what degree would be deemed to present a lack of novelty? It is known that clusters of similar but varied artefacts might in some cases be an exhibit of creativity in themselves – like for example the musical form of theme and variations, in which musical material from the theme is repetead in varied forms and with varied changes.

Wiggins's notion of Value adds a socio-economical component to creative products. This definition of Value can be compared to a definition of Usefulness in the context of creative problem solving.

After defining this terminology, Wiggins proceeds to define U as a universe of possibilities which contains all possible non-identical concepts. This universe of concepts is multidimensional, and contains both concrete and abstract concepts. Wiggins aims his proposal of $\mathscr{U}$ to be compatible to a state-space interpretation. Thus Boden's conceptual spaces are defined as $\mathscr{C}$, non-strict subsets of $\mathscr{U}$. No $\mathscr{C}$ can be equal to $\mathscr{U}$ as this would make transformational creativity unnecessary. Wiggins then defines $\mathscr{R}$ as the set of rules which constrains the space, and $\mathscr{T}$ as the set of rules which allows for the traversal of this space (i.e. a search strategy). Thus $\mathscr{R}$ represents the type of artefact to be created, while $\mathscr{T}$ is the way in which an artifact is produced by an agent.

Wiggins further defines $\mathscr{E}$ as a set of rules which allows evaluation. While not defining the work of $\mathscr{E}$, Wiggins then characterizes exploratory and transformational systems under this notation. Furthermore, he introduces the idea of unreachable concepts. Thus given $\mathscr{C}$, a concept $c \in \mathscr{C}$ might be unreachable – depending on the traversal strategy $\mathscr{T}$ which is being used. In Wiggins's account, traversal strategies are *dependent upon the properties of a given creator*. A discussion on changing the traversal strategy itself ($\mathscr{T}$ to $\mathscr{T}'$) prompts the author to consider Boden's boundary between exploratory and transformational creativity as ill-defined. Wiggins then proposes as interesting future work the stufy of the changes that happen in the rules of evaluation ($\mathscr{E}$), which might lead to adopting different constraints for artefacts ($\mathscr{R}$).

Wiggins offers a new definition of transformational creativity as acting at the meta-level of representation. He then uses this theoretical framework to propose how implementations and their properties could be described (and in a sense evaluated).

Ritchie's Typicality Criteria and the Inspiring Set

A way of assessing creativity which takes into account the *inspiring set* has been proposed by (Ritchie, 2001). An *inspiring set* is for Ritchie the union of explicit and implicit knowledge which is to guide the construction of the creative program. The process of program construction can then be viewed as a mapping from the inspiring set to a program. Such a program generally contains a generating procedure which maps initial data values into a set of basic items.

Ritchie uses then these formal definitions to propose fourteen criteria of assessing creativity, mainly in terms of typicality, quality and novelty.

Ritchie's criteria are the following:
1. Average typicality
2. The ratio of typical results to all results
3. Average quality
4. The ratio of good results to all results
5. The ratio of good typical results to all results
6. The ratio of good atypical results to all results
7. The ratio of good atypical results to atypical results
8. The ratio of good atypical results to good typical results
9. The ratio of results in the inspiring set to the inspiring set
10. The ratio of all results to the results in the inspiring set
11. Average typicality of new results
12. Average quality of new results
13. The ratio of typical new results to new results
14. The ratio of good results to results

These criteria are then further implemented in the evaluation of a poem generator (Wasp), a conceptual blender (Divago) and a sentence paraphraser (Dupond) by Pereira et al. (Pereira, Mendes, Gervás, & Cardoso, 2005).

Process, Novelty and Quality based Evaluation - Pease, Winterstein and Colton

Pease, Winterstein and Colton (Pease, Winterstein, & Colton, 2001) propose an evaluation of creativity which takes into account the input, output and process by which the output is achieved by the creative system. Using Ritchie's definition of an inspiring set, Pease et al. propose methods for creativity evaluation. These methods are related to novelty, quality and process.

Different types of novelty are considered, and measures proposed to deal with them:
- Novelty relative to a body of knowledge (e.g. a concept space) – a *transformation measure* is proposed
- Novelty relative to complexity – a *complexity measure* is proposed
- Novelty relative to an archetype – an *archetypal measure* is proposed
- Novelty as surprise – a *surprise measure* is proposed
- Perceived novelty – a *perceived novelty measure* is proposed
  The following types of quality factors and measures are proposed:
- Quality relative to emotional response – an *emotional response* measure is proposed, depending on intensity and type of such a response
- Quality relative to aim – a *pragmatic measure* is proposed

In terms of process, a measure of *randomness* is proposed. Evaluation in general is considered to be bipartite by Pease, Winterstein and Colton: they posit that part of the evaluation should deal with the *created artefact*, while part should deal with *the process of creating* the artefact. Thus, they propose an *evaluation of item* measure and an *evaluation of process* measure.

The FACE and IDEA Descriptive Models

The FACE and IDEA descriptive models where introduced by Colton, Pease and Charnley (Colton, Pease, & Charnley, 2011) as a computational creativity theory contribution inspired by the goals of giving a rigorous, computationally detailed and plausible account. These models are aimed at describing software, with no claims that they might have value in describing human behaviour.

In order to understand the FACE model, which describes creative acts, one needs to first take into account the terminology of the authors. Thus Colton, Pease and Charnley define:
(i) a *concept* as an executable program which can take input and produce output[9];
(ii) an *expression* of a concept is an instance of an input-output pair which results from executing a concept's program;
(iii) an *aesthetic measure* is a function of a concept-expression pair which outputs a real value between 0 and infinity and

---

[9] This is thus a very different use of the word *concept* than that presented by cognitive science, in which concepts are mental categories used to group objects, events and information.

(iv) *framing information* is natural language text comprehensible by people, which adds value to a generative act – for example a text which puts the item in cultural and historical context, or describes processes underlying generative acts.

Under FACE, a singular creative act is described as a a finite ordered list of generative acts. This list must contain at least one generative act[10], and will contain exactly zero or one instance of each of the following eight types:

The eight types of generative acts are:

1. E^g - an expression of a concept;
2. E^p - a method for generating expressions of a concept;
3. C^g - a concept;
4. C^p - a method for generating concepts;
5. A^g - an aesthetic measure;
6. A^p - a method for generating aesthetic measures;
7. F^g - an item of framing information and
8. F^p - a method for generating framing information.

The g and p superscripts differentiate between *ground* and *process* level acts. $\langle F^g, A^g, C^g, E^g \rangle$ denotes a creative act described by a 4-tuple of generative acts.

Colton, Pease and Charnley propose to use the FACE model in a variety of ways. A quantitative way to use it might be to compare the volume of creative acts between creative systems. A cumulative way might evaluate creative acts which produce an aesthetic and framing as more creative than the ones which only produce concepts and expressions. A comparative way would include orderings in which taking some generative act is seen as more creative than another, etc.

The IDEA model replaces the notion of value of solutions with that of impact of creations made by a computational creativity system. The IDEA model stands for an (I)terative (D)evelopment-(E)xecution-(A)ppreciation cycle, which includes the steps of engineering the system and its exposure to an ideal audience. Six stages of development are suggested. These depend on the difference between the knowledge information given to the system and the artefacts it generates. Two thresholds are used - a lower threshold which denotes too much similarity between given examples and generated artefacts, and an upper bound threshold which denotes too high dissimilarity which makes assessment impossible because of too little context. These stages are: (i) Developmental stage; (ii) Fine-tuned stage; (iii) Re-invention stage; (iv) Discovery stage; (v) Disruption stage and (vi) Disorientation stage.

Using a human assessment based on well-being (indicating liking or disliking) and cognitive effort, the IDEA model describes measures of disgust, divisiveness, indifference, popularity and provocation for the human assessment stage, followed by measures of the impact of the creative acts based

---

[10] In the definition of the authors, creative sets are non-empty set tuples of generative acts.

on provocation. These measures aimed to assess types of impact like: *acquired taste, instant appeal, opinion splitting, opinion forming, shock, subversion* and *triviality*. Thus the model defines *impact* as any other measure achieved than triviality.

These FACE and IDEA models were used by the authors to exemplify a comparison of mathematical invention and visual art computational creativity systems (like AM (Lenat, 1976), HR (Colton, 2012a), AARON (Cohen, 1995), the Painting Fool (Colton, 2012b), NEvAR (Machado & Cardoso, 2000)). These models were later used to build a poetry-based generation system which can be evaluated using all the FACE metrics (Colton et al., 2012).

5.3 Summary of Part I

In light of the literature examined in this part, the following points emerge as being of major importance when aiming to study, model or implement creative problem solving:

(a) Elaborating the definition of problem solving as to include creative problem solving processes;

(b) Developing unified cognitive frameworks, in which various different types of creative problem solving tasks can be analysed;

(c) The ability to implement types of knowledge representation which enable creative processes similar to those of humans, like association and restructuring;

(d) From a methodological perspective, the ability to evaluate artificial creative problem solving systems using tools comparable to those used to evaluate creativity in human cognition.

Here is why these are important.

Creativity and problem solving are often addressed separately in the cognitive and artificial intelligence literature, as seen in Sects. 2.1 and 2.2. The classical (AI) definition of problem solving needs to be updated to include the cognitive processes of creativity, and explain the phenomena of insightful problem solving (described in Sects. 2.3 and 2.4). As most problems in the world are ill-structured, a wider definition of problem solving should include the step from ill-structured to well-structured problems before proceeding to account for the classical problem-solving steps.

Because of the interplay between knowledge organization and process explained in Chap. 3, both knowledge representation and process have to be tackled together in an account of creative problem solving.

The field of computationally creative systems has started gaining considerable traction (Chap. 4), thus providing a great playground for computational models of creativity. However, current computational creativity systems do not have as a priority the modeling of cognitive processes. More cognitively inspired computational creativity systems are necessary, to help the further understanding of (human) cognitive creativity, and to provide the computational tools required to study it.

Multiple accounts of diverse creative cognitive processes exist. Ideally, we should move towards the level of unified cognitive theoretical frameworks. That is design frameworks which allow the possibility of building multiple systems, in which various types of creative problem-solving tasks can be studied (like the ones described in the human evaluation Sect. 5.1). Moreover, such a unified view should include the ability to study creative problem solving in a variety of modalities, because of the interesting roles visuospatial intelligence might play in creativity, as described in Sect. 2.5.

A cognitive systems implementation of such knowledge organization and creative process has to also take into consideration the various types of process which seem relevant to creative cognition - including association, use of structure and similarity, and re-representation, as shown in Chap. 3.

Finally, different types of evaluation are currently deployed to human participants (like the in creativity tests described in Sect. 5.1) as compared to computational creativity systems (Sect. 5.2). An approach aiming to be of use to both AI and cognitive empirical studies would need to implement a type of evaluation closer to human creativity evaluation for the cognitive systems it yields, but to which computational creativity types of evaluation might still be relevant. How can all these themes be integrated? How could an approach which benefits both AI and cognitive empirical exploration look like? A possible answer is proposed in part II.

Part II

One Ring to Creatively Solve Them All? In
Search of a Unified Cognitive Framework

As seen in part one, multiple strands need integrating in order to bring together (i) the topics of *creativity* and *problem solving*, and (ii) the disciplines of *human* and *computational* creativity. Besides this, creativity and creative problem solving refer to a multiplicity of tasks and processes, from coming up with new uses for objects, solving riddles to insight. A unified framework needs to find a way to tackle such tasks in a congruent, coherent manner. A unified framework should propose mechanisms which can lead to the solving of such a wide variety of tasks. For example, such a framework should allow for visuospatial intelligence to play a role in creative problem solving. And it should make something of the relationship between knowledge representation and process, which we discussed to be important. How is this possible, and more importantly, can it be done?

The part two of this book will focus on synthesizing, and finding a form to integrate all these principles in a framework. At the center of this integration we will aim to keep the idea that knowledge organization might highly influence the types of processes which are possible.

Here is a short summary of what each of the next three chapters builds towards this integration.

- **Chapter 6 – Cogs of a Framework** – pulls together the aspects which are desirable for an integrated approach to creative problem solving. First, how can we account for the transition from ill-structured to well-structured problem solving? This chapter starts by putting forward a definition of problem solving which allows for the transition from ill-structured to well-structured problem solving, and for creative problem solving in general. If one were to pick tasks as diverse as possible before setting on designing a general framework of creative problem solving, what would these tasks be? A variety of tasks which could be used to stretch the capabilities of a unified framework are explored in the rest of this chapter.

- **Chapter 7 – CreaCogs — A clockwork view of creativity** – looking at such diverse tasks as the ones proposed before, is there any way of seeing them as a coherent set? This chapter starts proposing a solution, by building a view on how creative problem solving can be seen. A metaphor is put forward to view the relationship between creative processes and knowledge representation. This metaphor, in which representations are seen as cogs in a creative machine, leads us to set up a theoretical framework in which knowledge representation supports creative processes. The way the various tasks proposed in the previous chapter would be solved in such a framework are theoretically explored.

- **Chapter 8 – The Cogs in motion — Navigating the knowledge in CreaCogs** – The types of mechanisms which can be instantiated in the CreaCogs framework are explored, and partially formalized. Multiple examples of how the knowledge organization in CreaCogs can support a diverse set of creative processes are given.

Some of the topics in this part have also been explored by the author in (Olteţeanu, 2016; Olteţeanu, 2014).

6

Gathering the Cogs of a Framework

A framework in which creative problem solving can be studied in a more general manner needs to take into account a set of factors:

(i) **Unification and Diversity** – the framework should aim to account for a diverse group of creative problem-solving tasks, and support the implementation of various systems under the same set of principles – this is related to Newell's concept of unified frameworks (Newell, 1994).

(ii) **Multimodality** – the framework should aim to account for creative problem solving in a multi-modal manner. For example, the processes which are used to explain and implement creative problem solving should have application both to visuospatial as well as linguistic stimuli.

(iii) **Cognitive Comparability of Process and Sparsity** – the framework should be based on a limited small set of processes, for which some cognitive comparative counterpart can be assumed. According to our investigation in previous chapters, some processes which would have such cognitive comparability should involve association, similarity, and the ability to structure and restructure the problem space.

(iv) **Cognitive Comparability of Results** – systems implemented under this framework should give comparable results to human answers in empirical creativity tests as to allow further development of hypotheses about creative process. And,

(v) **Computational Comparability and Evaluation** – systems should provide results which can be assessed in computational terms and compared with other computational creativity frameworks.

How diverse could a group of creative problem solving tasks be, and still manage to remain coherent? This question is the focus of the chapter. Before attempting an answer, it is worth having another look at the classical definition of problem solving, and making room for it to include creative processes as well.

© Springer Nature Switzerland AG 2020
A.-M. Oltețeanu, *Cognition and the Creative Machine*,
https://doi.org/10.1007/978-3-030-30322-8_6

6.1 Creative Problem Solving Redefined

The classical definition of problem solving presupposes an orderly initial state of the problem, and a corresponding problem space. This problem space includes all the states in which the problem can be put via operators, or moves acting on the existing state. However, we know that creative problem solving generally allows us to see a problem in new ways. This seeing a problem in new ways could be described as creative problem solving leading us to new "initial states". Some such new initial states are productive – that is they allow us to solve the problem, or to see with much more ease a path to the solution.

It may be that having a well defined initial state is a reflection of a well-structured problem. As problems in the real world are often ill structured, defining the initial state of some problems as well structured might indicate an oversight. It might forgo mentioning a previous but maybe not always entirely conscious step, of "structuring" an unstructured problem into some initial state, which is then perceived as well structured. This initial "structuring" might happen in the mind of the programmer or problem-solver or artificial intelligence scientist, before proposing a well structured problem. It might happen before studying how the solution to such a problem can best be found, or the solving optimized. Thus, this (well structured) initial state already contains all the objects, be it abstract or concrete, necessary to solve the problem, and a structure which is productive.

A revised version of problem solving which includes creative processes,and the tackling of ill-structured problems could look as follows. An initial (ill-structured) problem can be seen as an initial set of features. The goal of the problem, or what it takes to reach a satisfying solution for the problem, might also initially be somewhat ambiguous to the solver.

The problem solver brings an initial set of representations to the solving process. These are the representations in the knowledge base (KB) of the solver. Only a small subset of these representations are initially used in the solving: the ones which (i) the problem solver initially believes apply to the problem, or the ones that (ii) are naturally activated in their mind of the solver by the initial contact with the problem.

The problem solver represents the problem, from the initial set of features, into some initial state. This means interpreting the initial set of features, and translating them into representations of what the objects of the problem are, deciding what the salient or important elements of the problem are, and what the problem actually is. Such steps are a form of structuring the problem which aims to bridge the gap between an ill-structured problem and a well-structured problem, most likely using structured knowledge (and ways of structuring) which are already present in the knowledge base of the solver.

This interpretation/representation yields an initial state, with afferent problem solving operators and paths. Some such operators and paths are the ones afforded by this representation, and might not be immediately visible to the solver. Some depend on the operators known or strongly associated by the problem-solver to the chosen initial state, and its various associated or herein contained representations. From this initial representation and initial state, a set of states (a state space) opens. The next steps are applied as in classical problem solving. If the process is not successful, the problem solver can do various things, including the following

(a) she can *restart at the interpretation step*, that is re-represent features, problem objects, and generally what the problem is;

(b) she can *change currently held representations*, thus changing the knowledge base and structures she uses in structuring the problem and

(c) she can *bring new features in* the problem, in multiple ways - for example by reinterpreting initial features as being some different problem object, by deciding some new problem object which was not salient before is needed to solve the problem, etc.

After the problem has been reinterpreted, or re-represented, the steps posited in classical problem solving can again unfold. Whenever no solution is found, the problem can be reinterpreted or expanded, until a useful initial representation, a productive state space, a better goal definition and/or solving path are found.

A synopsis of the steps of creative problem solving can be seen in Fig. 6.1.

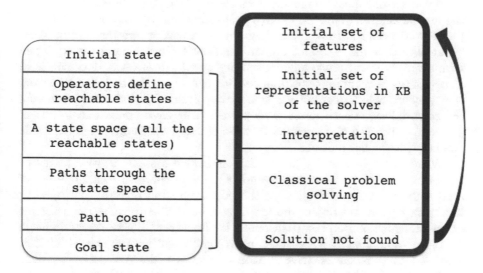

Fig. 6.1: The elements of classical problem solving on the left are integrated in the definition of creative problem solving on the right

6.2 Desiderata for a Framework of Creative Problem Solving

How varied are the tasks that a unified creative problem-solving framework could aim to solve? In this section we will talk about a set of diverse problems, tasks and processes, including visuospatial inference, creative use of affordance, concept generation and structure transfer, insight and re-representation.

6.2.1 Visuospatial Inference

What is visuospatial inference? According to (Sloman, 1971), a rational (but not necessarily logical) process of inference often performed by human beings. Here is an example: Fig. 6.2 depicts a mechanism of pulleys and levers. A human looking at this mechanism, and knowing where in the mechanism the motion is initiated, can infer the way the system will move and what type of motion the end tip of the right lever will perform. Try it for yourself: the arrow in the part (a) of the figure shows how motion starts. Then verify whether it is true that, like in the (b) part of the diagram, the right side of the right level will move downwards.

If you are like most humans, you can imagine the motion passing through the mechanism, and have no trouble confirming the (b) part of the diagram. In fact you would not need this diagram to be sure where the motion goes. What does that tell us about human cognition? That humans are equipped with a variety of inference-making sensory-based processes. It does not seem that such processes are propositional or "logical" in nature, and Sloman argues that they are not. A possibility is that such capacities for inference come from the sensorial experience humans have with their environment, that is from previously observed and encoded features of various natural or human made "objects", and their motion.

What would it take for an artificial cognitive system to solve Sloman's example? A system able to tackle such a domain will need to know types of motion for a variety of objects (in this case levers and pulleys). Then, using this knowledge about object motion, it should be able to somehow assemble or transfer such motion compositionally to the level of the entire mechanism.

Let us now imagine that such an artificial cognitive solver was, in fact, creative. What is the creative version of such a task? A creative problem solving variant is that the solver would receive an incomplete mechanism, and asked to fill in the various parts that are missing. Or that it would be asked to create its own mechanism from a set of parts, given that a certain type of motion was required. For example, like in Fig. 6.3 a creative agent capable of visuospatial inference could be given just the motion input and an expected motion output, and asked to construct a mechanism to produce it, using two of the available parts or more.

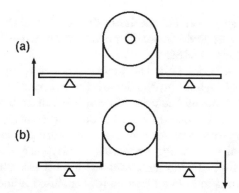

Fig. 6.2: A pulley and levers example from Sloman

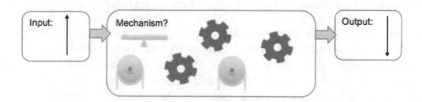

Fig. 6.3: A creative variant of a visuospatial inference task, like the one provided by Sloman

6.2.2 Creative Use of Affordance

Imagine that an agent needs a cup to pour water in, but there is no cup available. What does the agent do? If we are talking about a human, endowed with creative abilities, she might easily replace the missing cup with a bowl, a pot or, depending on how desperate the circumstances are, even a boot. This kind of problem is a problem of creative use of affordance, where affordances are things that can be done with the objects at hand[1].

Problems requiring a creative use of affordance can be generalized, in the physical domain, to the following definition: they are problems in which an agent x requires a specific tool or set of objects o_a to solve a specific problem. However, one of these required objects is not given in the agent's environment. Agent x must thus search the environment (or their own mind) for a creative substitute o_b.

At an abstract level, creative use of affordance reflects the ability of using different concepts which have the affordances you require for the problem at hand, when other concepts are not available or have somehow failed short. For example, the ability to use different constructs or concepts in mathematics to build a proof; the ability to use different words, parts of plot development or

---

[1] For more on the concept of affordances see (J. J. Gibson, 1977).

narrative style to yield a certain aesthetic flavour; the ability to use different experimental tools to study a scientific phenomenon, when the ones you have used before did not give a clear result.

Creative use of affordance in the physical domain, involving objects, is similar to the ability tested empirically by the Alternative Uses Test, when people are asked "Tell me all the uses you can think of for a brick" (previously described in Sect. 5.1). Because of this, introducing creative use of affordance as an ability in a creative problem-solving framework can be very useful possibilities: (i) artificial systems implementing creative use of affordance can be evaluated comparatively to humans, and (ii) hypotheses about how creative use of affordance works in humans can be implemented in models and falsified via computational experimentation.

6.2.3 Concept Generation and Structure Transfer

How are new concepts generated creatively? This question is linked to but doesn't entirely overlap theories of concept formation[2]. However theories of concept formation generally deal with categorization, and how a particular category, which ends up representing a concept (like the concept of *bird*), is parsed, acquired and understood based on experience. For example, if you ask someone to name a bird, they are more likely to name a sparrow than a penguin, therefore prototype theory proposes that some members of a category are more central than others.

Creative concept generation focuses more on the ability to generate new concepts out of new observations or old knowledge[3].

Various ways of generating concepts can be envisaged, however we will focus on only a couple of interesting processes which, if implemented by a framework, would prove headway in the direction of concept generation. For a reminder that concepts are not just equivalent to linguistic terms, but have multisensory flavour, we will stick to the visuospatial domain, and focus on the following processes: a) the use of visual templates and b) concept generation via overlap and synthesis.

a) Use of visual templates

Consider an instance of a *chain* object, like the one depicted in Fig. 6.4. Let us assume that a cognitive agent observing or representing this instance is able to understand its elementary components (the loops) and the relationship between them (a specific type of connectedness).

---

[2] For example prototype theory (Rosch, 1975), exemplar theory (Medin & Shoben, 1988), theory theory (Murphy & Medin, 1985).

[3] For related issues, see concept discovery (Dunbar, 1993), concept combination (Aerts & Gabora, 2005) and concept blending (Fauconnier & Turner, 1998), which are important themes in both cognitive science and computational creativity. The creative concept generation we refer to here is not identical with concept blending (Fauconnier & Turner, 1998), which can be considered a special case of concept generation.

Let us say that two other objects are known to this cognitive agent, which have similar features with the elementary components of the *chain*. These are: a *scissor* (part of its handle is loop like) and a piece of *string* (because its property of being easily twisted, a string can become a loop). Then a creative cognitive system should be able to transfer the specific template of connectedness from the chain object and realize it with the two new objects.

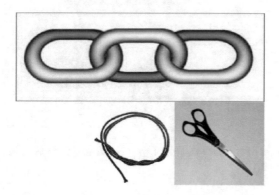

Fig. 6.4: An instance of a chain representation used as a structuring template

b) Concept generation via overlap and synthesis

Imagine that an agent has observed the relationship *bigger than* twice over the same object domain – for example between the trees in Fig. 6.5(a) and then between the trees in Fig. 6.5(b). A new concept, that of *growth*, could be derived if the representations of those instances are overlapped and reinterpreted as in Fig. 6.5(c).

The template of this inferred growth concept could be separated from non-essential features (like the objects to which it applies). The relationships between the object sizes are essential features of the growth concept, and thus part of the template. This template can be transferred to a new set of objects, like the ones in Fig. 6.6. The template can thus be used both to recognize the same relationship between new objects (classification) and to order new objects (productive use).

After being applied to multiple sets of objects, a synthesis of the *growth* concept can be re-represented graphically like in Fig. 6.6(c) in its essential features.

These are but a part of the concept generation mechanisms a creative cognitive system should be able to perform, and more of them will be discussed in Sect. 7.3.3.

As for the process of structure transfer, some of it is already observable in the cases of template transfer explored above. However, a unified framework for creative problem solving should provide types of knowledge organization

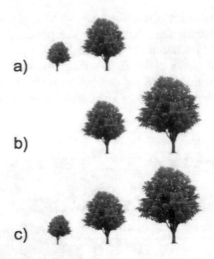

Fig. 6.5: Inference of a new relationship *growth* in c) via overlap of *bigger-than* instances a) and b)

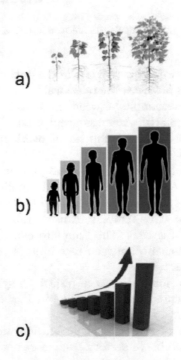

Fig. 6.6: a) to b) Adaptation of the growth template to a new domain; c) synthesis via compression to defining features

and processes which support ampler cases of structure transfer. This is necessary in order to account for processes in which structure transfer is already posited to take place, like making analogies (Gentner, 1983). However, structure transfer is much wider in scope. It is an essential feature necessary for transferring known problem templates to new problem spaces and the use of elements of such problem templates to create new templates. These abilities are necessary in order for creative problem solving to occur.

6.2.4 Insight and Re-Representation

Insight is based around the restructuring and re-representation of a specific problem. Such restructuring makes the problem center on different features, or see existing features in a new way, thus helping solvers look at the problem with a different mental toolset.

For example, think of the matchstick insight problem in Fig. 2.2, which requires the solver to see the signs as modifiable, and the matchsticks as parts which can be used to modify them, changing their meaning. Part of the problem – in this case the mathematical signs – need to be restructured in order for the solution to be possible.

Or take the four dots and nine dots problems from Fig. 5.2. They require the solver to abandon initial parsings of the 4 or 9 dots as a bounding box of the pencil moves, and re-represent the problem as including some of the empty space around the dots, and benefiting from its (to draw on) affordance.

Or take the two strings problem by (Maier, 1931), which is stated as follows: *A person is put in a room that has two strings hanging from the ceiling. The task is to tie the two strings together, but it is impossible to reach one string while holding the other. What can the person do to tie the two strings together?* A depiction of this problem is shown in Fig. 11.3.

The solving of this problem, which you will find in the next chapter, requires the ability of the solver to restructure and re-represent existing objects in the environment.

This makes structured representations and the ability to restructure them essential to the pursuit of modeling creative problem solving and insight in artificial cognitive systems.

Conclusion

Visuospatial inference, creative use of affordance, concept generation and structure transfer, insight and re-representation, these are a very wide variety of tasks, which can be generally assumed to be based on a great amount of participating cognitive processes. Instead of focusing on their differences, however, we will focus on what they might have in common. Such processes must be similar or build on a coherent toolkit, for us to harbour an integrative view of such tasks as creative problem solving. Is there a way to unify such a set of tasks under a common small set of principles, and better yet, under one intuitive metaphorical view of creative problem solving?

CreaCogs – A Clockwork View of Creativity

What would a framework look like, in which all of these tasks, from creative visuospatial inference, to insight problem solving, take place?

Let us return to our simple machines (levers and pulleys) example from the previous chapter, and explain creative visuospatial inference a bit further.

7.1 A Clockwork Metaphor

Creative visuospatial inferences with simple machines and motion

First let us have a look how the visuospatial creative inference variant we built based on Sloman's example can be solved. Say an agent will receive a problem like the one shown in Table 7.1 – Label 1 (L1): the agent is given a set of simple machines (middle rectangle). It is asked to come up with a mechanism which will produce a specific type of motion output (right rectangle), given a specific motion input (left rectangle).

First, the agent will bring with themselves some existing knowledge about motion, parts and mechanisms (Table 7.1 – L2). For example, looking at the parts you were given, you might use your already known mechanism made of two levers and a pulley (Table 7.1 – L3). If you are using this existing knowledge as a structuring device of the problem space, that will make the pulley and lever objects more salient to you (L4). You could try to put together some of these, however, you are missing a lever, therefore cannot reconstitute the mechanism from your existing knowledge in its initial form (L5).

You might attempt to replace the missing lever with other parts, by activating your knowledge of other simple machines (the Existing knowledge field of L6). You might use the motion resulting as an output from the partial match mechanism you created (circled in the Mechanism field of L7) to select applicable object representations from your existing knowledge. If you have triggered multiple such knowledge representations, you could select between them, by matching your knowledge of how motion flows through them to the

© Springer Nature Switzerland AG 2020
A.-M. Olteţeanu, *Cognition and the Creative Machine*,
https://doi.org/10.1007/978-3-030-30322-8_7

end of the partial mechanism you built, and to the output required by the problem. Thus some simple machines from your existing knowledge, like the ones circled in the Existing knowledge field of L7 will match the problem, becoming possible structural parts. You could use either of these parts (that match your existing partial construction and the output), and put together the entire mechanism, the entire chain of simple machine parts, from input to output. This will bring you to a successful conclusion.

However this is not the only possible course of action when given such a problem. You could instead compose from scratch a solution, based on the motion affordances of separate parts. You would thus start from a state similar to that depicted in L8. Then, based on the motion you know is given as the input, you could select a simple machine that matches that motion, like the cog circled in L9. Then you could look at the desired output. Based on the motion you have to obtain at the end (L10), you could select to use a cog a second time (L11). You will then put these two selected cogs in place, and realize that the motion cannot flow between them seamlessly. Thus you will have to fill in this space, circled in the Mechanism field of L12. This you could do again through matching the motion to existing knowledge of mechanism pieces (L13). Finding that another cog could "fill in" this space, you will obtained the mechanism circled in L14, and discard the other objects.

You could also use other known mechanisms to start solving this problem. In the end, whatever parts you use, they will be compositionally equivalent with a lever (L15). That is, the mechanism you will create would have the same input and output as a lever would. If the problem would not have specified a constraint to use two pieces, you could have used a lever to reach the desired output with the given motion input. It is to be expected that, given different sets of simple machines, multiple constructions with the same input and output would be possible, and thus equivalent.

Table 7.1: Creative inference with simple machines step by step.

Label	State
1	

Continued on next page

Table 7.1 *Continued from previous page*

Label	State
2	
3	
4	

Continued on next page

Table 7.1 *Continued from previous page*

Label	State

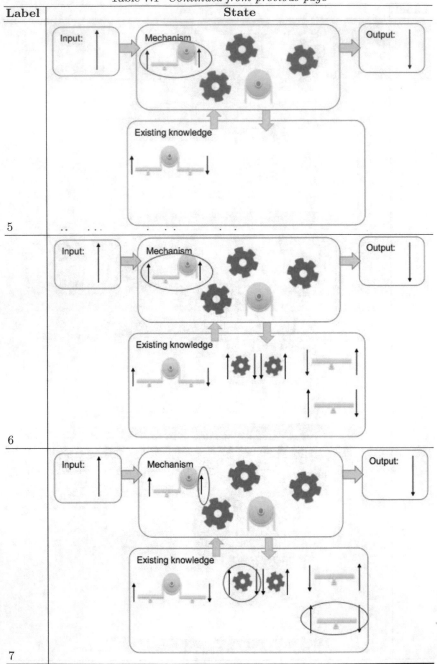

Continued on next page

Table 7.1 *Continued from previous page*

Label	State
8	
9	
10	

Continued on next page

Table 7.1 *Continued from previous page*

Label	State
	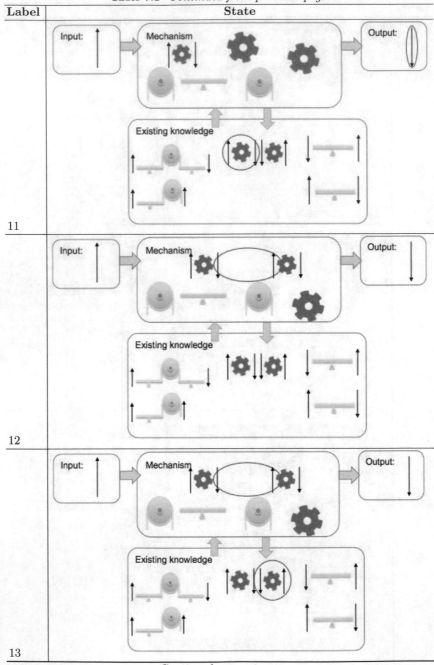
11	
12	
13	

Continued on next page

Table 7.1 *Continued from previous page*

Label	State
	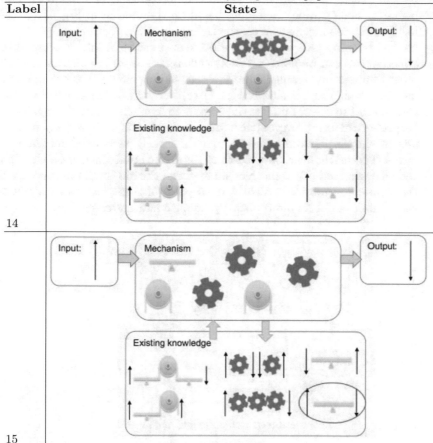
14	
15	

Simple machines principles

What are some of the principles that can be extrapolated from this creative visuospatial inference example? And **how would they look if we applied them to representations, rather than simple machines?**

- **Representation equivalence** – based on affordances. This is the observation that some mechanisms (set of parts or simple machines organized in a specific way) will be equivalent to other mechanisms, in terms of the kind of input and output motion they produce, and thus in terms of the affordance they have as mechanisms. For example, see the two mechanisms in Fig. 7.1(a).
- **Matching** based on affordance – a simple machine (or mechanism) that is needed can be selected based on its input and output motion, or on the

motion exiting from the mechanism that precedes it and has been built before it. For example, matching based on the motion in Fig. 7.1(b) left helps select the mechanism on the right side of the figure.

– **Re-using knowledge and knowledge structure**. A known template of a mechanism can be used to select needed parts from the environment, in order to direct and frame future problem solving efforts. For example, the mechanism at the left side of Fig. 7.1(c) is a knowledge structure which can be used to select and use the three simple machines on the right side.

– **Representation composition and substitution**. Based on motion, sets of simple machines can be compositionally assembled into mechanisms. The mechanism on the left of Fig. 7.1(d) and the cog on the right can be assembled into a mechanism in which the motion flows (because of their matching motion). Also, various parts of these mechanisms can be substituted based on affordance equivalence and matching (a-b).

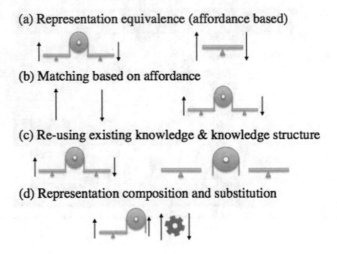

(a) Representation equivalence (affordance based)

(b) Matching based on affordance

(c) Re-using existing knowledge & knowledge structure

(d) Representation composition and substitution

Fig. 7.1: Creative visuospatial inference principles in the simple machines domain

We have thus observed principles that could be applied to solve this class of problems. Why does this matter? Can a connection be established between simple machines and motion on one hand, and solving complex creative problems (like insight problems) and affordance on the other?

The Two Strings Insight Problem and Ways of Solving It

If we think of the simple machines above in a generalized way, as representation parts, and of motion more as affordance, an interesting thing happens. The solving of an insight problem like the two strings problem can be framed in a similar way as that of the creative simple machine motion inference problems we looked at so far. How?

In the two strings problem, you are given as input the various objects in the room – the person, a chair, a jar of nails, pliers, etc. – and their relationships. You are asked to reach the goal of having two strings tied together, with the constraints that the person in the image cannot reach one string while holding on to the other. This can be seen in the top part of Fig. 7.2.

The solver also has access to their existing knowledge about how groups of objects function together, and how they have been previously used (this knowledge of course depends to a certain extent on the solver, and more generally on the culture they come from). We will call these representations of knowledge on groups of objects, interaction and results *knowledge templates* or *problem templates*. Existing knowledge can be seen at the bottom part of Fig. 7.2.

Applying various existing knowledge templates, you can organize the problem objects in different ways. For example, nails might remind you that they can be hammered into the wall. Thus, you might start looking for a hammer. As no hammer is available in the problem, you might then look for an object that can be turned into a hammer. Perhaps you could use the jar or the pliers *as a hammer*, to put the nail into the wall. Doing so will mean that you will bring a hammer, an object which did not previously exist, into the problem space.

You could however access another part of your knowledge, and organize the problem space in a different way. For example, you could remember that pliers can be used for manipulating wires. Strings look a bit like wires, so perhaps you could use these two – pliers and strings – together. Let us say you try to do this – holding the pliers in your hand and reaching for the wires gives you an extra affordance, it lengthens your hand. If your problem was that you could not reach the second string, perhaps now that you are reaching for it with another object, you will be successful. However, seeing the problem (and the pliers) in this way would preclude you from seeing and using the pliers as a weight.

If you would think of the pliers as a weight, and then attach this weight to a string, you could bring a pendulum and its affordances into the problem space. You could then swing the pendulum, setting it in motion, catch one of the strings and wait for the other to come to you (this is, by the way, the classical correct solution to this problem, though when one talks about creative problems, one must be able to be open to the possibility that multiple solutions might be correct).

Other existing knowledge could also be used to organize the objects and direct your problem solving efforts. You might go up on the chair, because this is an affordance that the chair allows. This will make you taller, able to reach higher, and thus able to grab the strings from a different point. This may or may not help in reaching both strings. You could use a combination of the nails, chair and a makeshift hammer, and try to nail one of the strings

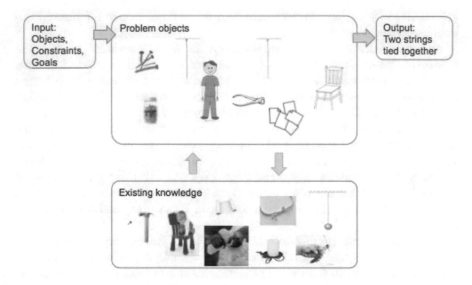

Fig. 7.2: Solving the two strings insight problem

to the ceiling, thus keeping it in place until you grab the other one. You could see the paper and remember its affordance of being rolled – you might then roll the paper in an attempt to make a tube. A tube looks like a string, and could be tied to one, in an effort to elongate one of the strings. You might "zoom in" on the person, realize that they are wearing other objects that you could use, "deconstruct" these objects, and then, for example, fold the shirt to elongate the strings, hoping to reach a configuration in which you can finally tie the strings together.

Various types of what I called problem templates, or even object templates[1] will be used and projected on the existing objects of the problem. This will give rise to various possible problem configurations, in the same way in which projecting known mechanisms onto given simple machines yields different groupings of (subsets of) the same problem elements. While these configurations hold, they might preclude others, and make specific solving paths easier or harder. We will call this problem restructuring.

The insight moment might very well be the moment in which your entire chain of inference snaps into place, and you have an organized set of actions that can take you from the input to the output. It might also be the moment when you discover a missing link in your chain of affordances (or problem solving action plan). Or it might be when you find a new way of seeing the problem under existing or emerging types of problem representation (which allow for new and hopefully productive chains of inference to happen).

---

[1] Knowledge about objects which can be decomposed and recomposed out of other objects.

In the case of the two strings problem, we can see how existing knowledge is thus used to compose a solution, structuring the existing objects, their parts, or grouping them together, deciding which parts are useful and which parts are useless. The objects of the problem (or their parts) can be put together in various ways, using existing knowledge. this sometimes includes creating new objects with new properties out of existing problem elements. It might be that not all such objects need to be put together, and that to compose a solution of some is to make other solutions impossible.

The Clockwork Metaphor – Simple Machines as Solving Insight Problems

The example we have explored above has implied us thinking of simple machines in a generalized way, as representation parts, and of motion in a generalized way as affordance. We have obtained a clockwork metaphor of representation: a view on how the creative problem solving process could proceed, using representations as the "mechanical parts".

In the simple machines example, we talked about a system which can compositionally solve the motion inference problem given a set of connected simple machines. This system could fill in a particular missing piece through knowledge of the simple machine components and their motion. Multiple solutions of filling in a missing piece can be applied. To translate this system to general creative problem solving, the simple machine elements in this example can be replaced with concepts. The motion ability of the simple machines can be replaced with concept affordances. Then various combinations of such machines can be thought of as problem templates used to achieve a particular end action.

In the simple machine examples, parts of the mechanism are present, and parts need to be filled in. At the general creative problem solving level, this can be seen as knowing some elements of a problem, while also needing to bring in different concepts, and their functionality, in order to obtain the desired affordance or end result. Not all the known or given problem elements are useful, nor is their productive combination initially known. Subsets of the given problem elements can be assembled and reassembled in multiple ways, together with other elements, brought forth from the agent's knowledge base. In this analogy, functional fixedness is the act of assembling such concepts in a way which is most comfortable and comes automatically to the mechanism assembler or clockmaker.

Some elements have to be used in some problems – they are part of the problem statement, problem general set-up, they are problem constraints or concepts around which a solution needs to be built or adapted. These elements correspond to the fixed points in a simple machine mechanism. Understanding what the truly fixed elements of a problem are might not however be as straightforward as expected. Problems of the creative kind can be ambiguous in their formulation. The agent solving the problem might find it natural to consider as fixed elements which are not truly so, because of the knowledge they bring to the problem, or because of assumptions they make regarding the problem statement.

Multiple different strands of known concepts can be organized around the fixed points. The fixed points can be looked at as being a possible part of multiple mechanisms. That is, a possible part of multiple ways of arranging existing knowledge (in potentially new forms) to solve the problem. The ability to restructure knowledge and one's problem space is equivalent to the ability to navigate between these compositional possibilities. The moment of solution is the moment in which all the elements fall into place, allowing the motion to be passed across the entire mechanism freely.

Simple machines can bind together when the motion of a machine can be carried on by the other (a locking point). Similarly, concepts can bind together when some of their features are similar, or in other ways "match" together. Simple machines can be replaced by other machines or groups of machines which afford a similar type of motion. Similarly, concepts can be set in place as possible solving parts; other concepts which share features and functionality with the existing ones can be searched for in the existing knowledge base. The newly found concepts can replace other concepts in the construction of a solution, or even of a view of the problem.

Various fixed points in the mechanism can have simple machine parts and motion inference strands organized around them in parallel. Different strands of motion might come together, fit, and organize a chain. At the creative problem solving level, different points of the problem might be operated on in parallel, putting together representations and their affordance chains around them. Such affordance chains might at some point come together to construct an ampler solution, and even surprise the solver in an insight moment. Various types of re-representation of the initial problem are possible, by making/constructing parts of the mechanism out of different representational cogs or simple machines.

This clockwork metaphor allows us to think of insight and creative problem solving in a piece-wise, as well as integrative fashion. This view, about how the creative problem solving process unfolds, is centered around how existing knowledge and problem elements are used, in order to produce new knowledge and be able to productively see and solve problems.

The cog to clockwork inspiration has warranted this framework the name CreaCogs. The name stands for Creative Re-Representation using Affordances in Cognitive Systems[2]. However, CreaCogs can also stand for Creative Cogs, Creative Cognition, Creative Cognitive Systems, etc. As it can be interpreted in multiple (productive) ways, the CreaCogs name tag is a small depiction of the principle of re-representation – a set of features can be represented and interpreted in multiple ways, each triggering their own associated meaning.

---

[2] Abbreviation CReACogS could have been used but its spelling has been deemed too cumbersome.

What is the breadth of creative problem solving mechanisms CreaCogs might serve? As this clockwork metaphor is centered around organizing and using knowledge, we cannot talk about the creative mechanisms, without first getting a better grasp of the clockwork itself.

7.2 The Clockwork

Discussing the clockwork means setting up the theoretical framework under which such wide creative problem solving processes could take place. Theoretical frameworks are, to start with, an exercise of the imagination. During this, we will cast our gaze on various points, trying to illuminate different parts of how such a framework would work out. After this initial intuitive view, the next chapters will describe the knowledge organization and processes of this framework in a more detailed way. We will then put these principles to the test of computational implementation and empirical evaluation. Until then, the purpose of this chapter is for us to get an overview of how the clockwork could be set up and such principles could work together, to support creative problem solving.

The theoretical framework proposed here is based on a way of encoding knowledge, which permits processes of fast and informed search and construction, for the purposes of creative problem solving. These processes take place conceptually at three levels, which are visually depicted in Fig. 7.3. What is the purpose of these three levels? Starting from the bottom level, let us examine in turn: L1 – Feature spaces; L2 – Concepts; and L3 – Problem templates.

*L1 **Feature spaces***
The first level is the subsymbolical level of feature maps or feature spaces. Whenever an object is observed, its various known sensory properties, together with its observed motion and actions (or actions that the agent can perform towards it) are encoded in the various feature spaces of the framework, based on their type. Thus, visuospatial properties like shape or color will be encoded in different feature maps, motion in another feature map, etc. These features can be organized based on their type. Thus, a particular colour will be encoded in the colour map close to another colour to which it is similar. The same holds for shape, motion and other features. Each observed or retrieved object (or concept in its more general form) will be an activation distributed over feature maps. This expresses a way of tackling the grounding problem in line with cognitive grounding theories (Barsalou, 2003; Barsalou & Wiemer-Hastings, 2005).

Such grounding does not only affect the way concepts are stored/retrieved, but turns out to have important uses for the creativity domain, which we will discuss later.

*L2 **Concepts***
Concepts represent the second level of this theoretical framework. The various known concepts are grounded in a distributed manner in organized feature

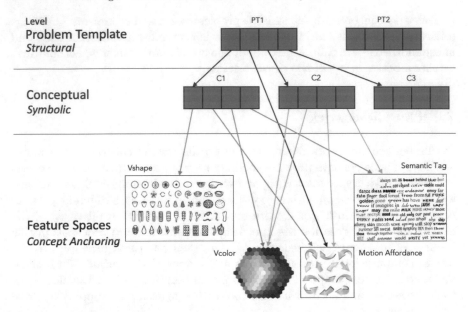

Fig. 7.3: A visual depiction of the theoretical framework

spaces. This type of grounding means that concepts with similar properties have points in common (or points in proximity) in various feature maps. This makes concepts which are similar on various properties efficiently accessible during search processes.

The name of the concepts is encoded in a different name tag map, thus functionally constituting another feature. This is plausible set up, as in humans the ability to name objects can be lost (anomic phasia - word selection anomia), while the ability to comprehend objects and concepts is independently maintained. With the name tag being only a feature, rather then the entire concept, and concept encoding being than an encoding concept names, this knowledge set up allows concept meaning to be recalled independently of name recall.

Thus a concept's meaning is the collection of features, properties, actions and relations over which that concept has been encoded. A concept can be identified or recalled by its name, but can also be triggered by other sensory properties (the way it looks, moves, etc.). Concepts do not need a name to exist in the mind that beholds them (though obviously that can impede fast communication about them). Grounded in feature spaces, concepts also act as a grounding layer for the next level of elements – that of problem templates.

L3 Problem Templates

The third level of the framework is comprised of problem templates. Problem templates are known ways of solving problems, or using existing sets or objects and concepts to produce a certain effect. They are structured representations which are encoded over multiple concepts, their relations, and the affordance the problem template provides.

A concept can be connected to and used by various templates, in which different parts of its features might be useful. For example, as shown in Fig. 7.4, a hammer encoded in a problem template with a walnut (top right side) will have its affordance of breaking things emphasized by the actions in the template context; meanwhile, when a hammer appears in a problem template in conjunction with a nail (top left side), the problem template will be about the affordance of affixing something to the wall or another surface.

Problem templates can also behave like concepts over time (when they are used multiple times, compressed or named).

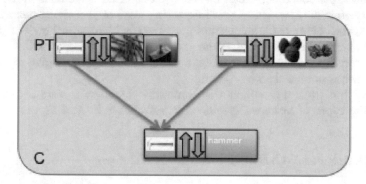

Fig. 7.4: Concept in multiple problem template contexts in CreaCogs

Knowledge organization principles – summary

The knowledge organization employed in CreaCogs has multiple advantages for the kind of processes required in creative problem solving, including:

a) *grounding downwards*; concepts are grounded in feature maps, while problem templates are grounded in concepts. This allows easy search and substitution of missing parts. If a needed object is missing, a similar object can be found by looking downwards in the knowledge base or comparing needed features with the objects present in the environment. This allows the agent to use a shoe when a hammer is not present (the shoe has a similar weight, a solid sole which affords hitting similarly to the head of a hammer, and a part which can be grasped).

b) *anchoring upwards* in context; concepts gain different meaning (and hold different relational roles) through the various templates they participate in.

c) *re-use of structure* (or structure transfer) because of structure and content being kept separately, but in relationship. The structure of a template can be used to recruit new concepts. The structure of a concept can be used to recruit new features. Also concepts and features can be reused in different structures.

d) use of *sensory experiences as structuring elements*. Thus the features of a visuospatial symbol representation (e.g. the Ouroboros snake) can be amplified into a problem template and replaced with other conceptual elements (e.g. the elements of the benzene molecule).

Besides the structuring and restructuring functionality, CreaCogs allows for the creation of new relations, concepts and templates via different forms of overlap. Some of these are residual of other activities, and can be viewed as generalizations over multiple correlations. For example, some features can be associated across multiple concepts (as some concepts can be associated across multiple problem templates). If a feature to feature overlap happens across multiple concepts, it can be strengthened and leave residual effects on the knowledge base, which trigger interesting ways of perceiving meaning. For example, the colour *red* is sometimes perceived as being somehow "related to" speed, violence, fire or energy. Some such residual correlations will allow for a rich play with features and meaning creation in the arts, and give some much less desirable potential to advertising.

Now, that we had a look at the framework, could such a framework allow for all the types of tasks we specified as desirable in Sect. 6.2?

7.3 Desiderata through CreaCogs's Lens

We have established a set of tasks as desiderata from a unified framework, In this section, we will check each in turn, aiming to establish whether and how CreaCogs could be used to support them.

7.3.1 Visuospatial Inference in CreaCogs

Visuospatial inference was the task in which a human, looking at a mechanism, and knowing where the motion in the mechanism was initiated, can infer the way the mechanism will move and its end motion. We developed a creative inference version of this task, in which the agent is supposed to construct a mechanism that will allow for a specific type of motion output, given the motion input. Can this be accounted for in the CreaCogs framework?

a) *Single case* – visuospatial inference with one object. Performing this in CreaCogs involves activating the knowledge of that object, and simulating the specific previously encoded motor affordance. Thus, with a lever, two motor inferences can be encoded – when the lever is pushed down on the left side, or pulled up on the left side – the effect of the resulting motion being that the right side of the lever will move up or down respectively.

If the visual features of a lever have been observed in the environment, and knowledge about the start of the motion is given, a CreaCogs agent will match this motion to one of the two motion simulation routines attached to that object; it will then simulate and anticipate the result of that motion.

b) Compositional case – In the case in which a mechanism is being observed, the system can deploy the same type of knowledge compositionally. Thus the motion inference made on the first object will be propagated into the beginning motion pattern of the second object. This can be applied sequentially to compositional cases of multiple objects. The agent can then simulate and follow the motion as it propagates through the mechanism[3] until the last inference has been made about the exit motion (motion at the end of the last part of the mechanism).

Let us explore such a compositional case, and how it would be solved in CreaCogs. In Fig. 7.5, top left, two cogs are given to an agent, together with an initial upward motion input, and the motion output is requested. The first of the two cogs is matched to the conceptual representation of a cog, with the initial upward motion (C level – down left). This knowledge is used to elaborate the representation of the given mechanism (PT level – up right, first three slots). The inference made about the motion of the first cog, obtained from previous conceptual knowledge, is then used to determine the matching affordance of the second cog. This is then projected on the conceptual level, to retrieve the resulting motion of a cog that was set in motion counterclockwise (C level – down right). Once this has been located, the problem representation is elaborated again and the end motion is inferred (PT level – up right slots 4-6).

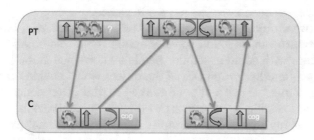

Fig. 7.5: Compositional visuospatial inference in CreaCogs

c) Creative case – This is the case in which a mechanism needs to be constructed, various stable points have been provided (as fixed machines), and a certain type of motion flow is expected. In CreaCogs, the piece-wise knowledge about the elements and previous experience with mechanisms (which can be encoded as problem templates) can be used to construct the mechanism. This

---

[3] This is a non-parallel, no-interference case. That is to say, in this case motion is assumed to flow on one strand, not on multiple parallel strands. Such parallel strands would ensue if, for example, the initial object would be connected to multiple different objects.

can be done in multiple ways, and we have shown many of these in Table 7.1 before transferring the simple machines example to the two strings problem. Some of the processes used in the creative case, besides motion inference, are template guided search or property guided search, filling in previously known templates, using replacement parts or equivalent sub-mechanisms until these sub-parts fit to allow for the expected end motion, trial and error, etc.

Visuospatial inference can theoretically be depicted both symbolically and subsymbolically, however, in the case of simple machines, as we do not have precise symbolic terms about motion, a subsymbolical implementation will probably be more expressive and direct (also a more accurate depiction of natural cognitive systems).

7.3.2 Creative Use of Affordance in CreaCogs

Creative use of affordance refers to the situation in which an agent requires a specific object (for example a cup). However, that object is not available in the environment, and the agent must find a creative replacement, that can enable the same affordance (a human could successfully use a bowl, a bucket or even a boot).

Creative use of affordance can be deployed in various ways in CreaCogs. Since in CreaCogs each object is represented as a distributed encoding in organized feature maps, various types of search can be performed to find replacement objects in case an object is not available. For example:

a) The affordance of each object can be used to link back to other objects that have been encoded over the same affordance.

b) If no other object is encoded with the same affordance, objects with a similar affordance can be found (nearby similarity search on affordance).

If no object with same or similar explicit affordance is found, the search can be focused on other properties of the object which enable that affordance – properties connected with the affordance in the given concept are just a start for such a search; some properties might be highly connected with the affordance over multiple other examples. Thus, a functional property or set of functional properties (which enable the affordance) might be found by an agent exploring in such a way their own knowledge. Once the properties correlated with enabling that affordance have been found, the agent can map these back into known objects which:

c) are anchored in conjunction of the functional property;

d) are anchored close to that functional property.

These objects can then be tried out as potential replacements, which may hold the affordance.

7.3.3 Concept Generation and Structure Transfer in CreaCogs

Multiple ways of doing concept generation and structure transfer are available in the CreaCogs framework. Here we will describe just a few to showcase this diversity, and proceed to lay down more formal concepts for these mechanisms in Chap. 8.

Diversification – A concept can become a template by refining its parts – i.e. a *stone* which is used for smashing things or driving wedges through things can be grasped. When this affordance is differentiated as a specific part, for example a *handle*, which is built and optimized for grasping, we get a *hammer*. This allows the expansion of a feature to a concept, a concept to a more complex concept or to a template.

Concept to concept overlap – Sometimes concepts overlap on certain features. Such overlaps allow or can trigger composition and feature exchange. The concept *sea* has a feature which involves liquid, and so does the concept *juice*. A creative concept obtained via their overlap would be a *sea of juice* – which is probably something children have thought about with pleasure before. Overlapping *sea* with another concept with fluid properties, *blood*, we obtain *sea of blood*, but also *sea water in its blood* – depending on which concept we use as a container template. More complex templates could be *sea in the blood*, *sea waving through its veins*, etc.

Some of these overlaps might seem like poetic licence, while others are well established in our spoken culture, like *pitch black*, a concept which could have been generated because of the feature *black* being so characteristic for *pitch*.

Such a type of concept generation via overlap can be observed over a variety of features, including type of motion, and sometimes involving deep conceptual structures. For example, the relatively new concept of a *meme* is meant to describe something that spreads in the world by moving like a virus but is actually an idea, or an element of a culture or system of behaviour. In this case, the movement of ideas or cultural elements must have seemed similar to that of a virus to Richard Dawkins (Dawkins, 1989), who coined the concept.

Some overlaps can come from previously unnamed correlations of features, and previously unnamed concepts. As a concept is, in CreaCogs, a correlation of features, it makes sense that further correlations will allow the generation of further concepts. Some of these overlaps are seemingly semantically unrelated previous to the overlap, however the CreaCogs framework allows for overlap via features to trigger these possible constructions, as well as overlap via concepts.

Using structure from a different concept – Some concepts come with their own set of relations and structure. One can use this set of relations to create a new concept, by projecting some of that structure on new elements. Take the following examples:

Ex.1 – chain
- The loops of the *chain* where sparkling.
- A *chain* of shops opened across town (deployment of the same structure over space).
- Something triggered this *chain* of events (deployment of the same structure over time).

Ex.2 – storing
- The warehouse *stored* various objects.
- The day *stored* various surprises for him.

Ex.3 – shines
- The sun *shines* over the people today.
- The luck *shined* over him wherever he went.

Ex.4 – flight
- The eagle *flew* over the valley.
- The wooden log *flew* from her hand in the direction of the animal.
- His hands *flew* over the keyboard.
- He had a *flight* of fancy over the events of the last few days.

In these cases, the new concepts or objects put in the template are made to play a different role than usual, depending on the structure of the previous concept or template which they fill in.

In CreaCogs such transfer can be done via overlapping features, like for example in Fig. 6.4, were the chaining template can obviously be applied to objects with similar properties. A loop of string and the eye of a scissor, due to the bendability of the first and the elliptical structure of the latter, can allow for the similar physical relation of chaining. After many transfers of such a template or relationship, the template itself becomes strong enough (and perhaps abstract enough) to be used in conjunction with other, less similar elements.

Synthesis – Concepts can sometimes be re-compressed into their representative features, as problem templates can be re-compressed by being named as concepts. This was exemplified in Fig. 6.6(c).

This allows the synthesis of a template to its essential features (like reducing the Tower of Hanoi problem to a movement heuristic which is required to solve it), or that of a concept (e.g. velocity) to its essential features. This permits fast external representation of concepts, through iconic means, and easy triggering of more complex elements.

Synthesis also permits transfers downwards from a template into a concept, and from a concept into a feature space. Such transfers enable templates to be compared to concepts, and concepts to be compared to features. Through this transfer, synthesis allows further productive connections with other elements of the knowledge base.

7.3.4 Re-Representation through Search and Construction in CreaCogs

Re-representation can happen in two main ways in CreaCogs: creative substitution of a problem template (or subparts of it), and generation of a new problem template (or subparts of it). These, in their higher forms of deployment, are proposed to roughly correspond to re-representation in insight and discovery (when a new useful template is found) and creative innovation (creativity dominated by construction processes).

Such high-level cognitive feats can be seen as applying the processes described above – of search of affordance, structure transfer and generation – at a larger and sometimes more abstract scale. We will exemplify this by describing these processes at the problem template level.

a) Creative search – The same creative use of affordance can be made for problem templates as for concepts, when searching for a particular template that can reach a particular result. In the concept case, the search focused on concepts or objects with the required affordance, or a similar one. In the problem template case, templates with the required affordance, or a similar one, are the target. The affordance itself is used to guide the search.

If no such templates are found, the agent can try to discriminate the concept (or even property) which enables the affordance. If such a concept which is functionally linked to the affordance is found, the search for a useful template can then proceed guided by this concepts, and leading into its connected templates. If no template has been found, constructive techniques can be applied to make a new template out of useful elements.

Thus a new problem template which affords the solution can be found via re-representation. Finding and applying a problem template brings about a new way of seeing things, of organizing the objects in the given problem. Such a template also brings forth new information from the knowledge base of the cognitive system into the problem space.

The insight effect, with the appearance of an entire new representation in the consciousness of the solver (a pop-up effect), might also rely on specific convergence mechanisms being at play. These will be further addressed in Chaps. 9 and 11.

b) Construction – New templates can be constructed in ways similar to concept generation. Various concepts or templates which overlap can be made into new templates, which will now yield affordances pertaining to both the initial concepts or templates, or qualitatively new affordances altogether. Some such templates could emerge via processes of overlap and repeated correlation, while others might take more overt effort to constructively develop. Construction might come at the cost of losing parts of the interacting concepts or templates, and parts of the affordances. The initial participating templates could also be kept in their separate form in the knowledge base, or discarded and replaced by their transformation.

Parts of a template can be substituted with other templates. An initial template can thus be enlarged and enriched. This latter process of construction as elaboration can be seen as the opposite of the process of synthesis, which compresses a larger representation structure to some essential features.

Finally, various relations between concepts get stronger over time and can organize themselves, when brought together, into a new template. This process does not apply only to concepts existing in the mind of the agent, but can be distributed across the mind and the environment of the agent. Thus concepts in the environment can keep on overlapping with concepts in the mind, or a template in the mind can receive interference from an object or layout in the environment.

In conclusion, the way various elements of knowledge organization (space, connectedness, representation structure) are used in this framework allows re-representation. Space and connectedness allow easy access to multiple other relevant elements, via explicit similarity links on the various feature spaces, and implicit similarity links when reaching for context (problem templates) in which concepts have participated, and taken up a certain role. This role can provide implicit similarity due to similarity of context.

Multi-feature representations allows for re-representing the object. Structured representations allow for re-representing the object as being formed by different parts (implicit re-representation). Explicit re-representation can be realized by trying to construct the possible templates which will fulfil the requirements for a certain problem solution.

CreaCogs is thus a spatially informed and organized theoretical framework. How do its elements and mechanisms look like in more depth?

The Cogs in Motion – Navigating the Knowledge in CreaCogs

Structured representation is a recurrent theme in both artificial intelligence and various theories of cognition. A hypothesis of CreaCogs, set in Chap. 6, is that the lack of useful structure in ill-structured problems must be compensated by a cognitive effort of restructuring. Thus such cognitive processes of restructuring are the precursors, or in some cases the very processes of creativity, in the context of problem solving.

For this reason, CreaCogs is a framework in which knowledge organization aims to enable (a varied set of) creative processes. Before delving into the general creative mechanisms enabled by CreaCogs, let us first focus on knowledge organization looking at the framework's elements: Feature Spaces, Concepts and Problem Templates.

8.1 Feature Spaces

Feature spaces are spatially organized sets of features encoded symbolically or subsymbolically[1]. They constitute the bottom level of the CreaCogs framework (see Fig. 7.3). The set of feature spaces (FS) in a knowledge base (KB) can be defined as follows:

$$FS = \{FS^1, FS^2, ..., FS^m\}, FS \in KB$$

Each feature space contains a set of features $FS^1 = \{f_1^1, f_2^1, f_3^1, ..., f_n^1\}$, so that the distance between features f_1^1, f_2^1 is expressed as $\delta_{1,2}^1$. The more similar some features, the smaller the distance between them in the feature map:

$$max\ (sim(f_x^k, f_y^k)) \iff min(\delta_{x,y}^k)$$

If a new concept C_z is learned, its features are compared to known features. This helps determine which of its features are already known, and which need

---

[1] A subsymbolic type of encoding would be more realistic from a sensory perspective

© Springer Nature Switzerland AG 2020
A.-M. Oltețeanu, *Cognition and the Creative Machine*,
https://doi.org/10.1007/978-3-030-30322-8_8

adding to the knowledge base (KB) before anchoring the concept in them. Let us say X is the set of unknown features of concept C_z, and Y is the set of features of C_z which are already known in the KB. Features from set X (unknown) are added to the KB by being encoded in their corresponding FS at the correct distance from other features they are similar to. Then, the newly encoded features from set X are connected to the newly acquired concept C_z. Known features from set Y, which are already present in the KB, are just connected to the C_z.

The feature space grounding makes possible measures of concept similarity on various features dimensions. It also provides the ability to creatively use a concept or object as a replacement of another one. An object will have features which are functional for particular affordances (they support them). When the distance (δ) between the functional feature(s) of the required object and another object are small, the latter might be used as a creative substitute.

8.2 Concepts

If KB is the knowledge base of an agent α, let $C \in KB$ be a set of known concepts, so that:

$$c_1, c_2, c_3, ..., c_m \in C$$

These concepts are anchored in the knowledge α has acquired via its various sensors, including properties, motor routines, linguistic tags and relations. These are encoded in the feature spaces (FS) we talked about above, where different types of such feature maps can be distinguished, and different points can be determined within them.

Thus, without defining all possible FS exhaustively, let V be a set of known visuospatial features[2], A a set of known affordances (motor actions that have been learned to be performed, or observed in the environment), and L a set of linguistic tags (names which the agent attributes to objects or it associates with other types of abstract patterns), such that $V, A, L \in FS$, and the elements of each specific feature space:

$$\{v_1, v_2, v_3, ..., v_o\} \in V$$

$$\{a_1, a_2, a_3, ..., a_n\} \in A$$

$$\{l_1, l_2, l_3, ..., l_p\} \in L$$

Each concept c_x known by agent α is grounded in a subset of the respective known feature maps:

$$c_x = (V', A', L'), V' \subset V, A' \subset A, L' \subset L$$

---

[2] We treat visuospatial sensory features together in this example for the sake of simplicity, but they can be differentiated in various types of feature maps, including shape, colour, orientation, etc.

and the set of known concepts C can be defined as a subset of the powerset of known features:

$$C = P(V) \times P(A) \times P(L),$$

Imagine two visual feature maps V1 (colour) and V2 (shape) could be differentiated. Concepts encoded in colour, shape, affrodance or action and linguistic tags feature maps would look like the following:

$$c_1 = \{green, round, to\ eat, apple\}$$

$$c_{15} = \{red, round, to\ kick, ball\}$$

In this example, only *apple* and *ball* are linguistic tags, the rest of the features are translated in their approximate linguistic description. This is evident as the *round* in c_1 is not the same as the one in c_{15}. In a self-organized shape feature space they would be in each other's neighbourhood. In translation to a symbolic description, much precision and expressivity is lost.

Not all concepts need to have a representative point on all the feature maps stored in the KB, in order for the concept to be encoded. Concepts can be encoded on a subset of feature spaces, even if no corresponding feature has been encoded on the remaining few. For example, c_x is encoded on the visuospatial feature map in features v_i and v_j, and on the linguistic feature map on feature l_i:

$$\exists c_x \in C, \quad c_x = (V', A', L') = \{v_i, v_j, \emptyset, l_i\}, \quad (\emptyset \subset V, \emptyset \subset A, \emptyset \subset L)$$

When a new element is observed as belonging to a concept known by α, this element is added to the concept in the knowledge base, e.g.:

$$Known: c_3 = \{yellow, round, to\ eat, grapefruit\}$$

$$Observed: c_x = \{pink, round, grapefruit\}$$

Then in KB: $c_3 = \{(yellow \vee pink), round, to\ eat, grapefruit\}$

These concept elements can be disjunctive in nature, the activation of one in a concept inhibiting the activation of another (e.g. a grapefruit being either yellow or pink).

Complex concepts (the grounding of which requires other concepts) and abstract concepts (concepts for which no good physical representation exists) are better modeled by more complex representation structures, which will be discussed in the next section.

An agent's comprehension of a presented concept, object or scene is thus the activation of the known elements from the scene in the agent's KB. If elements in the scene match elements in the KB, previous knowledge of that object can be brought forth, be it that the knowledge has been obtained in declarative, observational or interactive manner. After the objects have been identified, new knowledge present in the environment can be added to the KB. Thus knowledge is obtained, brought to bear on the problem at hand and updated in an interactive manner.

8.3 Problem Templates

Complex concepts and problem templates are kept in the knowledge base as activations over previously known concepts. They can include relations between concepts, actions, and results of those actions. Action results can consist of new relations between the initial concepts or objects, and transformations of the initial objects or their features. Previously solved problems, encoded with their solution in the KB of the agent, allow further use of their structure.

Given a set of relations R between concepts, relationship r_n is a relationship between concepts c_x and c_y, which can be expressed as follows[3]:

$$r_n(c_x, c_y), r_n \in R$$

$$\text{e.g. } onTopOf(table, glass), \ onTopOf \in R$$

Given a set H of heuristics or actions over concepts, these can be expressed as follows:

$$h_1(c_3, c_2) \in H$$

$$\text{E.g. pour}(water, glass), \text{pour} \in H$$

All problem templates PT are structured representations over: tuples of concepts (C), relations between concepts (R), heuristics or set of moves (H – which can be understood as the higher-order counterpart of motion affordances in concept encoding) and solution state representations (SOL):

$$PT \in P(C) \times P(R) \times P(H) \times P(SOL)$$

$$PT_x = (C', R', H', SOL'),$$

$$C' \in C, R' \in R, H' \in H, SOL' \in SOL$$

$$\text{For example, } PT_1 = \{c_1, c_2, c_3, r_1(c_1, c_2), h_1(c_3, c_2), sol_3\}$$

$$PT_1 = \{\{table, glass, water\}, \text{onTopOf}(table, glass), \text{pour}(water, glass), sol_3\}$$

$$sol_3 = \{\{table, glass, water\}, \{\text{onTopOf}(table, glass), \text{in}(glass, water)\}\}$$

When a certain type of solution is required for a particular problem, the set of solution state representations (SOL) can be searched for that result, in order to then trigger previously known templates in which such a solution state has been achieved. After such problem templates that can achieve the solution required have been found, an attempt to apply these templates to the current problem elements can be made.

Objects or concepts of the given problem can also trigger templates in which they have previously been involved in from the knowledge base of the solver. This allows for the natural modeling of functional fixedness: some

---

[3] Such relations can be expressed logically, but they do not have to be. They could also be expressed through an analogical or pictorial representation that has implicitly embedded the spatial relations themselves.

concepts in a problem can be associated with particular templates of the agent with a high activation strength.

Problem templates can be treated as concepts $PT_x \simeq C_x$ after a template has been strongly encoded, compressed and provided a linguistic tag which allows for its naming and easy communication.

Abstract concepts, which are not understood through direct action or physical representation, are considered a form of intermediary representation between concepts and problem templates. However, as their encoding is dependent upon previous experience and encoding of a set of other concepts, many more assumptions are made when communicating about them than about concepts which have been encoded with direct sensory experience, as their encoding might not be similar in two different agents.

This reflects communication difficulties which humans do encounter when dealing with abstract concepts – like *"justice"* or *"freedom"* – which can mean different things for different people. Deviation from a "common" meaning, if such a meaning exists, can be viewed as a product of the deviations of all other concepts used for encoding. On an individual level, each agent can provide their particular encoding case (with different objects and events) for abstract concepts, which manifests itself in individual differences of meaning.

Acquiring or communicating a similar PT to a different agent might have more chances of success when the contributing elements, relations and actions are explained from their anchoring concept level (bottom-up). However, even if these elements are communicated, the agent which does the listening might group them in different PT contexts, which are closer to the agent's already encoded PT set.

Agents have preference for certain actions and interpretations because of their expertise and familiarity with particular sets of actions, heuristics and templates (in the CreaCogs framework these are represented as stronger KB associations). At the representation level, heuristics can be built compositionally, as a set of actions over given objects, that are put in certain relations.

For example, cooking a favorite recipe like $h_{15} = $ *Pasta bolognese* is a collection of cooking actions like *mix, stir, chop, season, simmer* over the following set of concept ingredients: $C = \{c_1 - minced\ meat, c_2 - onion, c_3 - tomatoes, c_4 - mushrooms, c_5 - pepper, c_6 - basil, c_7 - oregano, c_8 - pasta\}$.

The set of actions required is:

$$\{h_1 - stir, h_2 - chop, h_3 - season, h_4 - simmer, h_5 - fry\},$$

Each of these a primitive cooking template. Such primitive templates are structured problem templates themselves, for which no heuristic can be further decomposed in other actions:

$$h_1 - stir = \{\{foods\{c_1, c_2, ..., c_n\}, pans\{c_{31}, c_{32}\}, stirrers\{wooden\ spoon\}\},$$
$$\{in(food, pan), in(wooden\ spoon, food)\}, stirring\ motion, stirred\}$$

For the template $h_{15}-$ *Pasta bolognese*, the *bolognese sauce* can act as a composition of previously known actions over given ingredients, as follows:

$$h_{15} = (stir(stir(fry(minced\ meat), chop(onion, tomatoes)),$$
$$simmer(5min), season(pepper, basil, oregano), chop(mushrooms)),$$
$$simmer(10min)), bolognese\ sauce$$

The summary of this template is thus a composition of previous templates:

$$h_{15} = (h_1(h_1(h_5(c_1), h_2(c_2, c_3)), h_4(5\ min), h_3(c_5, c_6, c_7), h_2(c_4)),$$
$$h_4(10\ min)), sol_5$$

We have looked at Feature Spaces, Concepts and Problem Templates. What kinds of creative mechanisms would be enabled by such types of knowledge organization?

8.4 General Creative Mechanisms

We will now have a look at the general creative reasoning mechanisms which can be deployed under the knowledge organization of CreaCogs. We will first look at how hypothesizing can happen using concept similarity. We will then focus on the creative use of problem templates and structured representations.

8.4.1 Hypothesizing by Concept Similarity

Due to the distributed encoding of concepts over features, concept similarity can be computed between concepts by comparing their elements. This can be done by checking (a) the similarity between the features of two concepts and (b) the features two concepts share. A third type of similarity is implicit: (c) being involved in the same structures.

For example, due to their common feature elements on the affordance (A) and visual (V) feature spaces, $c_1 = \{a_1, a_2, v_1, v_2, s_1\}$ and $c_2 = \{a_2, a_3, v_1, v_3, s_2\}$ can be considered similar.

Both these types of similarity ratings can be used for hypothesizing. In the following we will show a few examples of the element-based similarity hypothesizing.

Consider an agent that knows the concepts c_1 and c_2:

$$c_1 = \{a_1, a_2, v_1, v_2, s_1\}$$

$$c_2 = \{a_2, a_3, v_1, v_3, s_2\}$$

The concepts c_1 and c_2 overlap in a_2 and v_1.

$$c_1 \cap c_2 = \{a_2, v_1\}$$

Concepts c_1 and c_2 are associative synaptic bindings over their elements. The activation traveling across both of these concepts between the features a_2 and v_1 will strengthen the association between these features.

Now let us say that the same agent encounters a new concept, c_3, some features of which are observable, but the affordances of which are unknown:

$$c_3 = \{v_2, v_3, s_3, a_?\}$$

The agent will check the similarity of c_3 with concepts which it already knows. Let us say it notices some degree of feature overlap between the new concept and c_1 and c_2:

$$c_3 \cap c_1 = \{v_2\}$$
$$c_3 \cap c_2 = \{v_3\}$$

The features v_2 and v_3 thus overlap. The agent could then consider possible that some of the affordances which hold for c_1 and c_2 might also hold for c_3. There is no direct correlate affordance for the features v_2 and v_3 specifically. The system could propose that c_3 inherits the affordances of the concepts it has features in common with:

$$c_3 = \{? a_1, ? a_2, ? a_3, v_2, v_3, s_3\}$$

This would be a very coarse inference. However, because of the previously observed correlation between affordance a_2 and the feature v_1, this hypothesis can be refined one step further. As v_1 is not one of the observed features of c_3, only a_1 and a_3 will be proposed as possible affordances of c_3, to be tested in the real world.

This means that previously noticed feature associations cumulatively matter to the system. Such associations can become strong enough to be triggered whenever one or a subset of elements of the associative pattern are present; the system will thus try to retrace a previously known pattern (in a somewhat Gestaltic fashion).

These mechanisms can trigger further inferences in the system, from implicit information which gathers over time. This can lead to the birth of new substructures, including new concepts, and the functional fixedness phenomenon.

8.4.2 Creative Use of and Hypothesizing with Problem Templates

Previous problem templates, like the one for *Pasta bolognese*, can be used and re-used. Moreover, because of the posited type of knowledge encoding, the template can pop-up whenever an open search happens in the system for a general *cook* heuristic, with some of the conceptual elements (c_1 *mincemeat*, c_3 *tomatoes*) present in the fridge. The search can also be run over timing, and cooking pasta in general, depending on how strong the associations of the agent between these elements and that template are.

When creative solutions are proposed by the agent, or forced upon it by the absence of certain ingredients, similar ingredients to the missing ones will be sought. Thus *mince* can be replace with *aubergine, onion* with *leek* or *chalotte, red pepper* with *yellow pepper, chorizo* with other types of *salami*.

When trying to change or enrich such a recipe, it is reasonable to assume that "similarity" for an expert cook presupposes a set of observed, acquired and tested taste associations. These can be relations of food items that go well together, like (*courgettes* and *mushrooms*), (*red pepper* and *tomatoes*); or relations between specific templates and food items that give a specific taste (*chorizo, Parmesan, herbs, spices*).

Other problem templates than cooking ones can be used creatively in a similar manner, by using concept similarity to find and replace elements by others with the same or similar features.

Hypothesizing using problem similarity is also possible. Thus, different templates with similar elements can be used creatively. Subtemplates might be created via intersection, convergence, difference of previously observed templates. This can result in effects which look like mixing previously held templates or structurally sound parts thereof, to achieve a composed effect, or parts of effects from different templates.

Templates can be similar based on their components, relationships, heuristics or solution states. Replacement and creativity is possible across all these axes.

Some problem template hypothesizing requires mechanisms of creative search and is a precursor for mechanisms of creative reconstruction.

8.5 Creative Search and Substitution Mechanisms

In order to re-represent a problem, finding a problem representation which can yield the desired results is necessary. The search for a productive problem representation can be described as looking for a template: given initial problem objects c_1, c_2, c_4 and the need to fulfil sol_5, what mechanisms can you apply to reach a representation which affords the solution? What template $PT_?$ can the initial problem objects and the solution be part of?

In creative problem solving, the subset of objects required to solve the problem might not be predefined, closed, or restricted to only the salient objects or concepts offered by the problem. This subset necessary for solving might involve objects known by the solver, or objects which the solver could create.

Take the set of objects given in the problem to be O_P, the objects in the solution space to be O_S and the objects in the solver's KB to be O_{KB}. If in classical problem solving, $O_S \in O_P$, in creative problem solving $O_S \in \{O_P \cup O_{KB} \cup O_N\}$, where O_N are new objects constructed by agent α taking as input O_P and O_{KB}.

Intelligent search mechanisms need to take place over the knowledge base (O_{KB}) for computational explosion not to occur when searching for the objects required by the solution (O_S), for new objects conducive to a solution (O_N) to be produced and for a productive solving template $PT_?$ to be found. How would such search mechanisms look like in CreaCogs?

Such search mechanisms can be characterized in a variety of modes. The following characterisation is based on the initial direction the search takes relative to the concept level in the knowledge base: upward, downward and sideways.

8.5.1 Upward Search

This search goes up from the initial concepts in the problem template space. It checks for problem templates and other representational structures the given problem elements have been involved in. The problem templates known to have concepts which include the initial ones are searched for affordances which are similar to the solution required by the problem at hand. If a problem template with similar concepts and desirable affordances is identified, this kept as a representation structure relevant for the problem at hand. The solving of the problem can then be attempted using this representation.

In this mechanism, the search in the KB of the agent goes up from the level of the initial concepts to their projections in the problem template space, to check problem solving or general representational structures the concept or the structure has been involved in. A check is made to whether the affordances or solutions of the such found problem-templates are similar to the solution searched for the problem at hand. If similar affordances or solutions are yielded, the problem template is kept as a representation structure relevant for the problem at hand. The solving of the problem is then attempted with this representation.

This is presented in simplified form in Fig. 8.1, to help the visual understanding of the process. In this figure, the initial concepts of the problem are c_1 and c_2 (bottom left), and the required solution is sol_4. $PT_?$ is a template which needs filling in, to hopefully give a productive representation of the problem. The yellow arrows show the direction of the search: c_1 and c_2 trigger the templates they've been involved in from the problem template set PT_x. Some such templates will be triggered by multiple concepts of the problem. If the solution of any of these templates (sol_x) is similar or equivalent with the solution required by the problem (sol_4), then PT in which this has been found becomes a candidate representation of the problem. It can be used to structure the problem, and thus take the place of $PT_?$.

Let us say that PT_x stands in for templates the agent finds in her knowledge based, and PT_{sol} for template which could be used to solve the problem. The templates the agent finds can be in various relationships with the templates the agent ideally needs. The similarity between PT_x and PT_{sol} can be part of a variety of cases:

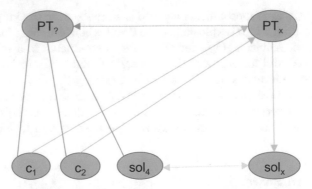

Fig. 8.1: Upward search in the framework

- PT_x and PT_{sol} overlap – templates found have common elements with the solving template. These common elements can include not just concepts but also relations and affordances (all this depends on how much of the end state is known or presumed, and some initial interpretations of the end state might be wrong or reflect biases). From the templates found in the knowledge base (PT_x), some of their elements might note be contained in the initial problem space. At some times, these elements are not crucial, and they can be ignored. At others, it is such elements that are responsible for the affordances which lead to solution. In this case, the reconstruction of these elements can be attempted in the problem environment.
- PT_x is a subpart of PT_{sol} – that is it demonstrates some useful affordances, but not all the ones required. Then PT_x can be kept as a useful subpart of future constructions, in an attempt to get closet to PT_{sol}, where other parts might need to be found. PT_x and other templates might be then used to construct PT_{sol}.
- PT_x contains PT_{sol} – the elements which are useful only need to be disentangled. In this case, a simplified version of PT_x, reduced to the elements relevant to the problem at hand, will be employed to re-represent the problem.

A special case of this mechanism is that of convergence. Some problem templates might be activated convergently by multiple problem elements. These might be a better match for the problem at hand. Other cases of convergence can exist. When various PTs are activated in the search for an appropriate template, these might have a subset of common elements (other than the given problem elements). The search for a suitable template could thus trigger different templates, which might convergently activate a subset of common elements. These elements could be particularly useful when attempting to initiate a productive re-representation, leading to a solution.

8.5.2 Downward Search

In this search mechanism, the agent goes down from the given "objects" to the feature level. It then tries to match these features to affordances required for the solution state.

This search mechanisms is shown in a simplified manner in Fig. 8.2. The yellow arrows show the direction of the search. c_1 and c_2 (middle left) are searched for elements that match (elements of) the required solution (sol_4). If useful elements have been found, they can be used all together (via abstraction / generalization strategies) or in different new combinations (constructive) to search for a useful template. The concepts these elements are part of might be used in solving the problem, or new concepts might be searched for that have been anchored in the relevant properties, and included in the problem space.

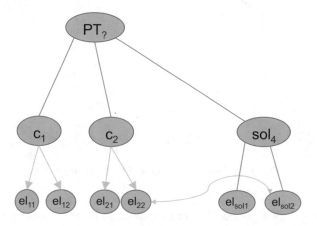

Fig. 8.2: Downward search in the framework

This type of search can be used as an eliminatory strategy – to make less salient the concepts or properties which do not work for a successful representation. It can also be used as a prioritization strategy – the essential properties are flagged for safe keeping, e.g. by an increase in their activation. In this way, useful elements which are already present are strengthened, and they can be used for searching for a potentially successful future structure.

8.5.3 Sideways Search

In sideways search, the agent uses the problem concepts to search for similar ones that can solve the problem (in its knowledge base and the environment). This is shown in a simplified manner in Fig. 8.3. The yellow arrows point the direction of the search. At the bottom left, c_2 triggers a similar concept,

c_x. The templates attached to c_x are searched for one which might yield the solution sol_4, or a state similar to it. If such a template is found, it might prompt using c_x rather than c_2 to attempt a solution. Variants of this are of course possible. For example, the agent could search for a concept that is similar to the solution, then check what templates this is part of, and whether concepts similar to the given problem concepts are functionally enabling reaching it.

Similarity can happen on the various feature spaces, or sets of spaces. However, some features will be functionally relevant for a particular affordance, while some will not be. If similar concepts relevant for the solution are found, they can become part of the solving template, or contribute a solving template through one of their connections.

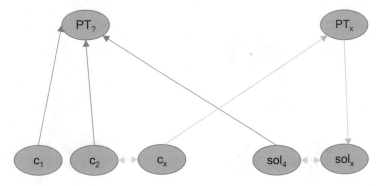

Fig. 8.3: Sideways search in the framework

Assuming that a potentially useful template or set of concepts have been found, how will this be used to represent and solve the problem?

8.5.4 Restructuring, Creation of New Objects and Re-Representation

Finding knowledge objects like a potentially viable PT_x, a set of concepts which might refine a viable PT_x and a concept c_x which overlaps the requirements of the problem (as shown in the previous three sections) helps restructure and re-represent the given problem, and sometimes recast some of the given objects as different objects (or concepts).

Given a concept made from a set of features, if a different concept can be found anchored in the same or a similar set of features, the initial concept and its features can be restructured as a the latter. For example, if c_1 is part of the problem set, and v_4 is similar to one of its features, one can attempt to re-represent its features as follows:

$$c_1 = \{a_1, v_1, v_2, s_2\}$$

$$v_1 \text{ sim } v_4, c_n \in KB, c_n = \{a_n, v_4, v_2, s_n\}$$

$$\text{Restructure } c_1 \text{ as } c_n = \{a_n, v_4, v_2, s_n\}$$

Presuming c_n does not exist, structure from c_1 and feature similarity can be used to attempt to create it.

Given a PT made from a set of concepts, if another template exists anchored in the same or similar subset of concepts, the first template and its elements can be restructured to the latter.

$$PT_1 = \{c_1, c_2, c_3, r_1(c_1, c_2), h_1(c_1, c_2), h_2(c_2, c_3), sol_3\}$$

$$c_2 \text{ sim } c_4$$

$$PT_n \in KB, PT_n = \{c_1, c_4, c_3, r_2(c_4, c_3), h_1(c_4, c_3), sol_5\}$$

Presuming PT_n does not exist, structure from PT_1 and concept similarity can be used to create it.

If an interesting PT is anchored in a a subset of the given concepts, but other elements from this template do not exist in the problem space, an attempt can be made to re-create these elements from the problem elements, in order to instantiate the template.

8.5.5 Discussion

After each re-representation, one can check if the new problem representation leads to the solution. If a re-representation was done specifically to obtain a certain affordance, which is required to satisfy part of the problem conditions, one can then attempt to solve the rest of the requirements.

Upward moves can be done automatically, triggering problem templates, or other structured representations and relations in which the concepts have previously worked together. This can bring about functional fixedness, as some salient templates are hard to avoid, and humans are not used to manipulating larger structures (like problem templates) quite as well as other smaller structures (like concepts), as possibly larger structures are harder to contain within working memory.

Riddles, Remote Associates Tests (Mednick & Mednick, 1971) and insight problems for empirical settings all seem to use predominantly search processes in this paradigm. Take the following riddle:

What can you catch but not throw?

The *catch* and *throw* concepts used in conjunction will initially yield sport templates, of type:

$$PT_{s1} = \{ball, catch(ball), throw(ball)\}$$

A search of context templates just over the linguistic tag *catch*, without the motion affordances, can yield the linguistic context template *catch a cold*. This verifies the problem condition *cannot throw*, however *throwing a cold* is not a usual pattern in thinking about colds. One might generally think of *giving someone else a cold*, and also *giving something to someone else* and *throwing something to someone else* have the same result, if the other person *receives* or *catches* that something. However, it is unlikely this similarity will be noticed, without having cast *catch* in the same context as the *cold* initially.

With remote associates, the search proceeds in parallel. Take the Remote Associates test item containing the words:

Falling Actor Dust

Let us say that $c_1 = Falling, c_2 = Actor$ and $c_3 = Dust$.

To find their remote associate, one needs to find a word c_4 so that the templates $PT_1 = \{c_1, c_4\}, PT_2 = \{c_2, c_4\}, PT_3 = \{c_3, c_4\}$ exist. When one has activated $PT_1 = Falling\ Star, PT_2 = Star\ Actor, PT_3 = Star\ Dust$, or at least two of them, and the third can be verified, one has converged upon $c_4 = Star$.

The classical candle insight problem (Duncker, 1945) is stated as follows: *You are given a candle, a book of matches and a box of thumbtacks. Fix the lit candle unto the wall so that the wax doesn't drip below.* Various saliencies draw initial attention. The template of a candle burning has effects like $\{light, wax, fire\}$. The template of fixing something unto the wall requires some material which can be *glue* or *nail*. *Wax* has *glue* properties, which probably explains why some people try to use wax to glue the candle to the wall.

The solvers need to focus on a representation of the kind $\{support, candle\}$, and find the support affordances of the *box* concept, which are not particularly salient in the *box of thumbtacks* representation. In the latter representation, the affordance of the object *box* are being already taken – $\{box, contains(thumbtacks), full\}$.

8.6 Creative Construction Mechanisms

Some of the mechanisms described above can be productive in themselves. Thus if the search is bringing two concepts together which have not been previously connected, new relations might be observed. Some of these relations might be interesting enough to be consolidated over time in the agent's memory. It is not hard to imagine that some transformational processes happen during this search (new templates are created, new relations are seen between concepts). However, we will refer here to mechanisms which are highly generative and productive by their nature (thus not accidental associations) – whether they developed out of initial search or whether they stand as mechanisms in their own right is an empirical cognitive questions, which requires empirical testing to answer.

In this framework we will differentiate between two processes of conceptual composition – cc_i and cc_{ii}. Assuming the simplified form of such processes, and that such processes use existing knowledge from two or more other concepts:

1. cc_i – maintains structure (which is common or aligned in both concepts) and imports features from both of them, to compose new concepts;
2. cc_{ii} – maintains features (which are common to both concepts), and imports and composes structure from both of them.

If some similar features exist, they can provide a locking point for the composition processes. Thus a third process of conceptual composition is using common features or templates as a locking point to construct a new concept. This is different from processes of generalization, or observations of a relation through synthesis.

Combination of problem-solving templates or representation structures larger than concepts is a step of higher complexity. However, similarity of the elements or the structure in problem templates can be used in a variety of ways:

(a) synthesis and generalization of new relations – keep the common elements of both templates and the relationships and heuristics which apply to both of them;
(b) hypothesizing based on already observed strong relations – if a template contains elements of already known templates, hypothesize that the results of those templates could be achieved as a consequence;
(c) chaining – If a template PT_1 presents in its solution set part of the elements of PT_2, then perhaps the two templates can be chained in $PT_3 = PT_1 \cup PT_2$;
(d) extending by replacement or via recasting – if part of the elements of PT_1 can be used for another template PT_2 without destroying them, extend PT_1 to include unknown information from PT_2;
(e) superset with emerging structure – keep all elements of template PT_1 and PT_2 and see if new relations appear when attempting to construct PT_3 which includes them both;
(f) keep existing common structure, while mixing elements from both templates, etc.

If some of these techniques can be achieved with search processes ((a) – (d)), others, like (e) and (f), are more likely to belong to the category of composition processes. Such representation construction processes can be defined as combining previously known representation structures and elements, to obtain new sets of affordances. While aiming for new representations, or aiming to achieve specific affordances, other associative and comparative processes might generate new concepts, relations and hypotheses.

Though an theoretical differentiation can be made between them, such construction and search processes can both be creative, and are likely to happen in tandem.

Multimodal and Concept to Template Transformations

Looking at the above described mechanisms, one could assume the type of feature map engaged in such operation is not of importance, and the mechanisms can apply in a general form to any sensory feature map. However, when characterizing a system with multiple sensory modalities, a creative interplay is also possible **between** the different modalities.

Thus, a concept of growth observed visually can be compared to or translated into a concept of growth based on auditory intensity, or pitch heigth. A concept experienced in a certain sensory modality, like *balance* – which is generally experienced through proprioceptive and visual modalities, can be transformed in a concept of balance in one's actions, as personally evaluated in various categories. A problem template could also bring multiple concepts from different modality domains in relation.

Besides multimodal transformations, complex sets of features can act as concepts or as problem templates themselves. This is shown best by the anecdotical examples of Kekulé using Ouroboros snake (iconic image) as a template for inspiring organisation of the benzene molecule, and Watson quoting dreams of spiral staircases (iconic image from a concept) as possible organizational (problem) template for the double helix discovery.

8.7 Discussion – the Relation between Imperfect Recognition, Constructive Memory and Re-Representation

It is worth noting that, in this framework, the process of object recognition itself does not require perfect matching of observation to pre-existing knowledge in the KB, and this reflects cognitive realities of operating in real-world environments. It is thus unlikely that an object in the environment will present itself to its observer bearing all identifying traits which the observer has encoded in its KB about the object. Recognition then operates by offering the best possible match in the KB, and switching to interactive learning soon after. That is, after the object has been recognized, based on a partial trait match, the agent can investigate to see if this particular object has new features that might be added to her knowledge base. This allows new traits of known objects to be learned from the environment.

However, this type of recognition also has as a consequence the bias that completely new objects from the environment will be initially compared to similar objects the agent has previously encountered. In this context, hypothesizing over the possible uses of new objects will be made by projecting pre-existing knowledge of already known objects, before a completely new concept will be built for that particular object.

Much recognition is therefore constructive – the agent assumes about an object, concept or type of event that certain properties (which the agent has already encoded) will be present. Such a type of operating is known as constructive memory (Schacter, Norman, & Koutstaal, 1998; Schacter, 2012). A negative effect would be influencing witness testimony, by triggering a template which overrides what they are remembering, or communicates expectations on what to testify. For example, (Dale, Loftus, & Rathbun, 1978) have shown that questions such as *"Did you see the..."*, *"Did you see any..."* and *"Didn't you see some..."* were answered yes more often than other question types which asked for the same information by preschool children.

On the positive side, constructive memory is an ability without which we could not navigate real world environments with any speed, as we would be required to retest all our assumptions about the world at all times. Constructive memory, with its less productive side effects, is thus a great mechanism of cognitive adaptation.

Imperfect recognition of objects and events, on which fast decision making and survival are based, might also play a role in creative problem solving. Sometimes, an imperfect match to our problem is all it takes (and all we get) to solve it. Such imperfect matches might provide new ideas and new materials for constructing new solutions.

Functional fixedness, the human tendency to apply and generally only see a certain set of known and familiar solutions to a certain problem, to the detriment of other, simpler or more productive solutions, is a side effect of having problem templates encoded in a tightly knit manner with their practically used solutions.

The process of re-representation is the ability to reconsider our direct assumptions, and re-encode the elements of the problem in a manner which is more productive. In a sense, the equivalent of this is to not take our functional fixedness premises for granted.

However, at the problem template level, this can be harder to do, as problem templates are ampler structures, and one has to inhibit such knowledge in order to regroup elements in potentially more productive templates, or create new productive templates as an adaptation of previously known ones. In human insight, an assumption about how this process of restructuring is enabled is that the incubation phase dissipates the functional fixedness, by diminishing the activation of normal patterns. This could allow for wider searches and new templates to be grouped together and applied, until one emerges which fits the problem, with all solution parts falling into place. This could constitute, at the representational level, the equivalent of the illumination stage (Wallas, 1926).

Insight and creative problem solving can thus be viewed under this framework as processes of memory management, with both associationist and gestaltic (template pattern-filling) underpinnings, and with processes of recasting and restructuring using resources from the memory and the environment.

So far, we have discussed theoretical matters. Let us see whether these mechanisms can be implemented in variate enough domains. Can these mechanisms be shown to work in practice, in a set of variate domains, and can they be brought in some measure of comparability to human performance?

Part III

Empirical and Computational Explorations

As seen in Part II, an integration of a wide set of principles in one framework may be possible. However, could cognitive systems be constructed on the basis of this framework? Would their performance be comparable to that of human participants? How could one evaluate such things?

The third part of this book focuses on applying the previous framework and processes in a set of practical cognitive systems cases, and developing a set of tools through which the performance of such systems can be evaluated similarly to that of human participants.

Here is a short summary of what each of the next four chapters explores:

- **Chapter 9 – What do Swiss, Cake and Cottage have in common?** – focuses on the first applied implementation of this framework: building a cognitive system that can make associations and solve problems like the Remote Associates Test (RAT). There is a bigger game at hand, as this test is used as a shorthand version of measuring insight. However we end up enjoying the RAT and even constructing a visual version of it. A point of comparative evaluation to human participants is found.
- **Chapter 10 – What could you use this object for?** – discusses the problem of creative object use, and the implementation of a cognitive system that can answer such problems. A parallel with some tasks in creativity testing is found, and various types of comparative evaluation are put forward.
- **Chapter 11 – Daily Eurekas about Candles and Strings** – makes the leap into approaching insight with the toolkit we have built so far. What if we transcended creative use of objects, and thought of creative use of problem templates instead? Also, what is the anatomy of an insight problem, and could we construct such problems in a domain which reuses our previous insights?
- **Chapter 12 – The journey thus far and the journey ahead** is a Janus two-faced chapter, summarizing what has been built overall in this book and where the next threads and hope of progress now lay.

Some of the topics in this part have also been explored by the author in the following scientific publications: cognitive AI solver for the Remote Associates Test (Olteţeanu & Falomir, 2015) and a visual version of the test (Olteţeanu, Gautam, & Falomir, 2015); a cognitive system that can solve the object replacement and composition problems (Olteţeanu & Falomir, 2016); an overview of approaches to some systems (Olteţeanu, Falomir, & Freksa, 2018) and approaches for insight problems (Olteţeanu, 2016).

9

What Do Swiss, Cake and Cottage Have in Common? – Computational Explorations of the Remote Associates Test

What do Swiss, Cake and Cottage have in common? An unlikely question to come by, unless you happen to be one of the participants in a Remote Associates Test, in the lab of Mednick and Mednick (Mednick & Mednick, 1971). The Remote Associates Test, affectionately referred to as the RAT from now on, is a form of a shortcut (RATs, mazes, shortcuts – they all associate). It's a shortcut to accessing creative abilities like the ones deployed while solving insight tasks.

Various psychological tests have been employed to measure creativity (Guilford, 1967; Kim, 2006), as you remember from Sect. 5.1 Some of these tests aim to empirically study what happens during insightful problem solving, by using insight problems (Maier, 1931; Duncker, 1945), like the ones shown in Sect. 5.1. Such problems, however, are quite hard and take a long time to solve. You cannot push insight to happen faster (or, if you can, that counts as a successful intervention, but you can only apply that to a group of participants, a control group and other intervention groups are generally still the case). As a participant might take half an hour to come up with a solution, it may be that the experimenter is only capable of addressing three or four, and in some cases only one single problem within a single experimental session. Because of insight problems take a long time to administer to humans, the experiments which use insight problems to explore insight can contain only a few problem items. This reduces the amount and variety of data coming from such experiments, and the inherent strength and generality of conclusions that can be drawn.

In this context, would it not be nice to have a test which measures insight, yet is shorter, and can be given in a large quantity of test items to your participants? Enter the RAT, which is thought to measure a similar ability as the insight tests: performing well at this test has been shown to correlate with the ability to successfully solve insight problems (Schooler & Melcher, 1995). How does it work?

The RAT gives participants three word items, like SWISS, CAKE and COT-TAGE. The participant has to find a fourth word, which can be associated with

© Springer Nature Switzerland AG 2020
A.-M. Oltețeanu, *Cognition and the Creative Machine*,
https://doi.org/10.1007/978-3-030-30322-8_9

all three of the initially given words. Mednick (Mednick, 1962) thought that, in order to be creative, one needs to be able to associate remote items, thus the RAT is designed to measure creativity as a function of this ability for association. The advantage of the RAT is that many items of this test can be administered relatively quickly. Thirty seconds is enough time to answer most RAT items.

So what do SWISS, CAKE and COTTAGE have in common? If you have not answered it by now, as you probably already had more than 30 seconds reading these paragraphs, I will have to spoil it for you. It is CHEESE (and perhaps now the RAT acronym makes even more associative sense – Cheese, RAT, mazes, insight shortcuts – they all associate).

But they all associate in specific ways. In the case of the above, Cheese is a valid answer because there are such things as Swiss Cheese, Cottage Cheese and Cheese Cake. However, not all test items in the RAT of (Mednick & Mednick, 1971) are equal.

Worthen and Clark (Worthen & Clark, 1971) remarked that this test contains a mix of *functional* and *structural* associates. Here is how they explain this differentiation: *Functional* associates elicit a functional relationship between them, like the one between *bird* and *egg* – birds are a function of eggs, or eggs are a function of birds, but eggs and birds are definitely in more than a language relationship. Functional items may or may not also be a language relationship, but the relationship between them definitely goes beyond it. *Structural* associates, on the other hand, are items generally associated together in language, by appearing in the same syntactic structure. For example, items like *sweet* and *tooth*; *black* and *magic*) appear together in language, but amongst these items a functional relationship does not really hold.

After making this differentiation, Worthen and Clark commented that using a set of queries which contains a mix of items, like Mednick's, might not be productive in finding out how creative processes relay on association, and that the two types should be separated from each other. Worthen and Clark also proposed a remote associates test based on functional associates (FRAT). However, the items of this test have been lost[1]. Currently, structural associates are the items which are most given to human participants. Structural associates are also called compound associates; this is because compound language items, like compound nouns (e.g. Band-aid, Rubber band), can be thought of as compound associates.

Could principles of the CreaCogs framework be implemented and used to computationally solve the Remote Associates Test?

To answer this question, we first focus on describing the Remote Associates Test in more detail. Then, we look at what CreaCogs mechanism might

---

[1] The items of this test were initially stored in the National Auxiliary Publications Service. Later on, they should have been sent to the Library of Congress, however the the Library of Congress mentions never having received them – personal correspondence 21st of July 2016.

be appropriate for RAT solving, and what its place is in the CreaCogs framework. We design a computational solver for the RAT – comRAT – based on this mechanism. Then, we have a look at whether comRAT works, how it performs, and what happens in the case of multiple possible answers. We compare answers from comRAT with answers given my humans, from a set of normative human data (Bowden & Jung-Beeman, 2003), that is data aiming to "norm" typical speed and accuracy.

Towards the end of the chapter, exiting the domain of cognitive modeling, and entering the one of computational creativity, we ask whether we could use comRAT to create new RAT queries, and if so, how. We then get hands on creative ourselves, trying to see whether the RAT task itself could be extended to the visual domain.

9.1 Meet the RAT (The Remote Associates Test)

The Remote Associates Test (Mednick & Mednick, 1971) is a test meant to measure creativity. The RAT has been widely used in the literature, both for creativity measurement (Ansburg & Hill, 2003; Cunningham, MacGregor, Gibb, & Haar, 2009) and in order to assess the relationship between creativity and other things, like sleep (Cai, Mednick, Harrison, Kanady, & Mednick, 2009) and synaesthesia (Ward, Thompson-Lake, Ely, & Kaminski, 2008).

As seen before, the test generally takes the following form: given three words, the participant has to find a fourth word which can be associated with all the given three words. For example, the following 3 items are given:

OPERA - HAND - DISH

In this case, an answer considered correct is *SOAP*, because of the following associates: *soap opera, hand soap and dish soap.* (Mednick & Mednick, 1971).

The Remote Associates Test has been translated and adapted to a variety of languages other than English (Nevo & Levin, 1978; Hamilton, 1982; Chermahini, Hickendorff, & Hommel, 2012). Of course, when we talk about translating the RAT we do not mean a direct translation: a query like Cottage, Swiss, Cake could only be translated in languages which already have the associates which would allow it to be solved: if the compound noun Cheesecake does not exist in a particular language, this query would be unsolvable in that language. Thus, translating the Remote Associates Test to another language might mostly involve generation of new queries which work for that language.

With each test consisting of only three words, and taking less than a minute to solve, the RAT makes possible the administration of 90 or more items for a normal testing session per participant, thus yielding a rich amount of data. A correlation in performance between insight tests and the RAT has been previously demonstrated empirically (Schooler & Melcher, 1995). If this correlation holds, then the RAT could be used to gather much more data and

tap much faster into mechanisms which are similar to the ones responsible
for insight. This makes the RAT worthy of modeling, and the following work
aims to set the precedent for an automated Remote Associates Test solver.

Could the principles of CreaCogs allow us to implement a solver for the
Remote Associates test?

9.2 Which Cogs Fit the RAT?

The process of solving the Remote Associates Test has some phenomenolog-
ical overlap with solving insight problems: participants attest to having a
solution to RAT queries come to mind instantly, the equivalent of the illumination phase in insight problem solving. Because of this we assume most of
the search process to happen "under the radar", or "under the hood", that
is, unconsciously.

How is the RAT solved, to obtain such effects?

Here is the hypothesis that we will follow. The various words that are
given as part of a RAT item have pre-existing associations in the memory of
the agent. When three terms are given, the associations of these three terms
are activated. Amongst these associations, some terms may be activated by
all three of the given items. A form of convergence could thus happen, upon
such items. Common items are found via such a convergence, which manifests
itself as an overlap of activation. This convergence makes a term pop-up from
the long-term memory of the cognitive system. Various constraints or boost-
ers could be applied to this activation, or to its strength, depending on the
familiarity of that compound term to the user, whether the associated terms
are related semantically or not, etc.

The process required to implemented this hypothesis is represented in the
CreaCogs framework by the general mechanism of creative upward search.
This mechanism widely argues that creative problem solving is at times the
search for the right problem elements to focus on; or the search for the right
problem template through which to represent or re-represent the problem at
hand in a productive way. This is shown in Fig. 9.1: various concepts are
given, like c_1 and c_2 at the bottom left of the figure, together with a goal or
solution (here sol_4). The participant attempts to solve the problem.

This solving mechanism proceeds by searching for the associated problem
templates in which the initial concepts were involved. For example, c_1 activates
problem templates PT_a, c_2 problem templates PT_b, and sol_4 activates set PT_c.
The process then converges in templates which might be common to the given
concepts, or that might have elements in common with the required solution.
The activated template set converge in PT_x. As the RAT is used to study
insight, this CreaCogs mechanism posited for creative problem solving should
have applicability on the RAT as well.

A refinement of this mechanism which applies to the RAT is presented in
Fig. 9.2. Concepts activate all the problem templates in which they have been

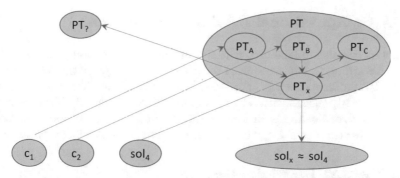

Fig. 9.1: comRAT search mechanism as pertaining to previous formalization. C stands for concept, PT for problem templates, and the tip of the arrows shows the direction of the activation

involved. In the RAT context, words activate compound or joint compound nouns in which they have appeared. This activation of contexts of course means activating multiple associative terms with which compound and joint compound nouns are formed. The overlap of activation sent to a concept from multiple compound terms is the convergence. This convergence helps find the answer term. Concepts which are activated from two or three of the given concepts will automatically pop to attention because of stronger activation.

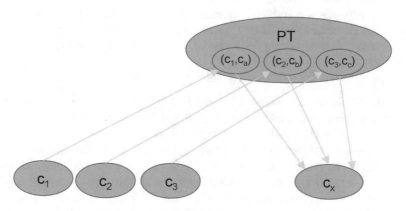

Fig. 9.2: Adapted search mechanism for the RAT, as pertaining to previous formalization. C stands for concept, PT for problem templates, and the tip of the arrows shows the direction of the activation

Could this mechanism work to solve actual RAT queries? In the following, the implementation of this mechanism as an automated solver – comRAT – will be described.

9.3 A Computational RAT Solver (comRAT)

No system can be implemented without knowledge. In the following, we will focus on obtaining the data required for the system and preparing it specifically for the RAT. This is called knowledge acquisition. The CreaCogs framework posits knowledge organization to be important in supporting the creative process. Thus after dealing with knowledge acquisition, we will focus on knowledge organization, to set up the process of solving the RAT computationally.

9.3.1 The RAT Knowledge Base

In order to build the RAT Knowledge Base (RAT-KB), language data of compound terms was needed. We aimed for a computational cognitive system, that is a system inspired by the type of knowledge, knowledge organization and processes that natural cognitive systems (people) use. We thus wanted to use knowledge that people are actually likely to have. We found a potential knowledge sources in the form of n-grams. N-grams are contiguous sequences of n items of text of speech, used in computational linguistics. The sentence before this is a sequence of text, and *"used in computational linguistics"* is thus a 4-gram. 2-grams (or bigrams) are thus sequences of two words in text or speech. *"Or speech"* is a bigram, and so is *"text or"* For the KB of comRAT, 2-grams of the publicly available, genre-balanced Corpus of Contemporary American English (COCA)[2] have been used.

These 2-grams are indexed on part of speech according to a lets of tags – the UCREL CLAWS7 Tagset[3] and contain data on frequency of use. A line of data on three-grams from the COCA corpus might thus look like the following:

$$569 \; like \; a \; baby \; || \; ii \; at1 \; nn1,$$

where *ii*, *at1* and *nn1* are part of speech tags (for example *nn1* stands for singular common noun), *like a baby* is the 3-gram itself and 569 is its frequency, that is how many times the 3-gram appears in the corpus.

The steps for acquiring and preparing the data were the following. First, the 1 million most frequent 2-grams of this corpus were acquired. Based on the part of speech the data is classified as, a pruning process was applied, in order to remove items not relevant for the RAT task. For example, it was unlikely that data on proper nouns (*IBM, Andes*) or articles (*a, an, every*) will be required. The items categorized with the tags displayed in Table 9.1 were kept as possibly relevant for the RAT task. As a result of this tag-based pruning process, approx. 200 000 bigrams were obtained.

[2] Corpus of Contemporary American English (COCA): http://corpus.byu.edu/coca/.
[3] For a complete list of the UCREL CLAWS7 Tagset see: http://ucrel.lancs.ac.uk/claws7tags.html

Table 9.1: Tagset used for extraction of items from 2-grams of the Corpus of Contemporary American English

Tag	Description	Example
FU	unclassified word	
FW	foreign word	*chateau*
JJ	general adjective	*blue*
ND1	singular noun of direction	*north*
NN	common noun, neutral for number	*sheep, cod*
NN1	singular common noun	*book, child*
NN2	plural common noun	*books, children*
RA	adverb, after nominal head	*else, galore*
REX	adverb introducing appositional constructions	*namely*
RR	general adverb	*down*
RT	quasi-nominal adverb of time	*now, tomorrow*
VB0	be, base form	finite, imperative, subjunctive
VVG -ing	participle of lexical verb	*giving, working*
VVN	past participle of lexical verb	*given, worked*

We did not seek to obtain a priori evidence whether this set will contain the necessary or useful data to solve the RAT before the experimentation phase. This is because we wanted to check whether the type of knowledge organization and process we were proposing was going to work without us pre-selecting a favourable knowledge set.

9.3.2 Knowledge Acquisition and Organization by Association

comRAT-C is endowed with three types of knowledge structures (or Classes): Concepts, Expressions and Links. In this implementation, Concepts are one word lexical items, Expressions are the equivalent of a representation structure containing two Concepts (words), and Links are bidirectional connectors between Concepts and the Expressions they are part of.

For knowledge acquisition, comRAT-C is presented sequentially with each of the 2-grams from the set pruned from the corpus. When a 2-gram is presented to the system, an item of the Expression class is constructed for it. The system then checks if it "knows" the Concepts contained in this Expression – that is if it already has these Concepts in its KB. For example, if comRAT is presented with the 2-gram *"Self-Defense"*, it will check to see if it knows the Concepts of *"Self"* and *"Defense"*. If one or both of the Concepts are unknown, the unknown Concepts are added; then a Link is constructed between them. If both *"Self"* and *"Defense"* are known, comRAT-C just adds the Link between them. This Link is bidirectional, so that comRAT can get from *"Self"* to *"Defense"*, and the other way around. After a while, each Concept is thus connected by Links to all the other Concepts it has formed an

Expression with, each Concept thus forming a hub of incoming and outgoing connections.

Word like *"Blackboard"*, *"Healthcare"* and *"Toothpaste"* are called *joint* compound nouns, or compound words in closed form – that is two words that have melded together into one word. By contrast, open form compounds show the words next to each other – for example, *"Bandwagon"* and *"Rubber band"* are a joint and an open compound word respectively, each containing the noun *"Band"*.

Some of the RAT queries might refer to compound nouns existing joint compound nouns. For example, in such a query, HEALTH might be one of the words of the query, while CARE is the answer. This means that, in order to solve such queries successfully, comRAT-C needs to take the word *"Healthcare"* as an Expression, with the Concept *"Health"* being linked to the Concept *"Care"*.

Joint compound words are not marked by the tagset in Table 9.1. After talking to a couple of linguists, we were not many steps closer to a reliable dataset of joint compound words. We thus needed to provide a computational solution to this problem. To surpass this issue, after all the Expressions have been acquired, comRAT compares each Concept with the other Concepts it knows. If comRAT recognizes a Concept as *part-of* another Concept, for example *"Health"* as part of *"Healthcare"*, it assumes *"Healthcare"* might be a compound lexical unit. It will then try to match the remaining part or the word, in this case *care*, to the other Concepts it knows. If the match is successful, this joint compound word which was initially considered a Concept, is also added as an Expression, and Links are set between its composing lexical units. Not all such items will provide a joint compound though - for example, the word *absolute* might be matched to the potential initial part *abs*, but no word will provide a match for the second part. This is only a partial computational solution, as in some rare cases the two parts of a word might be matched to Concepts, but those Concepts might not constitute a meaningful unit together. This process thus currently constitutes just a shortcut to getting to joint compound concept parts.

This concludes the knowledge acquisition and organization process. Now the system is ready to accept queries.

9.3.3 Solving the Compound RAT (cRAT) Queries

What is then the process used to solve the compound RAT? This process is fairly straightforward, and heavily helped by the type of knowledge organization obtained in the previous step.

Whenever a 3-item compound RAT query is received, comRAT-C searches its KB for Concepts matching the query words. If found, these Concepts are activated. All the Concepts which have been Linked to these 3 query terms via previous Expressions are then activated, as shown in Table 9.2. This happens independently of whether the given query items were initially experienced in the first or second position of an Expression. The other item in all 2-item Expressions which contain the initial query items become active. Thus *cake* activates both items in which cake is the first term, like *cake batter*, and items in which cake is the second term, like *carrot cake*.

Table 9.2: Example of activation of linked items for the query COTTAGE, SWISS, CAKE. ∗ acts as a wild card which can take other values.

(Cottage ∗) OR (∗ Cottage)	(Swiss ∗) OR (∗ Swiss)	(Cake ∗) OR (∗ Cake)
cottage **cheese**	Swiss Alps	cake batter
cottage garden	Swiss army	cake decorating
cottage industries	Swiss ball	cake flour
cottage ...	Swiss chard	cake layer
... cottage	Swiss **cheese**	carrot cake
... cottage	Swiss chocolate	**cheese** cake

Going back to CreaCogs, we can see how such queries elicit the conceptual and the problem template layer. This is shown in Fig. 9.3, where the bottom part represents the concept level, and the top part the template level. The initial three concepts trigger a series of compound templates. The templates thus activated implicitly activate a variety of concepts[4], like the ones in the bottom right half of Fig. 9.3. Of these, some will be activated only one time (by one of the initial items), like *garden* and *Alps*; some will be activated by two items, like *chocolate*, and some by three, like *cheese*. comRAT-C checks for answers by searching for the most activated concepts, and converging upon the answers.

For a clearer understanding of the search process, rather than keeping in mind the CreaCogs levels, have a look at the visual depiction of this mechanism at the concept level alone in Fig. 9.4. Here, the three given query words are shown in green. The activation spreads from these to the concepts linked to them in various previous templates, thus activating the concepts in blue. The term *chocolate*, shown in yellow, is activated by two of the initial query items. The term *cheese*, which constitutes the answer, is activated by all three.

An interesting thing to note is that multiple results coming from a 3-item convergence are also possible with this process. Normative data for human performance like the one offered by Bowden and Jung-Beeman (Bowden & Jung-Beeman, 2003) only offers one correct answer. To have comparability to such data, in the cases in which convergence might yield multiple results, comRAT-C is set to initially offer as an answer the first Concept found with activation coming from all 3 items. However, as multiple items might be acti-

---

[4] Such templates are in a sense only a way of meaningfully organizing or grouping knowledge.

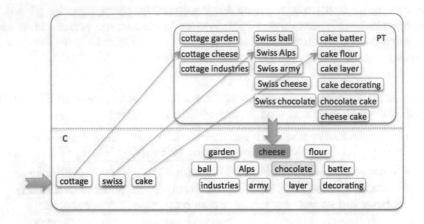

Fig. 9.3: comRAT-C process in terms of CreaCogs

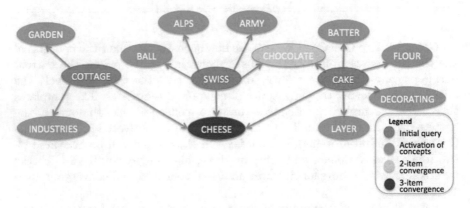

Fig. 9.4: Visual depiction of the activation during a comRAT query

vated from all three concepts, comRAT-C could also offer a different though still correct answer to that mentioned by the normative data.

Furthermore, some of the compound terms known by the human participants which solved the queries in the normative data (Bowden & Jung-Beeman, 2003) might not be known by the computational solver. Thus other 3-item convergence answers could be offered by comRAT-C compared to those offered by humans, due to differences between their knowledge bases. If no 3-item convergence is found, the system will propose the first encountered word on which 2-item convergence has happened.

The knowledge organization makes this process quite fast. However, this implies that knowledge organization – a pre-ordering of all the concepts and their links based on the expressions in the knowledge base – happens before the process, like in a natural cognitive system.

As multiple answers are sometimes possible, an interesting question is why humans might prefer a certain answer over another, and whether the frequency of compound items might have an influence on this preference. Readers not enjoying formal descriptions can skip to Sect. 9.5 to see the comRAT-C solver in action.

9.4 Formalizing Preferred Answers and Item Contribution

To have a shot of answering, in the future, why an answer might be preferred over another, we need to first ask: how do the various query items contribute to the answer?

We define all known words in our knowledge base (KB) as set W, and all known two-word expressions as set E, so that:

$$w_1, w_2, w_3, ..., w_m \in W, \quad W \in KB$$

$$e_1, e_2, e_3, ..., e_n \in E, \quad E \in KB, e_k = (w_x, w_y)$$

As our known words are acquired from bigrams, for each known word w_x there exists at least one expression which w_x is known to be part of, be it that it is the first or second term in that expression (for each $w_x, \exists$ $e_x \in E \mid e_x = (w_x, w_y) \vee e_x = (w_y, w_x)$. Both expression forms can also exist. Compound words or expressions made from the same words in a different order are not equivalent, as it is made clear by the example of the compound words *boathouse* and *houseboat*, thus:

$$(w_x, w_y) \neq (w_y, w_x)$$

For now, whenever we refer to term w_x as being part of e_x, it can appear in either positions - (w_x, w_y) or (w_y, w_x)[5].

Any RAT query is of the form:

$$q_{abc} = (w_a, w_b, w_c),$$

and its result, an intersection of the expressions triggered by each word, will be set S_{abc} (which includes the empty set):

$$w_x \in e_a \cap e_b \cap e_c, \quad w_x \in S_{abc}, \quad S_{abc} \in W$$

For our further analysis, we assume the probability of the three initial query terms to participate in finding a solution to be equal[6]:

---

[5] Ordering influences will be addressed in Sect. 9.10.

[6] We start from this case as a non-biased hypothesis. If a researcher chooses to entertain a particular hypothesis referring to which of the initial words will have a higher influence, this can easily be modelled by giving different weights to these terms.

$$P(w_a) = P(w_b) = P(w_c) = \frac{1}{3}$$

For each of the given terms – w_a, w_b and w_c – the set of expressions they participate in with other terms can be defined as e_a, e_b and e_c, e.g.[7], so that for example:

$$e_a = \{(w_a, w_1), (w_2, w_a), (w_3, w_a), ..., (w_a, w_m)\}$$

$$e_b = \{(w_b, w_1), (w_{12}, w_b), (w_{30}, w_b), ..., (w_b, w_n)\}$$

$$e_c = \{(w_c, w_9), (w_{12}, w_c), (w_{22}, w_c), ..., (w_c, w_k)\}$$

Each of the expressions the given terms participate in will have associated with them a frequency in our corpus. The total frequency of expressions (fr) in which the given terms participate is calculated as:

$$\sum_{i=1}^{m} fr(e_a) = \sum_{i=1}^{m} (w_a, w_i) \tag{9.1a}$$

$$\sum_{i=1}^{n} fr(e_b) = \sum_{i=1}^{n} (w_b, w_i) \tag{9.1b}$$

$$\sum_{i=1}^{k} fr(e_c) = \sum_{i=1}^{k} (w_c, w_i) \tag{9.1c}$$

For all possible answer terms $w_x \in S_{abc}$, the likelihood that they will be the preferred answer, if frequency of use is the factor deciding the preferred answer, is calculated as follows.

The probability formula is: $P(x) = \dfrac{\text{Favourable cases}}{\text{Total cases}}$.

The probability that each answer should appear is computed using the number of favourable cases that answer appears in combination with each of the items ($fr(w_a, w_x)$, $fr(w_b, w_x)$ and $fr(w_c, w_x)$); and the number of total cases of each of the given query terms ($\sum_{i=1}^{m} fr(e_a)$, $\sum_{i=1}^{n} fr(e_b)$, $\sum_{i=1}^{k} fr(e_k)$).

This becomes:

---

[7] The indices don't increment by one unit because that would imply every one of the given 3 words to be connected with all the others. Instead w_b might only be connected to w_1, w_{12}, w_{30}, etc.

$$P(w_x \mid w_a) = \frac{fr(w_a, w_x)}{\sum\limits_{i=1}^{m} fr(e_a)} \qquad (9.2a)$$

$$P(w_x \mid w_b) = \frac{fr(w_b, w_x)}{\sum\limits_{i=1}^{n} fr(e_b)} \qquad (9.2b)$$

$$P(w_x \mid w_c) = \frac{fr(w_c, w_x)}{\sum\limits_{i=1}^{k} fr(e_k)} \qquad (9.2c)$$

The total probability that w_x should be the preferred response based on frequency of expressions is:

$$P(w_x) = \frac{P(w_x \mid w_a) + P(w_x \mid w_b) + P(w_x \mid w_c)}{3} \qquad (9.3)$$

This is then done for all possible answers. Thus, given possible answers w_x, w_y, w_z, with $w_x, w_y, w_z \in S_{abc}$, the preferred answer based on frequency will be w_p, where:

$$w_p = max(P(w_x), P(w_y), P(w_z)) \qquad (9.4)$$

Bayes's theorem is then applied a posteriori to see how much each of the given terms contributed to finding preferred answer w_p:

$$P(w_a \mid w_p) = \frac{P(w_a) \times P(w_p \mid w_a)}{P(w_p)} \qquad (9.5a)$$

$$P(w_b \mid w_p) = \frac{P(w_b) \times P(w_p \mid w_b)}{P(w_p)} \qquad (9.5b)$$

$$P(w_c \mid w_p) = \frac{P(w_c) \times P(w_p \mid w_c)}{P(w_p)} \qquad (9.5c)$$

For each solution (preferred or not) in S_{abc}, a triple $c_{abc,x}$ can be calculated for the contributions of each initial term w_a, w_b, w_c to solution w_x. Thus for the preferred solution w_p:

$$c_{abc,p} = (P(w_a \mid w_p), P(w_b \mid w_p), P(w_c \mid w_p)) \qquad (9.6)$$

and the maximum contributing item is $max(P(w_a \mid w_p), P(w_b \mid w_p), P(w_c \mid w_p))$.

9.5 comRAT-C Experimentation and Results

Systems need to have their performance evaluated. As comRAT-C is a cognitive system, chose a comparability approach, in which the performance of the system is evaluated in comparison to human performance.

For human performance, the normative data from Bowden and Jung-Beeman (Bowden & Jung-Beeman, 2003) has been used. This data has gathered the average response times and accuracy of human participants to 144 RAT queries.

The results, as can be seen in Table 9.3, show that out of the 144 items used in Bowden and Jung-Beeman's test, comRAT-C answers 64 of them correctly without using any data on frequency.[8] Out of these, 64 correct answers, for 47 of these, all three initial RAT query words were known in conjunction with the answer. That is, for 47 of these queries, the three expressions needed to answer the query – $E_1 = c_1 c_x$, $E2 = c_2, c_x$, $E3 = c_3, c_x$ were known (where c_1, c_2 and c_3 are the given query words, and c_x is the correct answer from the normative data). The accuracy of the system is thus 97.92% when all three expressions are known, without using any frequency data or complex activation mechanisms. This performance is based on associative convergence principles alone.

Table 9.3: Analysis of comRAT-C's performance in relation to known items

Number of Expressions known =>	0 E	1 E	2 E	3 E	Total
Correct Answers	0	0	17	47	64
Plausible Answers	2	11	12	1	26
Not solved	4	23	27	0	54
Total	6	34	56	48	
Accuracy			30.36%	97.92%	

Among the answers comRAT-C gave, some were not correct, but not incorrect either. We called these answers "plausible answers", as can be seen in Table 9.3. These answers are not the answers given as correct in the normative data. However they could be considered as interesting or good enough answers from the human perspective.

Some such plausible answers arise from data regularity, converging upon items which are common to the three query items and possibly to many others, for example adjectives like *great, big, small*. Other plausible answers are more interesting, surprising and can be considered more "creative" from the human perspective. Examples of such interesting plausible answers are shown in Table 9.4. They offer as response a noun or another word which is indeed a specific remote associate of this particular 3 words tuple, rather than a word which might be a common associate to multiple tuples. (e.g. words like easy, small, black, etc).

---

[8] Correctness in this case is considered as the exact answer provided by the system on its first try.

A more rigorous description of the two cases might be that interesting items are items with which the 3 elements in the query form new concepts, while the "common" items are attributes which are perhaps characteristic of many items (or form with the second element an attribute-concept pair). In this case, taking into account the frequencies of such items or their part-of-speech tag might endow the system with the ability to differentiate between surprising and regular plausible answers.

Table 9.4: Some of the plausible answers obtained by the computational RAT

No.	w_1	w_2	w_3	$Answer_1$ (Bowden & Jung-Beeman, 2003)	$Answer_2$
1	High	District	House	SCHOOL	STATE
2	Health	Taker	Less	CARE	RISK
3	Cat	Number	Phone	CALL	HOUSE
4	Chamber	Mask	Natural	GAS	DEATH
5	Self	Attorney	Spending	DEFENSE	BILL
6	Fight	Control	Machine	GUN	POLITICAL
7	Off	Military	First	BASE	PAY
8	French	Car	Shoe	HORN	COMPANY
9	Cry	Front	Ship	BATTLE	WAR
10	Change	Circuit	Cake	SHORT	DESIGN
11	Child	Scan	Wash	BRAIN	BODY
12	Mill	Tooth	Dust	SAW	GOLD
13	Home	Sea	Bed	SICK	WATER

In order to accurately assess the performance of the system, the knowledge in the KB-comRAT needs to be compared to the knowledge required to solve the items in the normative data (Bowden & Jung-Beeman, 2003) test. For some queries in Bowden's data, the system simply did not have enough knowledge to respond. As Table 9.3 shows, in the cases where comRAT-C had all 3 items in its database, its correctness of response when compared with normative answers was at 97.92%, while when comRAT-C only knew two of the given expressions, it was finding the correct answers in 30.36% of the cases. The fact that comRAT-C can solve some queries correctly even in the absence of knowledge regarding one of the terms is encouraging, since humans are normally assumed to know all the three items when answering a RAT query correctly, or to at least be able to verify whether the 3rd expression is a valid, meaningful one.

9.6 Preferred Convergence – Empirical Analysis

As comRAT-C shows that multiple answers are possible for some queries, a question that follows is why do humans prefer certain answers over other possible answers? To explore this, we will look at the items with multiple answers from our current dataset.

Four queries from the normative dataset where answered correctly and had multiple interesting answers. These queries, and their correct answers from the normative data, where the following:

1. HIGH DISTRICT HOUSE. *Answer:* SCHOOL
2. CHAMBER MASK NATURAL. *Answer:* GAS
3. SELF ATTORNEY SPENDING. *Answer:* DEFENSE
4. BACK STEP SCREEN. *Answer:* DOOR

comRAT-C found multiple possible answers for these queries, as shown in Table 9.5. The table also shows frequency-based probability for each answer of the four queries, calculated as shown in equations 9.2 and 9.3. The answers are arranged in decreasing order of probability (with the maximum probability item to the left side). In all four cases, the first answer (A_1) which offers the highest probability is also the one which is considered correct in the normative data.

Table 9.5: Frequency-based probability for the multiple answers of four queries

Query	A_1	A_2	A_3	A_4	A_5	A_6	A_7	A_8	A_9	A_{10}	A_{11}
High District House	School	Court	Historic	U.S.	Officials	Office	Water	State	Suburban	Light	Church
Answer Probability	0.1850	0.0306	0.0069	0.0061	0.0046	0.0034	0.0033	0.0027	0.0012	0.0012	8.8E-4
Chamber Mask Natural	Gas	Death									
Answer Probability	0.1162	0.0240									
Self Attorney Spending	Defense	Bill	Personal	Private							
Answer Probability	0.0767	0.0146	0.0059	0.0056							
Back Step Screen	Door	Porch									
Answer Probability	0.0485	0.0063									

This shows that items with highest frequency might be the ones preferred by humans. Only four items are obviously not enough to settle this matter, but comRAT-C makes such a hypothesis testable, as we will discuss later.

The contribution of the three items to the preferred responses is shown in Table: 9.6. The highest contributing item is shown in bold. As seen here, the position of the highest contributing item varies across these four queries.

Table 9.6: Contribution of the three items to various answers

Query	Answer	Item 1	Item 2	Item 3
High District House	School	**0.60**	0.40	0.00
High District House	Court	0.07	**0.83**	0.10
Chamber Mask Natural	Gas	0.24	**0.43**	0.33
Chamber Mask Natural	Death	0.45	**0.50**	0.05
Self Attorney Spending	Defense	0.25	**0.47**	0.27
Self Attorney Spending	Bill	0.32	0.03	**0.65**
Back Step Screen	Door	0.34	0.02	**0.64**
Back Step Screen	Porch	**0.66**	0.19	0.14

The contribution of the three query items[9] is important, as it can help the further study of the preferred answer. A possibility is that, if the contribution of the items is important, then perhaps one can manipulate the preferred answer by changing the order of the query words. Showing the strongest contributing item to one answer or the other first might influence the preferred answer. This might only hold if the two responses are close in average probability. Such investigations are made possible by comRAT-C and the data it provides, but are left open for future investigation.

For now, we will focus on comparing the difficulty of the queries for humans and comRAT-C.

9.7 RAT Difficulty for comRAT and Humans

Analysing the data on these four queries, we observed a correlation between comRAT-C's probability of answering queries and the difficulty of the RAT query for humans. The number of participants that could solve a particular test item decreased with comRAT-C's probability to trigger that item. The time taken to solve a query by human participants increased the lower the probability for comRAT-C to find the answer item.

Table 9.7: Frequency-based probability for the multiple answers of four queries

Query	Probability	% of participants solving (15 s)	Mean Solution Time (s)
High District House	0.1850	55	5.59
Chamber Mask Natural	0.1162	53	5.86
Self Attorney Spending	0.0767	4	8.42
Back Step Screen	0.0485	0	-

After making this observation on the limited set of multianswer queries (shown in Table 9.7), we wanted to check whether this correlation holds on all the queries from Bowden's data. In practice, we could actually check for correlation on the queries which fulfilled the following three conditions:
(a) comRAT-C could answer them correctly;
(b) comRAT-C had knowledge of all three expressions formed by the RAT query items and the correct answer (this allowed us to have frequency data available for the probability calculations), and
(c) normative data was available in the Bowden paper.

Fourty eight items fulfilling these conditions were found. The same correlations held: (i) the higher probability of an answer by comRAT-C, the more people could solve that test item; (ii) the lower the probability of an answer by comRAT-C, the longer people spent before giving a good answer. A summary

---

[9] This has been calculated as shown in equations 9.5 and 9.6.

of correlations and significance for all the 48 correct answers is shown in Table 9.8, for participants being given 7, 15 or 30 seconds to solve the problem.

Table 9.8: Correlation between probability based on frequency and human data, and its significance. MST stands for Mean Solution Time, and % PS stands for Percentage of participants solving

Measure	% PS - 7s	% PS -15s	% PS -30s	MST - 7s	MST - 15s	MST - 30s
Correlation $P(w_x)$	$r = 0.45$	$r = 0.41$	$r = 0.49$	$r = -0.39$	$r = -0.3$	$r = -0.52$
Significance	$p < 0.002$	$p < 0.004$	$p < 0.002$	$p < 0.007$	$p < 0.04$	$p < 0.001$

We then checked to see whether the same correlation held between human answers and the probability of finding the answer given each of the three terms, not just the average probability. Upon this analysis, the correlation was due to the first two terms – $P(w_x \mid w_a)$ and $P(w_x \mid w_b)$, with the third term $P(w_x \mid w_c)$ not being correlated to human performance. The term based correlations are shown in Table 9.9. This table also shows a significant medium size correlation between the added probabilities of finding the first two query items and human performance data.

Table 9.9: Correlation between the probability of finding the answer given each of the three terms, accuracy and response times. $P(w_x \mid w_a)$, $P(w_x \mid w_b)$ and $P(w_x \mid w_c)$ is the probability given each of the three terms. % PS stands for Percentage of participants solving. MST is Mean Solution Time

Measure	% PS - 7s	% PS -15s	% PS -30s	MST - 7s	MST - 15s	MST - 30s
Correlation $P(w_x \mid w_a)$	$r = 0.38$	$r = 0.33$	$r = 0.4$	$r = -0.29$	$r = -0.25$	$r = -0.33$
Correlation $P(w_x \mid w_b)$	$r = 0.40$	$r = 0.44$	$r = 0.53$	$r = -0.43$	$r = -0.26$	$r = -0.33$
Correlation $P(w_x \mid w_c)$	$r = -0.11$	$r = -0.18$	$r = -0.07$	$r = 0.11$	$r = 0.04$	$r = 0.05$
Correlation $P(w_x \mid w_a) + P(w_x \mid w_b)$	$r = 0.47$	$r = 0.45$	$r = 0.51$	$r = -0.41$	$r = -0.30$	$r = -0.41$

Thus comRAT-C can successfully solve RAT queries, shows important aspects of the RAT that have not been explored before (like the issue of multiple answers, and answer preference). Furthermore, the computational solver shows correlation to the human data, which means it can be used as a tool to model the process of solving the RAT, and further explore refined aspects of this process.

But can a computational solver of a creativity task, such as the RAT, be made even more useful, by being turned into a tool for making more RAT queries?

9.8 What Does It Take to Be a RAT? – Generative Abilities of comRAT

A creative way of looking at a system like comRAT implies wondering whether it might hold potential for reverse-engineering. Thus, could comRAT be turned from a system which can find convergences between given items of a query, their known expressions and possible RAT answers, to a system which proposes queries that can be solved by humans?

An exhaustive initial idea on how this could be done is to check for convergences between all 3 items possibilities. This would go as follows: w_a, w_b and w_c would be taken as variables. They would be replaced in turn with all the words in the corpus. comRAT-C will keep on trying to solve, chewing through all these very many queries. The RAT queries which have at least one convergent term w_r, would be saved as potential new RAT queries.

This process is computationally exhaustive. Its costs depends on the initial size of the knowledge base (n), with a full run amounting to specifically $n * (n-1) * (n-2)$, thus approximately n^3. Then all these generated queries might need to be checked to remove very common attributes (like *little, great, only, big* etc.), or the entire process could be restrained to nouns.

However, upon further thought, smarter ways of generating rather queries exist, which rely on the exact same strength that comRAT uses to solve queries: it's knowledge organization. Let us say that instead of searching for potential queries, we consider potential answers. Literally any word can be an answer to a query, if it has at least 3 links. Thus, taking each word as a potential answer w_r, whenever a w_r has more than three links, these can be considered as query items $w_a, w_b, w_c, w_d..., w_n$. With the cost of one pass through the entire KB (n), we can then find all the answer to potential query items mappings. Some such examples are shown below (and more can be seen in Table A.4 of Appendix A):

1. *Answer:* **Star**.
   RAT query items: movie, rock, pop, neutron, formation, basketball, power, football, witness, film, system, clusters, cluster, player, track, tennis, shooting, guest, anise, child, etc.;

2. *Answer:* **Glass**
   RAT query items: doors, door, windows, window, ceiling, wall, beads, case, plate, window, wine, bowl, water, bottles, jar, walls, shot, jars, panels, cases, martini;

3. *Answer:* **Silver**
   RAT query items: medal, lining, sterling, bullet, hair, screen, medalist, tray, spoon;

4. *Answer:* **Table**
   RAT query items: breakfast, pool, card, water, night, dressing, operating, side, bargaining, end, dining-room, corner, buffet, tennis, defense, top, lamp, salt, manners, oak;

5. *Answer:* **Box**

   RAT query items: office, ballot, dialog, boom, lunch, press, jewellery, music, glove, shoe, metal, jury, deposit, cigar, litter, set, tackle, office, spring, plastic, toe.

The process of creating queries is not yet complete, but it gets us pretty close to the solution, at low costs. Queries can then be made out of various combinations of these items – for example, we can opt for query MOVIE, ROCK,CLUSTERS ro get to the answer STAR; or for query FOOTBALL, FILM,POP, to get to the same answer. Or we could simply use the highest probability or frequency to get the strongest links.

This technique can further use the frequency data to generate, for each answer item, queries with different probability (as weighed by the first two terms). This can be used to generate RAT queries fast to check whether the correlation (between difficulty of query for humans and the probability of the first two items) holds over a larger body of data. Generating RAT queries with comRAT and then gathering human data on them can be used to further check this correlation.

Furthermore, in such an experiment one could measure whether indeed the frequency of the first two expression plays a decisive role independent of the frequency of the answer item w_r. This is because one can yield multiple queries with the same response item, keeping w_r as a stable variable, and only manipulating query items via their frequency.

This technique can also be applied to generate tests with multiple correct answers, of different probabilities. This then can be used to check to what extent the preferred answer can reliably be predicted using frequency data.

The semantic domain of the query items might play a role in the difficulty of the query, and in making the query more interesting, or the answer to be considered as more creative. Thus, in the second example of the list of queries generated above from answers (answer: Glass), items like "door" and "window" taken together, or "martini" and "wine" taken together are part of the same semantic domain. They thus triggering the same interpretation of the response word "glass". This means that they might not qualify for a *convergence across semantic domains*. A more interesting query in the context of the same example would be "door", "wine", "case". Such experimentation would need that the knowledge of semantic domains is formalized and automatized.

The general premise of the RAT deals with the principle of "remote" association. "Remoteness" could be understood in a variety of ways, including as difference of semantic domain. However, remoteness could also be expressed, taking into account our current data, as low of frequency of expressions. RAT items with lower probability to be answered might not just be harder for human participants, but also considered more creative by them. A set of such queries could be generated to check this hypothesis, by asking human observers to judge high frequency and medium frequency items in terms of some designed scale, which could include how interesting the items are. This would shed light on whether such quantitative means of assessing frequency correlate with qualitative judgements of creativity.

In summary, such generative techniques enabled by comRAT and its knowledge organization allow the further exploration and manipulation of variables in the new Remote Associates tests. This constitutes a great tool, which can enable the cognitive scientist, psychologist or linguist to further experiment with the task and disseminate the processes which take part in its solving. Some possibilities for such further work are, but are not restricted to:

→ Verifying on a larger scale whether difficulty of answer is correlated to the probability of the first two query terms. Also checking if this is independent of the answer term, by keeping the answer the same.

→ Gathering further data on the probability based preferred item hypothesis.

→ Checking to see whether lower frequency items make for what is considered more creative RAT queries and answers.

→ Determining the impact semantic domain has on solving such queries.

9.9 Not a Blind RAT – Expanding the Remote Associates Test to the Visual Domain

The RAT can thus be solved using the CreaCogs principles in the language domain. However, would such principles apply to a domain which is not linguistic? Could the processes used by the comRAT hold in a different domain? And could there even be a Remote Associates Test that is not linguistic?

Exploring these principles in a non-linguistic domain would bring about a variety of advantages, including the following:

(i) The ability to dispel some fears in the literature that performance in the RAT might reflect language fluency performance more than creativity, by providing a way to reliably differentiate between the two components of such performance;

(ii) The ability to study a cognitive process in different domains, thus ensuring both domain independence and an ability to study domain influences;

(iii) The ability to give a creativity test in two different domains (such a test currently does not exist; test batteries like the TTCT have sections which address visual creativity and others which address language, but a test that can transfer across domains is not yet present in the literature);

(iv) The ability to deal in a more unified manner with creative processes, thus make stronger cross-domain and more refined intra-domain claims about process.

However, a visual version of the Remote Associates Test did not exist in the literature, thus we had to attempt to create our own.

9.9.1 Making the RAT Visual

What is the Remote Associates Test at its core, and how could this core be transported to a different domain? Let us look at our previous formalization of the RAT, and try to cross is linguistic domain boundaries.

In the linguistic RAT, the solver is given a 3 item query in which w_a, w_b and w_c are the query terms, and w_x is the answer term. For a participant to be able to solve the query, three items (w_a, w_x), (w_b, w_x) and (w_c, w_x) or their reverse – (w_x, w_a), (w_x, w_b) and (w_x, w_c) – must exist and be known to the solver[10].

Let us now assume that it is not necessary that the building blocks of the RAT are linguistic. Let us for example take the query items w_a, w_b and w_c to be visual representations of objects, rather than words. (w_a, w_x), (w_b, w_x) and (w_c, w_x) would thus be objects which co-occur in images or experiences for the solver, rather than words which appear in close succession in written or spoken language. w_x would thus be a visual representation of an object which can be given as answer.

A visual query constructed on these principles is shown in Fig. 9.5. Thus items HANDLE, GLOVE and PEN are given, and a potential correct answer, which is associated with each of these objects, is HAND.

Fig. 9.5: Example of a visual RAT question. This query shows the participants visual entities HANDLE, GLOVE and PEN. The answer is HAND

This construct makes the assumption that the solvers would count on experience with said objects and visuospatial schemas to trigger visual associates and converge upon the answer object. In the visual context, the order of entities might be irrelevant, or at least irrelevant in the same terms in which it mattered in language: if the objects have been seen co-occurring, they were present at the same time, rather than in a sequence, like in language[11].

Thus in the visual form of the RAT we consider each initial object of the query to have a variety of visual associates in the mind of the participants, in

---

[10] Knowing two out of three items might be enough for a human solver if they can discover w_x using the known items, and then assess whether the third term and w_x form a meaningful (though previously unknown) construct.

[11] However spatial position of items may be relevant. This will have to be settled in future work.

a similar manner as language terms would have word associates in the original language-based RAT. In the visual query depicted in Fig. 9.5, the visual associates HANDLE, HAND), (GLOVE, HAND) and (HAND, PEN) are necessary in order to solve the query.

Now we had a potential formula of creating visual RAT items, we needed to create more such items, and check whether human participants could solve them.

9.9.2 Giving the Visual RAT to Human Participants

In order to run the newly designed vRAT variant with human participants, 22 visual RAT queries were created. These queries can be seen in Appendix A, in Table A.4. Out of these queries, two were used for training and 20 as main test queries.

In order to solve these visual queries computationally (with comRAT-V), we required knowledge about visual associations of objects, rather than n-grams, like for comRAT-C. We thus set up a process to acquire this knowledge from a cognitive source - that is from people. We decided to ask participants to this study to also provide visual associates to some of the objects in the test.

However, if participants solved a particular query including a set of objects, they could not be asked to provide associates to the same objects, because they might have been biased by their own pervious answer. For example, requiring a participant to give associates for the object HANDLE after this participant has previously solved the query shown in Fig. 9.5 might bias her to give HAND as a first associate, whereas previously she might have said DOOR first.

Similarly, asking participants to solve queries after providing associates might have biased them in query solving, and changed their response times. For this reason, we needed to make sure that participants give associates to objects which were not part of the queries they solved. To ensure this, the study was split in two parts. The first part provided training examples for the visual RAT and the testing queries themselves. The second part gathered the associates. Participants were assigned in four random groups, to make sure that they give associates to objects they have not seen in queries during the testing phase. In the following, the two parts of the study and the four group design are explained.

Part 1 – Training and Test

The 22 queries each showed 3 visual stimuli each, be it objects or scenes. Fig. 9.6 shows a query in which the first two stimuli are objects and the third is a scene. Two training queries showing both objects and scenes were initially provided, instructing the participant how to solve them (these are shown in Figs. 9.5 and 9.6). Thus 5 objects and 1 scene where presented in training, and 54 objects and 6 scenes in the test itself.

Fig. 9.6: Second training vRAT query showed to the participants items BATH-
TUB, GLASS and BEACH. The answer is WATER

Participants were split into four random groups. All participants were
instructed that they will be presented with three objects or scenes and required
to provide a fourth element related to each of them.

While being shown the two training examples, participants were also instructed to self-assess how they first perceived the answer. They could choose
between (i) Visual imagery (if their self-assessment was that they imagined the
answer), (ii) Word (if they thought they first perceived the answer verbally)
or (iii) Other (case in which they had to specify).

Participants were then instructed to provide an assessment of each query's
difficulty, on a Likert scale, ranging from 1 (Very Easy) to 7 (Very Hard). After
these instructions were provided in the context of the training examples, the
participants where given to solve 15 of the 20 visual RAT queries. These
queries different according to the group, as will be described below.

The objects in the remaining 5 queries (also different for each group) were
meant to be used in the knowledge acquisition phase.

Part 2 – Knowledge Acquisition

In the second part of the study, the participants were asked to contribute
visual associates to a set of 15 objects (that is, each of the three objects
from the five unseen queries, in random order). The task was explained in the
following manner:

> *"Visual associates are things you see when you imagine a particular
> object. These might be other objects, which are situated next to the
> object that you are imagining in some circumstance, or specific parts
> of the object you are imagining."*

Examples of various visual associates were then provided for some objects:

> *"For example, visual associates for "glove" might be: hand, thorns,
> snow, scalpel, hot pan, bike, dirt. Visual associates for "pen" might be:
> paper, notebook, letter, test, form, cheque, desk, ink, drawing, writing,
> pen holder, ear, pen case, pencil, etc."*

The instruction for the participants when given an object was to *"Imagine each item, and then write the visual associates that come to mind"*.

In order for all objects to be given visual associates to, while also having a good number of participants answering each of the queries, the test was set up to be administered in four groups, via four different Google form surveys. The participants were allocated to groups by using a coin randomizer[12]. The participants would flip two Euro coins in this randomizer, and receive a heads and tails position combination. The image thus obtained via the randomizer was used to guide the participants to one of the four forms of the survey.

The 20 test questions were split in four 5-question groups. Each of the four groups of participants was (a) shown the two training queries, (b) asked to solve 3 sets of questions (15 queries) and (c) to provide visual associates for the objects in the remaining 5 queries[13]. The queries per group design is shown in Table 9.10. Thus, Group 1 was shown queries 1-15, and provided visual associates for objects in queries 16-20. Meanwhile, group 2 solved queries 1-10 and 16-20, providing visual associates for objects in queries 11-15, etc.

Table 9.10: The four groups and their assigned tasks. "Q" denotes a question, and n the number of participants in each group

Study items	Group 1 $n = 8$	Group 2 $n = 15$	Group 3 $n = 8$	Group 4 $n = 12$	Answers per item
vRAT Training Examples	Yes	Yes	Yes	Yes	Shown to all
vRAT Q1-5	Yes	Yes	Yes	No	Gr. 1, 2, 3 $(n = 31)$
vRAT Q6-10	Yes	Yes	No	Yes	Gr. 1, 2, 4 $(n = 35)$
vRAT Q11-15	Yes	No	Yes	Yes	Gr. 1, 3, 4 $(n = 28)$
vRAT Q16-20	No	Yes	Yes	Yes	Gr. 2, 3, 4 $(n = 35)$
Visual associates for objects in questions	Q16-20	Q11-15	Q6-10	Q1-5	all objects across groups

Thus, visual associates were provided by human participants to all the objects and scenes in the vRAT. These visual associates were further used by the knowledge base of comRAT-V.

9.9.3 Solving the Visual RAT Computationally – from comRAT to comRAT-V

In the comRAT-C solver of compound RAT queries, n-grams (specifically 2-grams) from a language corpus were used to generate the template knowledge (the Expression class), and to form the associative links between concepts. Furthermore, frequency data from the same corpus was used in the probability

---

[12] https://www.random.org/coins/?num=2&cur=60-eur.germany-1euro
[13] Note that the objects stimuli for visual associates were presented in an alternate order, as not to trigger the convergent associate which would be the answer.

based algorithm in order to select the preferred answer in cases of multiple possible responses, and this correlated with difficulty from human normative data.

In the visual expansion version (comRAT-V), the visual associates provided by human participants were used in the same way as n-grams in comRAT-C. Thus visual associates for the 60 objects were used to provide an equivalent to the "Expression Templates" in comRAT-C. They informed the knowledge base of comRAT-V, which again organized its knowledge in Concepts, Links and Visual Templates[14] (which replaced Expression Templates).

The frequency with which the participants provided a certain visual associate was used as a base for the same probability algorithm in order to break possible ties, and check for correlation with difficulty. This amount of data is of course too small to draw strong conclusions, and different ways to extract larger amounts of such data will be discussed in Sect. 9.10. However, the current expansion provided satisfactory results in terms of adapting the RAT to a visual version. Before looking at how comRAT-V did when solving these queries, let us see how the human participants fared when solving the visual version of the RAT.

9.9.4 Human Participants Results When Solving the Visual RAT

A total of 43 participants completed the study, 30 male and 13 female. The age of the participants ranged between (btw.) 20 and 60 years old (y.o.), as follows:

- 6 btw. 20-30 y.o.
- 19 btw. 30-40 y.o.
- 14 btw. 40-50 y.o.
- 4 btw. 50-60 y.o.

The English proficiency level of participants was (as declared by participants):

- Intermediate - 9
- Advanced - 21
- Proficient - 10
- Native - 3

Human participants solved on average 63% of the vRAT queries, as shown in Fig. 9.7. Their performance on the different queries varied between 6.45% (Q5) and 97.1% (Q20). Queries can thus be classified in different levels of difficulty based on this performance, with Q5, Q13 and Q16 being the most difficult, and Q8, Q18, Q20 the easiest queries.

In terms of self-assessed perception of the answer, participants considered they first perceived the answer mostly visually (56.6%) or as a word (38.9%), with some participants choosing the Other category. Out of the Other category, some participants specified that they perceived the answer via a different

---

[14] Visual Templates can also be seen as a form of visual context.

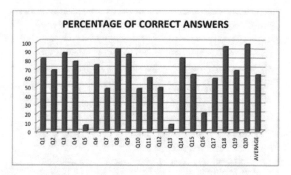

Fig. 9.7: Percentage of correct answers per query, as solved by the human participants

sense modality (0.16%). For example, a participant reported first *"perceiving the feeling of heat"* when the answer was *fire*.

Responses on how the answer was perceived are shown in Fig. 9.8 per query item. Thus the last 7 queries where perceived as much more visual on average than queries Q5, Q10 and Q13.

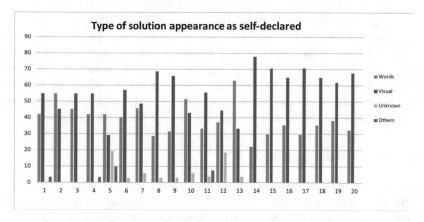

Fig. 9.8: Type of solution appearance as self-declared by participants per query. The query number is shown on the x-axis

Participants were asked to rate the difficulty of the problems on a 1-7 Likert scale. The results of this rating are shown in Fig. 9.9, together with the standard deviation (SD) of the ratings. Participants rated problems at an average of 3.41 difficulty on the Likert scale. They rated problems Q5, Q12 and Q7 as being the hardest, and problems Q18, Q14 and Q19 as the easiest, in the respective order.

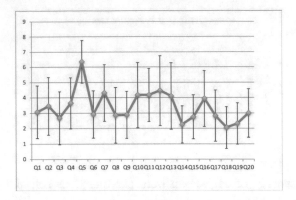

Fig. 9.9: Difficulty ratings for the 20 problems, as expressed by the human participants

Perception of difficulty might be individual or biased by intrinsic experience, and thus not reflect the actual average difficulty of the problems. To check whether the average of subjective difficulty ratings was related to actual average difficulty of problems (as expressed by percentage of participants solving the problem), We wanted to check whether the subjective difficulty ratings were related to the actual difficulty of the problems, that is to what percentage of participants manage to solved the problem. We correlated these two values for the 20 problems. A negative high correlation of -0.78 with significance of $p < 0.001$ was found between percentage of solvers and difficulty ratings. In other words, the more participants solve the problem, the lower their average subjective rating of difficulty. Thus it seems that participants can, on average, estimate actual difficulty of a visual query quite reliably.

9.9.5 Results with comRAT-V

The visual associates provided by human participants to objects were used to build the knowledge base of comRAT-V. The knowledge organization and process of computational query solving was similar to that of comRAT-C.

With this knowledge and process, and without use of frequency, comRAT-V was already solving 63.64% of the queries. After calculating frequency, the accuracy of comRAT-V responses increased to 72.73%. The relation between knowledge items specifically required by the queries in comRAT-V's knowledge base and comRAT-V's performance is shown in Table 9.11. comRAT-V answered correctly 16 out of 22 queries. Most of the correct answers (13) were found via 3 items convergences; no answer was found in the cases in which only one useful visual associate was known, and 3 correct and 3 plausible answers were produced in the cases in which two useful visual associates were known.

Table 9.11: The relation between comRAT-V's response accuracy and useful knowledge coming from visual associates

	1 item known	2 items known	3 items known	Total
Correct	0	3	13	16
Plausible	0	3	0	3
Not solved	2	1	0	3
Total	2	7	13	22
Accuracy	-	42.86% (85.71%)	100%	72.73%

comRAT-V proposed two or more possible answers to a few queries. For example, for Q8 (COW, KNIFE, GRILL – as can be seen in Figure A.1, Appendix A), the two answers proposed via three item convergence were CHEESE and MEAT. Both answers are plausible, and the CHEESE answer might be more salient with participants that do not eat meat. In the case of Q21 (COMB, RAZOR, SHAMPOO), a larger set of four possible answers is found via three item convergence: WATER, BATHROOM, HAIR, MIRROR). The expected correct answers were chosen in both cases by comRAT-V using the frequency-based likelihood.

comRAT-V also offered different plausible solutions to items which it answered correctly. For simplicity, we did not include this data in Table 9.11. This table includes only the highest probability-based items, and plausible answers when no correct answer was found. A total number of 10 other plausible answers appears in comRAT-V's solution spaces.

As expected, the knowledge in comRAT-V's KB is a powerful influencer of performance. As shown in Table 9.11 and presented in a visual manner in Fig. 9.10, current performance when all three query word-answer pairs were known was 100%. Note that high performance is not a necessity when having all the required knowledge, as other plausible items might have a higher frequency than the expected correct answers. This means that it is possible for the level of performance to decrease when aiming to answer computationally a set of queries with a larger knowledge base, unless this is based on cognitive associations and frequencies.

A correlation between the likelihood that comRAT-V would find an answer and the difficulty ratings of vRAT queries as provided by humans was observed. A moderate-high negative correlation $p = -0.64$ with moderate-high significance $p = 0.01$ was observed between the two values. Thus, the more likely comRAT-V is to solve a query, the lower the difficulty expressed by human participants when rating the same query. The percentage of solvers showed a positive yet non-significant correlation ($r = 0.41$) with comRAT-V's likelihood of finding a solution. More data is needed to check whether this could become a significant relation. However, altogether these results show that comRAT-V's likelihood algorithm and the CreaCogs convergence by association process captures something about the difficulty of the process of

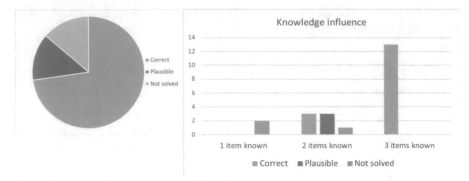

Fig. 9.10: Visual representation of the influence of knowledge on answer accuracy.

solving these queries, in the same manner in which the results of the same algorithm, applied in comRAT-C, showed an interesting relationship to human data.

Our initial set of visual queries and number of participant is of course small to draw any strong conclusions. However, it shows possibility in using the same mechanism to solve the RAT in two different modalities.

9.10 Discussion and Further Work

In this chapter we explored the Remote Associates creativity test, implemented a computational solver for it, explored its relations to human performance. We then expanded the principles learned along the way to make possible a first prototype of a visual Remote Associates Test, gave this test to people and showed the same mechanisms can be applied to computationally solve it. In this section, we will take a big-picture view of our findings, reviewing:

(i) the place of comRAT in CreaCogs, the cognitive processes implemented and the artifacts of implementation;
(ii) comRAT-C's performance and limitations;
(iii) the preferred item selection hypothesis and the correlation with human data on difficulty;
(iv) the application of the same process with visual stimuli; and
(v) comRAT's future perspectives, including using different data sets and its generative abilities.

(i) comRAT's place in CreaCogs and cognitive processes implemented

As an implementation, comRAT is a step further towards the automation of the CreaCogs framework. Specifically, comRAT explores the use of associative links for problem solving via convergence, and the upward search mechanism proposed in Chap. 8. comRAT models a convergent way of finding an answer, with a pop-up effect of such an answer. In cognitive terms, the query elicits the knowledge of the agent, an implicit search over that knowledge base happens, and the answers come up as a result of convergent activation from different initial concept points.

This process is not a classic problem-solving search process. It is rather a form of search in which the next possible states are proposed via association. These states are the items associated with the objects offered in the query – which is taken to represent the initial problem state. The problem space becomes the cognitive space of all the associations the agent can find to the initial problem state in its knowledge base. In this case, three different lexical items find the fourth element (answer) because they converge on it by associative power. The initial items can act as initial constraints of the search, because of the way the knowledge base of the system is organised.

In RAT, the pop-up or the "aha!" effect from more complex insight problems can be represented by the "sudden" appearance of the solution item (or a possible solution item) in the attention of the agent. comRAT-C assumes that this pop-up happens via a convergence of the associative mechanism. CreaCogs posits that this is what also happens at higher levels of complexity, and with much deeper constraints, in insight problem solving which involve sets of objects or concepts and possible actions or affordances.

The set-up of the knowledge base in comRAT is currently symbolic. This is not a theoretical commitment that cognitive processing in such cases would take part on a symbolic level alone, but an artifact of this particular implementation. The proof of concept presented here uses lexical symbolic information because of ease of access to both training data (lexical corpuses) and human performance data in the literature (the RAT normative data). The principles used in comRAT-C are assumed to be applicable to other types of data, as will be discussed in point (iv).

(ii) comRAT-C's performance and limitations
After the initial implementation of comRAT-C, its performance in answering compound RAT queries when given enough knowledge was high (97.92%), even if frequency was not used to select the best answer. This suggests that the type of knowledge, knowledge representation and convergence processes used are enough to automate such a task. Furthermore, comRAT-C proved robustness when dealing with incomplete knowledge, by finding the answer in some cases in which only two expression terms were known. This is consistent with expectations from robust and adaptive cognitive systems, which might rely on existing knowledge to solve problems, when the exact required knowledge is not within their grasp.

The limitations of comRAT-C are related to the amount of knowledge in its knowledge base. comRAT will most likely fail to answer well if it only knows one query word-answer pair. However, this is to most likely be expected for humans too.

The humans have a definite advantage in the cases in which two query word-answer pairs are known to them. In these cases, humans can have a guess whether the third item "fits" the answer converged upon with the known two items. For example, if given the query COTTAGE, SWISS, CAKE, and only knowing about SWISS CHEESE and CHEESECAKE, humans can make a more informed decision as to whether CHEESE could be the answer, by evaluating whether COTTAGE and CHEESE are likely to fit together. The automatic solver does not yet have a mechanism to decide whether such an answer is absurd or can work in the context of the third item. In the example above, if comRAT-C knows about SWISS CHEESE and CHEESECAKE, and also about SWISS CHOCOLATE and CHOCOLATE CAKE, it cannot yet estimate that COTTAGE and CHEESE are more likely to fit together than COTTAGE and CHOCOLATE. Various mechanisms could be put in place to make such a judgement, including going for a second level of associations, or clustering such associations to get and estimate of semantic domain. We will however not get any deeper in these matters here.

The comRAT system has an ability to generate different plausible answers or multiple correct answers. This computational ability creates the opportunity for further study into what answers are preferred by humans and what answers are considered as more creative or more interesting. Regarding the plausible answers, some of them are interesting from a cognitive perspective. Part of them are semantically-related to the "correct" answer offered by Bowden and Jung-Beeman (Bowden & Jung-Beeman, 2003), like items 1, 2, 3, 11, 13 in Table 9.4. Such observed relations are semantic similarity (11,13); opposition between the correct and the plausible answer (3), between one expression and the plausible answer (2) or just semantic neighborhood (1). This points at a possible inherent structure of the associative knowledge base, which requires further study.

The comRAT-C system was not built to specifically answer the Bowden & Jung-Beeman set of queries which we used for normative data. comRAT-C's knowledge was compared to the knowledge required to solve this set of normative queries only post-factum. The system was built in a general enough manner as to be able to attempt to answer any other normative datasets of queries on similar tests which are given to human participants. The only restrictions come from the nature of the associations made by the system – thus structural associates queries will have a higher likelihood to be answered – and from the limitations of the knowledge base. Any other n-gram corpuses can be implemented as a source for comRAT-C's knowledge base.

(iii) preferred items selection hypothesis and correlation with human data on difficulty

As comRAT-C can come up with multiple results for a RAT query, a frequency based mechanism of exploration for the most probable answers was proposed. The highest probability results coincided with the answers preferred by people in all four multiple answer cases. This indicates that the same mechanism can be used in the future for a wider investigation on what answers are preferred by human participants.

Data was also obtained on the contribution of each item in the RAT queries to each answer. Such data might in the future be used to determine whether the contribution of specific items or their order is what influences answer preference. Complete data on item contribution and probability for the 49 correct items is provided in Table A.3 of Appendix A.

The generative capabilities of the comRAT system can be used to devise more RAT tests with multiple answers. This will allow for the preferred item hypothesis to be fully verified in a statistically significant manner. More language data can also be added from other corpuses, to allow comRAT to give multiple answers to more queries, thus allowing for further validation.

A moderate correlation with strong significance was observed between the probability of comRAT-C answers and the percentage of participants solving the respective queries. That is, the higher this probability, the more participants were solving the query. An inverse moderate correlation with strong significance was observed between the same probability and response times. Thus, the higher the probability, the faster the participants were solving the query. As observed in Table 9.9, this correlation was mainly due to the probability of the first and second terms of the query.

The significance of these observed correlations indicates that, in the future, comRAT-C can be used as a basic tool to build more refined modeling and predictive mechanisms of human response times and accuracy (or query difficulty) for the compound RAT. Other RAT queries can also be generated with comRAT and then given to human participants, in order to check if this correlation holds in other experiments.

(iv) application of process with visual stimuli

We explored the transfer of the comRAT process to visual stimuli; this required expanding our previous formalization of the RAT to include visual objects, and the construction of a visual form of test. These investigations had the purpose to check: a) whether a creativity test can be applied on multiple modalities and b) whether the CreaCogs convergence process can be applied independent of modality.

Based on the current results, humans can solve such queries, and different levels of difficulty can be envisaged. The difficulty of the visual queries can be reliably estimated by humans. Future work related to the visual RAT will relate to creating a larger set of queries, testing such queries on a larger number of participants, gathering response time data and difficulty data. However, the initial small set of queries in vRAT shows promise in terms of administering the RAT test in two different modalities. A developed form of the visual RAT can be used to check how modality influences performance.

This is the only creativity test to date to have been given in two different modalities, as the visual or language creativity tests that exist (in TTCT) are separate tests, which do not aim to account for the application of the exact same process. The ability to investigate this process further across modalities will offer cognitive psychologists the possibility to understand the remote association process further.

The comRAT-V system solved visual queries based on visual associates collected from human participants. comRAT-V's performance was promising, despite the limited amount of visual associates data. In the future, more such data needs to be gathered, either from human participants or by setting up a computational mechanism to extract such visuospatial relations from existing data – for example from images depicting scenes. However, the initial correlation of comRAT-V's results with human difficulty shows that comRAT itself might be successfully applied in both domains, with the process it embodies presenting some important similarities to that employed by humans when solving such queries.

(v) comRAT's future perspectives, including using different data sets and its generative abilities

We will discuss comRAT's future perspectives on four lines:

a) other categories of RAT problems;

b) creativity and interestingness of RAT answers and problems;

c) semantic influences in the RAT; and

d) generative abilities of comRAT and modeling of further hypotheses.

a) other categories of RAT problems

The comRAT-C system solves compound types of RAT problems. The system can easily be used with other language corpuses, to solve the same types of problems with different knowledge bases, using the same knowledge organization and process.

However, other types of RAT tests could also be solved by comRAT in the future. The functional Remote Associate Test (FRAT) could be solved, if comRAT would be given functional associates data. Such data could be extracted from ontologies (category relations, part-of relations, etc).

If context plays a role in the organization of knowledge or the strength of connective paths between different knowledge items[15], then this test should be adaptable to different sensory domains. For example, in the visual RAT test, the stimuli are aimed at testing context based associations of visual items. The visual RAT can further be enhanced by controlling for and removing verbally connected items. Such investigations could throw further light on the influences of context on memory organization. They could also show whether memory storage is organized in a sensory dependent manner, by tapping into it with modality-specific stimuli.

Visual or other versions of the RAT can benefit the empirical understanding of human performance; to our knowledge, no other studies on remote visual associative memory (or other sensory types of remote associative memory) exist to date. However, cross or multi-sensory associative processes and memory might play a role in various domains of creative problem solving and scientific discovery.

---

[15] Context is not assumed to be the only element that plays a role.

Thus tests carefully controlled to study structural versus semantic items, and language/visual interplay could be modeled using comRAT, and enrich our knowledge about principles of convergence and association, in the context of the Remote Associate Test.

b) creativity and interestingness of RAT answers and problems
The ability of comRAT to find different plausible answers enables future work on what constitutes a creative or interesting answer from the human perspective. Further studies in this direction could for example determine whether high or low frequency answers are considered more interesting, or whether other factors, like semantic domain, play a major role in such assessments. A generative form of comRAT would also enable the study of which queries are considered more creative or interesting.

The ability to find other plausible items also makes comRAT a likely assistive companion for humans when solving RAT queries or for trigerring convergence processes in general.

c) semantic influences in the RAT
The frequency of expressions might not be the only item having an impact on the memory of RAT solvers. A second possibly contributing factor is the membership of two or all three of the query items to the same semantic category; or conversely, the lack of semantic category overlap. RAT's knowledge base(s) could be semantically parsed to answer such questions in the future.

d) generative abilities of comRAT and modeling of further hypotheses
The generative abilities of comRAT are yet to be fully explored and have great potential in creating Remote Associate Test items controlled on various parameters. Examples of such parameters are: the number of multiple answers; frequency of the answer word; frequency of the query word - answer pair; probability based on each query item, etc.

Further analyses on what makes RAT problems difficult using these tools could help integrate quantitative (frequency factors) and qualitative principles (semantic and ordering factors). This could enable comRAT to automatically categorize different levels of problems. Such a categorization, and control over query parameters, could make possible the modeling and prediction of cognitive difficulty.

9.11 Conclusions

The comRAT-C system implements a previously formalized upward search process in CreaCogs. This process is applied to computationally solve the compound Remote Associate Test (RAT), using a knowledge base of language data.

The experimental results showed that, out of Bowden and Jung-Beeman's set of 144 RAT queries, and using the COCA corpus, 64 items are answered correctly; that is, for 64 queries, the first answer provided by comRAT-C matches the answer deemed as correct in the Bowden and Jung-Beeman set.

Besides this, over 20 of the other response items are plausible answers – that is responses that a human may deem viable. The accuracy of response of the system is at 97.92% in the cases in which the system has all 3 items in its knowledge base, and 30.36% in the cases in which the system only knows two of the given expressions. Humans are normally assumed to answer correctly the queries for which they know all three items, so this showed that associative principles can add robustness to the system and help find solutions even in the cases in which knowledge is lacking.

A preferred answer hypothesis has been put forward, based on probability and the frequency of expressions in the knowledge base. Promising first results where obtained towards this hypothesis, however a full validation is still required.

A moderate, statistically significant correlation has been observed between the probability of finding the answer and the cognitive difficulty of solving queries, as expressed by response times and percentage of participants solving the queries.

A visual version of the RAT test was created and given to human participants. Visual associates where gathered from human participants as to be used by a computational solver – comRAT-V. Human participants solved 63% of such queries and declared they perceived the answer visually in 56.6% of the cases. Participants showed an ability to reliably estimate difficulty of queries on a Likert scale. The comRAT-V adaptation using visual associates in its KB solved 72.73% of queries, and showed a moderate-high correlation to difficulty of query as expressed by human appraisal. More data is needed to make any strong claims on comRAT-V's ability to correlate to human performance.

The successful solving of the RAT test shows the principles posited by CreaCogs are valid and worthy of further investigation. The comRAT system has great potential for becoming a tool for cognitive modelers to further investigate the human cognitive processes used to solve the Remote Associates Test. Furthermore, comRAT-C can be used with other corpuses, and its principles can be transferred to other types of data (functional RAT, visual RAT, etc.).

We now know that a CreaCogs mechanism can be applied to computationally solve the Remote Associates Test. How about other CreaCogs mechanisms, and other creativity tests? More importantly, could CreaCogs mechanisms be used to solve creative problem solving tasks encountered in the day to day?

What Could You Use This Object for? – Object Replacement and Object Composition in a Computational System, and the Alternative Uses Test

When a human needs something to drink from, and no cup is available, he is able to use a bowl, a bucket or even a boot for such purposes. The human is thus capable of *creative object replacement*. When needing to feed herself next to a river, a human might attempt to make a fishing rod out of whatever stick, piece of string and makeshift hook she can attach some bait to. The human is thus able to do *object composition*. How do such cognitive abilities work, and could we replicate them in a computational system?

Various objects in an everyday object domain are **similar**, over different types of features:

- a *spoon* is similar to a *bucket* along a *concavity* feature.
- a *surfboard* is similar to a *tabletop* along a *thickness* feature.

Still, a *tabletop* is similar to a *door* along a *shape* feature. However, these objects are dissimilar in terms of inclination and context.

Human creative thought and problem solving might employ such similarity relations. However, existing computational approaches do not cover, nor do they automatically classify this kind of similarities and relations, on multiple feature spaces. They also do not encode how various types of feature subgroups make things similar. CreaCogs proposes encoding and using such similarity relations.

Some objects have complex **structure**, which cannot be expressed via a single shape feature (the same stands for material and other features). However, knowledge of such structure could greatly benefit a system which aims to be able to compose objects on its own. CreaCogs proposes encoding structure by differentiating between simple and complex concepts.

Finally, similar objects can have different roles depending on the **context** within which they are encountered:

- a *tabletop* on legs of lower height, with a couch nearby, is generally not used for working, but has coffee table affordances;

© Springer Nature Switzerland AG 2020

A.-M. Olteţeanu, *Cognition and the Creative Machine*,

https://doi.org/10.1007/978-3-030-30322-8_10

- a *tabletop* on legs of a higher height, with an office chair nearby and a computer on top is probably used for working;

- a *tabletop* that is somewhat higher and has a coffee machine on it is probably found in a kitchen and used as a preparation table for cooking.

Such relations are essential to understanding the affordances, roles, uses and sometimes the very nature of everyday objects. CreaCogs aims to encode context via its problem templates at the macro level (above concepts) and through complex concept structure at the within concepts level.

Thus the CreaCogs framework of knowledge organization seems theoretically qualified to deal with all these, by taking into account the similarity of objects and concepts on different types of features, the structure of these concepts and the problem templates they engage in.

Could a conjunction of CreaCogs principles be implemented in a system that showed creative use of objects? Could such a system manage even simple abilities of object replacement and object composition (OROC)? Before attempting to answer this question computationally, let us first get a flavour for cognitive principles of knowledge retrieval and encoding, and start imagining what OROC would need to do.

10.1 Cognitive Knowledge Retrieval and Encoding

Knowledge retrieval and encoding have special properties in human cognitive systems. If you are touching a small cube that is very cold, what could it be? A possible guess is an ice cube. A human is able to recognize an object, or have a guess at what the object is, when shown only part of its features. How would a similar ability look like in OROC?

A pen is similar in length and shape with a pencil and a stick; similar in material with a plastic peg; similar in colour to a chair. Encoding similarity on various features brings about complexity. How could we describe such multi-similarity spaces in a simple way? What would the various feature spaces obtained after such knowledge organization look like? Let us try to build some answers for these questions.

10.1.1 Multi-Feature Object Recognition

Humans can recognize objects by a variety of features. For example, let us say that a human is looking at an object they never encountered before, in a foreign country they do not speak the language of, and is told the object is called a *"xanadu"*. The object also happens to be shaped like a *ball*. The human will make assumptions related to object function based on the features this object has, and already held knowledge of objects. The human might thus assume they could kick and roll this object, in the same way they would a ball. The same might happen if the human was just touching such an object, without seeing it, and with no knowledge of how it's called.

The same concept (*ball*) can be triggered in a human mind via a variety of sensory modalities. However, sometimes more than one feature is necessary to extract the exact object something could be from the memory. If you just know that it's round, is it a ball, a snow ball, a Christmas tree globe? Guesses can be made at what the object is when various features are presented to the conceptual memory of the subject.

In the following, let us imagine the subject is an artificial cognitive system, called OROC, which brings knowledge to bear on its activities from its database KB. Let us assume that OROC lives in environment E. Various situations are possible in this environment ($Env_x \in E$). Agent OROC has to do its best to understand any of Env_x presented, by using its knowledge base KB and making inferences.

Perception in OROC works in the following way: OROC receives a feature or a set of features from the environment. These can be a name (if OROC receives verbal input), shape and color (if it receives visual input), material (from touch and vision), affordance (if OROC sees someone doing something with an object, or does something with an object itself).

This means that by just hearing a name, seeing an object shape or a type of motion in E, OROC should retrieve and object from its KB, or a subset of objects which are candidate hypotheses for what objects might be present in Env_x. The hypothesis (or hypotheses) built by OROC from elliciting knowledge from KB to understand Env_x is stored in the working memory of the system – WM. This process is shown in Fig. 10.1[1]. For example, if a cup is presented by the environment, the agent might retrieve knowledge about a high convexity shape, the fact that such an object could be made of a ceramic material and useful for a *"to drink from"* action. On the other hand, if told the affordance *"to drink from"*, the agent will come up with objects that can be used for that – for example a *Cup*, a *Glass* or a *Bottle*. If a material like *paper* is perceived by the agent, it might retrieve from its knowledge base objects or concepts like *Newspaper*, *Book* and *Notebook*.

A few more examples of possible given stimuli in a variate Env_x, and the knowledge retrieved in the WM of the agent from its KB are presented in Table 10.1. The hypotheses made by OROC on what the object might be can elicit its entire knowledge base. For example, when something of paper is touched (and no other information is present), OROC hypothesizes that it might be touching: (a) a book, made of paper, with thick rectangular shape, with covers, the affordance of which is "to be read"; (b) a newspaper, made of paper, with thin rectangular shape, (larger but thinner than the book), the affordance of which is "to be read"; (c) a paper towel, made of paper, which can

---

[1] The working memory seems to be displayed in Fig. 10.1 a separate, smaller knowledge base. However, this is only for visual clarity purposes. Working memory is to be understood as the bounded activation of a set of features or objects in KB. Only such a limited subset can be payed attention to at one time (working memory generally has constraints in natural cognitive systems).

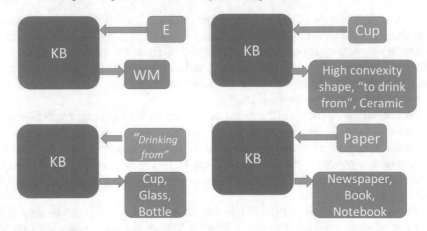

Fig. 10.1: The Environment (E), knowledge base (KB), working memory (WM) elements, in a cycle of knowledge retrieval (a) and examples of this cycle in action (b to d)

have different rectangular or square shapes, and different degrees of softness, the affordance of which is "absorbent", "to wipe with"; (d) wallpaper, large very thin and generally rectangular, used for decoration.

Stimuli from E	Concepts ellicited in WM
Paper	Book, Newspaper, Paper Towel, Wallpaper
Long Narrow Rectangular	Shelf, Surfboard, Table top
Wood	Shelf, Table, Desk
"to wipe with"	Sponge, Towel
Sharp	Blade, Pen
"to write with"	Pen, Pencil, Chalk, Marker

Table 10.1: Results for multi-feature object recognition

The elicited knowledge and a need for differentiation (as to understand exactly what object is being sensed) can help guide future behavior, by guiding the senses of the agent to retrieve a new property. For example, finding out the shape and size of an object made of paper will narrow down the possibilities on identifying what the object is. The most efficient feature or feature set that can be retrieved from the environment in order to minimize the number of hypotheses the agent comes up with, can be determined in advance. We will call this feature or set of features the *the maximum discriminant*. Ideally, the maximum discriminant will reduce the hypotheses the agent comes up with to 1.

This maximum discriminant could generally be calculated based on the knowledge present in the KB of the agent, and the features already presented to the agent. The maximum discriminant would thus be individual for each system, depending upon its knowledge base. It is possible that regularities in the maximum discriminant exist for agents which inhabit similar spaces.

Once the maximum discriminant has been calculated, the agent can guide its behaviour based on this in order to clarify what the object is. Using the maximum discriminant, the agent can go retrieve this data point if the discriminant is only one feature, or the next most important feature, if the discriminant is a subset. Retrieving more discriminant features will allow for a mapping of the object in E to a smaller and smaller set of objects in the KB, and in some cases to one object, and its recognition.

10.1.2 Multi-Feature Similarity

Triggering associated possible objects from the KB based on one or more noticed features in Env_x helps OROC hypothesize about what the perceived object is. OROC hypothesizes what the perceived object is by exploring its feature spaces (FS) – concept (C) links. For example, when perceiving a specific feature, or feature set, OROC can examine its knowledge base to check which concept or sets of concepts are anchored in those features.

However, the same link between concept and its anchoring in feature spaces can be used to determine similar objects. Object that share features they are anchored on are similar in some way. This brings about the following consequences:

a) similar subsets of concepts can be determined, depending on each feature map. As seen in Table 10.2, objects like *Book, Newspaper, Magazine* and *Notebook* might be similar on the *Material* feature space, by being anchored in similar features in it (paper and paper like materials). Similar concepts can also be determined not just for each feature map, but for each feature point – for example, in the *Material* feature space, other concepts than the ones mentioned above will be similar based on the material feature *ceramic.*

Thus concepts similar on that feature space (FS) are all n concepts encoded in that point or nearby.[2]

b) a concept can be similar to other concepts on *each* of the different feature spaces it is encoded on. Thus *book* can be classified as similar:
  – on a *material* feature space with *newspaper, magazine, notebook*;
  – on the *affordance* feature space in point "to be read" with *newspaper, electronic book, website, memorial plaque*;
  – on the *shape* feature space with *notebook, chopping board*, etc.
Moreover, a concept can be similar to other concepts on two or more feature spaces, with a match on all feature spaces meaning identity for the given agent.

---

[2] Some such relationships can also be partially ordered, like *Chair* < *Table* < *Wardrobe* on feature: *Height.*

Objects classified as close or similar	Feature Space (FS)
Book, Newspaper, Magazine, Notebook	Material
Cup, Glass, Bottle	Affordance
Cup, Bucket, Flowerpot	Shape
Wardrobe, Door	Height

Table 10.2: Object similarity on different feature spaces

Various feature spaces can be envisaged for objects: size (height, depth, width), orientation, color, material (primitive or composed), shape (primitive or composed), name, etc. The more such feature spaces, the more groupings of similarity can be yielded. Let us assume γ to be a variable which represents the number of such similarity connections in a particular feature space. The first column of Table 10.3 shows the number of feature spaces a given agent classifies objects into. Let us consider the first row, in which an agent classifies objects in two feature spaces, for example *colour* and *material*. In the second column, row one, we observe that two types of similarity on one feature space exist. That is, objects could be similar because they have (a) similar *colour* or (b) similar *material*. The third column of the first row thus shows objects which are similar on both these feature spaces, might also be equivalent for the agent.

Let us now see what happens if an agent classifies objects on three different feature groups – like in the second row of Table 10.3. Let us say these feature spaces are *colour*, *material* and *shape*. As seen in the second column, the agent might experience three types of similarity on one feature space. Objects could be similar in terms of *colour*; they could be similar in terms of *material*; and they could be similar in terms of *shape*. Now what would happen if the agent would look for objects that are similar on at least two feature spaces? Three combinations are possible: objects which are similar in terms of *colour* and *material*; *material* and *shape*; or *colour* and *shape*. A variable number of similarity connections (γ) could be established in each of these feature space combinations. If, given that the agent has three feature spaces, similarities are observed on all three feature spaces, the objects can be equivalent.

FS no.	Sim 1 FS	Sim 2 FS	Sim 3 FS	Sim 4 FS	Sim 5 FS
2 FS	$2*\gamma$	Equivalent	-	-	-
3 FS	$3*\gamma$	$3*\gamma$	Equivalent	-	-
4 FS	$4*\gamma$	$6*\gamma$	$4*\gamma$	Equivalent	-
5 FS	$5*\gamma$	$10*\gamma$	$10*\gamma$	$5*\gamma$	Equivalent

Table 10.3: Similarity degrees and their combinations. The rows show agents with different numbers of feature spaces. The columns show similarity on different number of feature spaces

Therefore the number of similarity groups, depending on the KB, can be calculated as a function of x, where x is the number of feature maps and k is the number of feature maps similarity is searched on (this constantly increasing until it reaches the concept equivalence case of similarity on all feature maps):

$$f(x) = \frac{x}{k!} + \frac{(x*(x-1))}{(k+1)!} + \frac{(x*(x-1)*(x-2))}{(k+2)!} ....$$
$$+ \frac{(x*(x-1)*(x-2)*...1)}{x!} \tag{10.1}$$

Also, remember that each such type or group of similarity connections will have a variable number of mappings (parameter γ), depending on the KB and the concepts represented. Thus, for 6 feature maps, the number of concepts would be a function $g(x)$:

$$g(6) = \frac{6}{1!}\gamma + \frac{(6*5)}{2!}\gamma + \frac{(6*5*4)}{3!}\gamma + ... + \frac{(6*5*4*3*2*1)}{6!}\gamma \tag{10.2}$$

For 6 feature spaces, this yields 120γ possible similar items with range of γ between 0 and the size of the particular feature space being considered.

Due to the CreaCogs knowledge organization, these subsets of similarity relations can easily be retrieved as a function of spatial arrangement. Thus, any or all these sets of similarity relations can be retrieved by going down the anchoring links or up the context links in this framework.

Let us see the various feature spaces obtained for OROC in the current implementation.

10.1.3 The Various Features Spaces Obtained

In our initial prototype implementation, when being presented with objects, OROC learns their properties and organizes them in its feature layer. Thus, after learning a set of objects, OROC's feature space of known materials will contain, for example: "Ceramic, Paper, Plastic, Porcelain, Wood, Glass fiber, unknown, Wax, Metal, Cardboard, etc [...]".

These features can be reorganized based on similarity metrics – for example "ceramic" can be moved next to "porcelain", "cloth" next to "paper", etc. If these features are spatially reorganized, the pointers of the Concepts to the feature space (which ensures concept anchoring) will be moved too. A possible improvement to the current prototype system would be to obtain such similarity metrics data. This can be done using sensory science data or setting up some form of knowledge acquisition (from the web, from human answers, etc).

Contextually, various material features can be grouped together in various ways (e.g. in groups like "can burn","texture", "absorbent", "tearable", "breakable"). In OROC, such groups can be inferred from object properties and object affordances. Thus if an object with certain properties can do something, other objects with similar properties can be inferred to be able to do it too. For example, if the agent observed that a ceramic cup has been broken, a general inference can be made about all the other ceramic objects that they are breakable. To be accurate, such inference require that some accurate functional link between a feature and an affordance has been established. If a feature is repeatedly correlated with an affordance, the system could for example learn that this feature-affordance pair might be one to attempt inferences on. If multiple objects made of cloth are observed to have the affordance of absorbing water, an agent might try to infer that other new objects made of cloth can be used for the same purposes.

Before looking whether OROC has indeed object replacement and object composition properties, let's have a look at its implementation.

10.2 OROC Implementation

The prototype OROC system takes as knowledge base an .xml file in which 200 object concepts have been defined on various feature spaces. Some of these are complex object concepts which have other objects as parts. As mentioned before, OROC's knowledge base is organized on feature spaces. This allows us to use features as search keys in the various feature spaces.

So, in light of what we discussed above, let's see how OROC inserts a new object in its concept knowledge base, how it recognizes an object, and then how it leaps to object replacement.

For each new concept it receives as an input, OROC checks its feature spaces knowledge base, to see whether those respective features are already known. If the features are already known, the concept can be linked to them. If they are not known, features can be inserted in the maximum similarity point that can be determined.

The recognition of a concept in OROC is done by finding the concept with the most matching features, via a matching algorithm. From object recognition to object replacement there is only a step. Instead of searching its KB for objects which match the features observed in the environment, in order to recognize the object, a search with a looser threshold is applied. Instead of trying to find matches on all features, OROC accepts (i) matches on some features and similarity on others, or (ii) matches or similarity on a subset of features that is relevant for the affordance at hand[3]. Is this enough to leap

---

[3] Currently similarity of concepts based on matching of features is implemented, as feature similarity would require either cognitively acquiring such metrics, or a subsymbolic layer. This is above the scope of this current prototype, which aims to test whether processes of the theoretical framework can be implemented with results that are creative, and comparable to human results.

towards creative object replacement, from object recognition? Let's set up the scene for some experiments.

10.2.1 Object Replacement Question Types and Proof of Concept

Various types of questions could be answered by a system able to perform object replacement. In the following, we will discuss three such question types, and present results which OROC provides to some of them. It is worth noting that the answer to all these questions can be given in OROC (and CreaCogs) by using a small set of algorithms and principles of search.

Question type 1

A possible setup is to give OROC a known affordance (like *"to tie with"*), and a set of objects in the environment (like *a sponge, a hammer, an electric chord*). The we could ask OROC which of the given objects can be used to provide this affordance.

This can be solved under the CreaCogs framework by going from the specific affordance to objects in the agents KB that are known to have it. For example, objects like *strings, rope* might have been used for tying and are known to the agent. Common properties of these objects can then be searched for, to generalize what properties seem essential for that affordance based on experience of affordance-property co-occurence.

The properties of the objects currently given in the environment are then observed or matches to known objects that have the *"to tie with"* affordance. The most similar object in the environment (in terms of this particular affordance) is then chosen. In this case, the electric chord is chosen, which is also thin, long, bendable).

Question type 2

A second type of question would be to give OROC an object, and ask it to find all the objects in its knowledge base that are similar to it, on it's different features. We could also ask OROC what are the objects it knows of a certain given degree of similarity to the given (for example degree of similarity 2 for two feature spaces, degree 3 for three, etc.). Thus, given object a, find all objects which could replace a for each feature space f_x or with a degree of similarity n.

In human terms, such a question would be phrased as the following: given a cup, find all objects that are similar to a cup in terms of its various properties.

To solve this type of question in the CreaCogs framework, OROC would go down from its knowledge of the concept c_a representing object a into the features on which such knowledge is represented. Then, it would search for mappings of all the other objects in that feature, or in its neighbourhood. The same can be adapted when searching for objects with a similar feature, using a distance metric for the similarity in the feature space.

In OROC, such a question produces results like the ones shown in Table 10.4.

Table 10.4: Finding objects similar on various feature spaces with OROC

Given object	Similar objects
Cup	sim to Bowl on material
	sim to Flowerpot on material
	sim to Can on shape
	sim to Candle Holder on material
	sim to Container on shape
Coat brush	sim to Bucket on material
	sim to Toothbrush on material
	sim to Toothbrush on shape
	sim to Shoe brush on material
	sim to Shoe brush on shape
	[...]
Table	sim to Shelf on material
	sim to Wedge on material
	sim to Desk on material
	sim to Desk on affordance
	sim to Doorstop on material
	sim to Hammer Handle on material
	[...]

Question type 3

A third type of question which could be answered with OROC under CreaCogs is what kind of other affordances might apply to a particular known object. This question can be defined as: given a object a (and a particular KB), make loose inferences about what affordances you can creatively use object a for. OROC obviously has to rely on its knowledge about other objects, their affordances and their similarities to the current given object to answer this type of question.

We initially set OROC's object replacement algorithm to select the $2nd$ degree similarity matches on shape and material. This can also be done with any other combination of features considered to be relevant[4]. Using shape and material as the features considered relevant, OROC came up with uses like the following:

- *"Maybe Cup can be used to carry water"*;
- *"Maybe Cup can be used to put flowers in"*;
- *"Maybe Cup can be used as food container"*;
- *"Maybe Cup can be used to hold earth and plants"*;
- *"Maybe Cup can be used to cook in, etc.*

---

[4] Relations between functional property and affordances could be also determined via co-occurrence in a larger data set. However, in the object domain, shape and material seem to be particularly important features for affordance, as will be shown in Sect. 10.3.4.

Table B in Appendix B presents a longer list of alternative uses generated by OROC.

How this mechanism of loose affordance inference fits into the CreaCogs framework? An object, which is a concept in the CreaCogs framework, triggers its known properties in the KB. In Fig. 10.2, the concept of a Cup triggers knowledge about cup material, cup shapes, and the affordance associated with a cup – here *"to drink from"*. These properties trigger other concepts anchored in them (or similar properties in the neighbourhood can trigger other concepts). For example, the material and shape of a cup trigger objects like a Pot and a Vase. In the next step, OROC infers that the affordances of these objects might also apply creatively to the initial given object. Thus if *"to cook in"* is a known traditional affordance of the object Pot, then OROC infers that it might also apply as a creative affordance to the object Cup, because of the shared material and shape properties of Cup and Pot. If *"to keep flowers in"* is a known traditional affordance of the object Vase, OROC infers it might also apply as a creative affordance to the object Cup, etc.

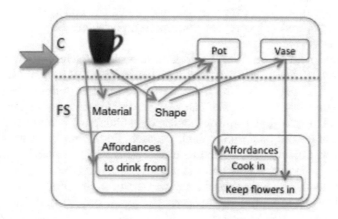

Fig. 10.2: OROC's loose inference mechanism in CreaCogs

This type of question, about inferring what kind of other affordances might apply to a known object, is similar to a creativity test which asks participants to come up with as many alternative uses for an object as they can think of – the Alternative Uses Test (Guilford, 1956, 1967). This means that the computational implementation of this question in OROC can be evaluated in comparison to human participant answers.

Before exploring how OROC's results for a set of objects can be evaluated, and compared to human results, let us see whether object composition is in principle also possible using this approach.

10.2.2 Object Composition Question Types and Proof of Concept

The second part of OROC uses the structure of known objects and objects similarity in order to attempt to generate new composed objects[5]. What types of questions could be asked about object composition? In the following, we will discuss three types of such questions, the processes they reflect in CreaCogs, and present results of the prototype OROC for question type 3.

Question type 1

This question takes the following form: *"Given a set of objects, what other objects could you make from them?"*. Thus in this type of question, the composing parts are known, and a set of composed objects is expected. An ample set of resources is presented by the composed objects already stored in the knowledge base of the agent.

This translates in CreaCogs mechanisms into: given a set of concepts $c_1, c_2, ..., c_n$, applying templates of known composed concepts $cc_x \in KB$, infer what new composed concepts can be created. In the current case we deal with the restricted domain of everyday objects. Thus the concepts which we refer to are objects, and the complex concept templates are objects composed of multiple parts[6].

For example, this question could look like the following: *"Given a wooden pole, a piece of string, a bottle and a paperclip, what objects could you make of them?"* The search in CreaCogs would proceed as follows: from each of the given concepts, an associationist search would start into the known object templates. Objects that contain (something similar to) a wooden pole and a piece of string could be found in such a search. For example, knowledge about a fishing rod object could be found convergently by the search started from the wooden pole and the piece of string. After having found this potentially useful template, the agent would try to realize it by filling it with existing objects. The agent would thus search the given objects for a hook. As no hook is given, a hook replacement will also do. Finding a hook replacement would involve a downward search of overlapping properties – the paperclip could thus be determined as the closest thing to a hook that exists in the room.

Please note that, in this form of the question, part of the challenge is to find what objects can be made out of the existing objects. A more restrained form of this question would be the following: *"Given a set of objects, which of these composed objects could you make from them?"*. This would involve

---

[5] This could be also used to generate new structures, and hypothesize about their composed affordances.

[6] Templates for objects composed of multiple parts are anchored in the set of parts that create them, the relations between those parts and the affordance of the composed object. This is similar to the way in which problem templates are anchored – in objects, relations between objects, actions and solutions – as shown in Chap. 8.

merely comparing properties of parts of objects in the complex objects with the properties of the given objects. However, in the initial form, no objects to compare to are given as part of the question. This creates extra difficulty as the templates to be applied (e.g. the fishing rod) are not pre-given. CreaCogs proposes to solve this by using the initial objects as seeds to trigger potentially useful templates.

Question type 2

This question is of the following form: *"Given an object, what objects that you know of could you compose it from?"*. For example, the agent could be given the fishing rod, and asked to come up with objects from its knowledge base to compose it. In a restrained form, this question asks: *"Given a set of objects, can you make a specified object out of a subset of them?"*.

This type of question translates in CreaCogs to the following: given a complex concept cc_x, the parts of which are known (thus which can act as template PT_x), what set of other known concepts $c_1, c_2, ...c_n$ can be mapped to it? The search can start from the template by activating the set of its composing parts, and then further proceed to finding replacement of those parts as known objects with similar properties. Similar objects can be found via property based replacement, as explained in the previous section.

Question type 3

The third type of question is of the following form: *"Given all known objects, what new objects can you compose?"*. This is a loose inference form of the two types of questions above: it asks in a sense for all known objects to be projected as possible parts into all the known composed objects in the KB. This question encompasses questions 1 and 2, constituting a directed search based on every object or on every template (whichever set is smaller should direct the search). If the templates are guiding the search, this is for replacement parts based on similarity. If the initial known objects are guiding the search, this is a search for templates these objects (or objects similar to them) have been part of, then a search for other objects to fill in that template.

Here are some object compositions obtained using OROC in such a search:

- *Use sharp stone and branch to make a knife with handle.*
- *Use salad tongs and hairband to make a slingshot.*
- *Use tree stumps and shelf to make a table.*
- *Use jar and candle to make candle with support.*

This search used object templates as the seed, and it shows that the principles posited above can be applied to do object composition.

In loose inference mode, the number of composed objects created is equal to the number of known structures, times the number of variable replacements combinations in that structure. Thus, the larger the knowledge base, the higher the number of (i) composed objects and of (ii) object replacements that can be performed with composing object parts. This is why associative and similarity based principles can help this search and composition process by directing it on paths which are potentially productive. Currently, OROC's knowledge base does not have a large amount of complex object templates. We intend to increase this part of the knowledge base in the future.

Theoretically, a type 4 set of questions is also possible: involving both assembly and disassembly techniques. Such a question would be of the form: *"Given a set of objects which in turn can be regarded as composed objects with various parts, what objects can be made using knowledge of their parts"*. It is clear that the same processes as above could be applied by OROC to solve this question type as well. In conclusion, we believe that the CreaCogs principles can be applied to issue results in object replacement and object compositions on this entire scale of question and task types.

However, whilst we practically showed that such results can be produced, how would they compare to results produced by humans? The object composition capabilities of OROC could be used in their current form in empirical comparison to an object composition test given to human participants. A creativity test for evaluating this ability does not exist in the literature, but could be designed.

Until such a test for object composition is designed, let us refocus on a previous lead. OROC's object replacement results were similar in form to answers given by humans to the Alternative Uses Test (AUT). Could the object replacement part of OROC be evaluated using the AUT?

10.3 Evaluation of Performance with the Alternative Uses Test

In order to evaluate the performance of OROC and further illuminate cognitive creative processes, a creativity task normally given to humans that could be solved by OROC needed to be found. The tasks that came to mind were the Alternative Uses Test (Guilford, 1967), and the Wallach-Kogan (Wallach & Kogan, 1965) creativity task. What follows is an account of OROC's performance evaluation in solving the former.

To attempt such a comparative evaluation, we first needed to construct an evaluation procedure.

10.3.1 Constructing an Evaluation Procedure

The Alternative Uses Test (Guilford, 1967) is a creativity/divergent thinking test. In short[7], the participants to the AUT are given an object, and a certain amount of time in which they are supposed to come up with alternative uses for it. The uses the participants came up with are then scored on Fluency, Flexibility and Originality or Novelty (sometimes also on Elaboration).

---

[7] For an ampler description of the AUT see Sect. 5.1.

We assumed OROC was able to come up with answers to the AUT by using its ability to make loose creative inference of affordance. The process worked as follows: given an object x, OROC will check its known properties (features $f_1, f_2, ... f_n$). These properties will then be inspected for other objects which are anchored in them – for example objects y and z might also have properties f_1 and f_2, which belong to the initially given object x. If a set of significant features are the same or similar between the given object o_x, and objects o_y and o_z, then the affordances of objects o_y and o_z might apply to given object o_x. Thus OROC proposes those affordances as potential alternative uses for object x.

Concerning comparability, could the same evaluation procedure originally applied to human answers, be applied to OROC's answers? The Fluency and Flexibility of OROC's answers could be easily assessed: Fluency by counting the number of alternative uses proposed, and Flexibility by counting the number of different semantic categories these alternative uses span over.

However, Originality could not be assessed: this metric requires the comparison of a particular answer to the answers produced by a population of other agents, in order to qualify answers as original or highly original if they have been produced by a small amount of the population (e.g. 5% and 1% respectively). We could compare OROC as an agent against different human individuals. However, normative data for individual human participants was not available, thus we opted for using the Novelty metric instead[8].

Novelty is generally assessed by using human judges. That is, human judges have a look at each proposed alternative use, and rate how novel they consider this use to be on a Likert scale. We could thus give the alternative uses proposed by OROC to a set of human judges, and ask them to rate the Novelty of the answers. For comparability to evaluations of human answers from others (Gilhooly, Fioratou, Anthony, & Wynn, 2007), we decided to use a 1 to 7 Likert scale. On this scale, 1 represented a use considered *"not at all novel"* by the judge, and 7 represented a use considered *"highly novel"*.

In order to further investigate how OROC's answers would be rated by human evaluators, we also chose another two other metrics to ask the judges for ratings on. These metrics were Likability and Usability. The rating for each of them was also expected on a 1 to 7 Likert scale. By asking the judges for these extra ratings, we also tried to ensure that tacit Usefulness and Likability assessments will not interfere with the judges' assessments of Novelty. For example, we did not want judges to give a low Novelty assessment to a proposed alternative use because they thought the object might not have much usability in that alternative capacity; or to give a high novelty rating to an object because of an aesthetical preference for it. We thus made Useful-

---

[8] We could also produce different artificial OROC-like agents, with different knowledge bases, and slight variations of process, and get the Originality metric by inter-comparison between them. However, we leave this to further work, as the comparison between OROC and human results is the more important initial step.

ness and Likability judgements explicit. Next, we needed to set in place the experimentation procedure.

10.3.2 Experimentation and Evaluation with Human Judges

Five objects from the household domain were given to OROC to make inferences of alternate uses on. These objects were: CUP, NEWSPAPER, TOOTH-BRUSH, CARPET and DENTAL FLOSS. Objects were chosen as not to overlap in shape category, in order to produce alternative use answers that did not overlap. Thus, for example, the object VASE was not chosen, because of its high-convexity shape which overlapped with that of the object CUP.

An online survey was set up using Google forms, for human judges to evaluate OROC's answers[9]. The survey contained two initial examples of alternative uses to be rated. Then, the actual rating process began. Each alternative use was presented as a sentence, followed by the three rating choices which the judge had to make. This looked as follows:

Statement: "A shoe may be used for putting a nail in the wall"
Novelty Rating: *not at all novel* 1 − 2 − 3 − 4 − 5 − 6 − 7 *highly novel*
Likability Rating: *I do not like it* 1 − 2 − 3 − 4 − 5 − 6 − 7 *I like it a lot*
Usability Rating: *not useful at all* 1 − 2 − 3 − 4 − 5 − 6 − 7 *very useful*

The 30 alternative uses produced by OROC on the five given objects were thus rated by 34 participants − 24 male and 10 female (ages 20-70). To ensure the judgements were not biased by the opinions the judges had on machine creativity, the judges were not informed that the answers they were rating were produced by an artificial system.

Fig. 10.3 shows the ratings human judges made on all three factors − Novelty, Likability and Usefulness − across the 30 alternative use statements. Mean Novelty appraisal for all uses was 3.79, with a mean (across statements) standard deviation (SD) of 1.69. Mean Likability appraisal for all uses was 3.31 SD = 1.68. Mean Usefulness appraisal for all uses was 3.77, SD = 1.7. Each sentence's mean rating can be seen in Table B, Appendix B.

We were curious to see which of OROC's generated alternative uses will obtain the highest ratings from the human judges. Over all objects and uses, the highest ratings were obtained, on each of the three metrics, by the following statements:

- Highest Novelty: *"Dental floss may be used to hang clothes to dry"* (statement no. 22, mean rating = 6)
- Highest Likability: *"A cup may be used to keep objects in"* (statement no. 20, mean rating = 4.79)
- Highest Usefulness: *"A cup may be used to hold a candle"* (statement no. 29, mean rating = 5.59)

The highest Novelty and Usefulness combined score, and the highest Novelty (N), Likability (L) and Usefulness (U) combined score were achieved

---

[9] http://goo.gl/forms/snaqh4bOLH

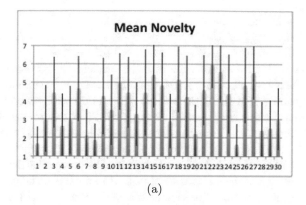

(a)

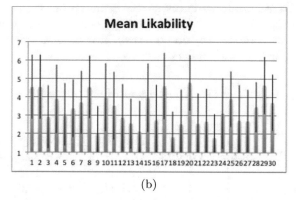

(b)

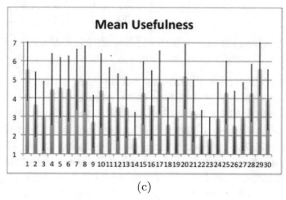

(c)

Fig. 10.3: Ratings on a Likert 1-7 scale across 30 object use statements: (a) Novelty Ratings; (b) Likability Ratings; (c) Usefulness Ratings

by the same use: *"Dental floss may be used for sewing"* (statement no. 15, $(N+U)/2 = 4.85$; $(N+L+U)/3 = 4.56$).

An overview of the evaluation for each object, including Fluency, Flexibility, Novelty, Likability and Usefulness metrics, is shown in Table 10.5. Average Fluency over all 5 objects is 6; average Flexibility is 4.4.

Let us now look at a study with human participants and compare. In the study of (Gilhooly et al., 2007), participants were split in two groups – a think aloud group and a silent group. They came up with an average of 27.25 alternative uses for the think aloud group, and 26.43 responses for the silent group, for 6 objects. This is currently comparable to OROC's total Fluency rating of 30 for 5 objects. However, this might change with the addition of more objects to OROC's KB if no time simulation mechanisms are put in place (the human participants are time bound in such a setting, while OROC is not). Also, some measure of association and similarity could be put in place to bound OROC's initial inferences to the strongest ones.

Unfortunately, Gilhooly et al. do not present normative data per each object, for us to compare to, nor do they give accounts of the Flexibility ratings of the participants'answers.

Table 10.5: Evaluation of OROC on Fluency, Flexibility, Novelty, Likability and Usefulness

Item	Fluency	Flexibility	Novelty Mean	SD	Likability Mean	SD	Usefulness Mean	SD
Cup	7	5	2.61	1.47	4.30	1.72	4.80	1.76
Newspaper	7	5	3.34	1.72	2.84	1.50	3.61	1.61
Toothbrush	5	3	4.29	2.08	2.85	1.80	2.98	1.83
Carpet	6	5	4.00	1.71	2.86	1.64	3.60	1.63
Dental floss	5	4	5.32	1.56	3.25	1.75	3.53	1.71

Novelty, Likability and Usefulness ratings per object are shown in Fig. 10.4. As can be seen here, the alternative uses for Cup received the lowest Novelty ratings, while the alternative uses for Dental floss received the highest Novelty ratings. This might be because Dental floss is a relatively newer widely distributed invention. If people had more time to be creative about the uses of cups, not much may seem new to them. However, the alternative uses for Cup were rated highest on the Likability and Usability scale.

A positive correlation with strong significance was observed between the ratings on Likability and Usefulness of all judges. This indicated that the more judges considered an alternative inference to be useful, the more they liked it. For all items, the mean correlation between Likability and Usefulness was 0.63, $p < 0.005$. This correlation ranged across statements between 0.35 and 0.93, as shown in Fig. 10.5. Thus for statement no. 24, *A cup may be used to cook in*, the Likability-Usefulness correlation was at its highest (0.93). For statement no. 21, *A carpet may be used as a bed cover*, the Likability-Usefulness correlation was at its lowest.

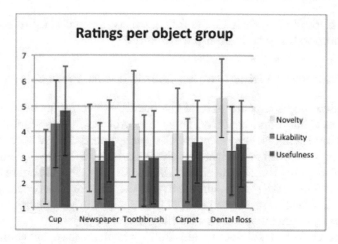

Fig. 10.4: Ratings per object group

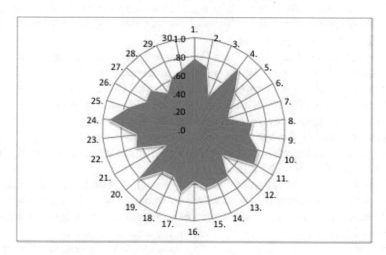

Fig. 10.5: Correlation between Likability and Usefulness for each alternative use sentence. The 30 alternative use statements are shown clockwise around the dial. The center of the dial represents no correlation (0.0), and the edge of the dial a perfect correlation (1.0)

In order to check whether the human judgement offered a useful, generalizable form of evaluation, various measures where applied to check for the inter-agreement of the judges, and the correlation of individual ratings to mean ratings. Applying these measures confirmed that using human judges for evaluation is a reasonably reliable form of evaluation.

What have we thus established as comparability so far? We have seen that the *answers* produced by OROC can be evaluated in the same ways as human answers to the AUT, and that they are comparable. What about the *process* employed in producing such answers? Can this be evaluated establishing some form of comparability to human participants?

10.3.3 Evaluation Using Human Think Aloud Protocols

A tool which might capture part of the cognitive process at work in various tasks is the think aloud protocol. In such a protocol, participants are asked to think aloud while solving a particular task. Standard methods for protocol analysis have been established in the literature (Ericsson & Simon, 1993; Someren, Barnard, Sandberg, et al., 1994). Usually, the thoughts produced verbally by the participants while solving the task are recorded, and then transcribed. These transcripts are split into short phrases (called segments). The resulting segments are then classified into categories.

The paper from (Gilhooly et al., 2007) which we used for comparability in the previous section applied such a protocol to the Alternative Uses Test. This enabled the closest thing to a comparison of process we could come up with: comparing Gilhooly's analysis of human think aloud protocols during the AUT to OROC's processes.

After classifying the transcribed think aloud segments, Gilhooly et al. built 18 categories. Such categories were seen as describing different processes by which human participants came up with answers. Gilhooly et al. describe the first 15 categories of process related segments. These categories each contain more than 1% frequency of the transcribed segments (a residual "Other" category accounting for less than 1% of the segments is also built).

Out of these categories, four seemed of particular interest to OROC. These categories are described as follows:
- **Disassembly Uses** (no.6 in Gilhooly's list) – (The participant) states a way of decomposing the target item and using the resulting components. For example, *"Remove laces from shoe and use them to tie your hair up"*. 80% of participants, 5.5% +/-1.3% of segments.
- **Property** (no.8) – States property of object. For example, *"Bricks are heavy"*. 55% of participants, 3.4% +/- 0.7% of segments.
- **Property Use** (no.11) – Explicitly indicates property which enables the stated use. For example, *"A pencil is sharp so can be used to poke holes in paper"*. 48% of participants, 2.9% +/- 0.7% of segments.
- **Context** (no.14) – Mentions context in which target object is often found. For example, *"You often see tyres in garages"*. 40% of participants, 2.9%, +/- 1.2% of segments.

As it can be seen above, a wide range of participants used these categories of processes, from 40% of participants producing segments in the Context category, to 80% of participants thinking aloud in ways classified under the Disassembly Uses category.

The rest of the segments and their corresponding categories are not as informative when trying trying to establish comparability to OROC. Some of these are: Unmediated use (mentioning a possible use without an explanation) – 33% of segments, Item naming (repeating the name of the item – perhaps to enhance search activation processes) – 11.66%, Episodic Memory use (remembering previous creative use, so not novel to their experience) – 9.2%, Use query (Re-asking themselves what else the item could be used for) – 5.9%, etc.

Returning to the four categories of interest, let us see how they relate to OROC. The Property and Property Use categories are both reflected in OROC's processes. Properties are the equivalent of object features in OROC. Property use is the equivalent of making a feature-affordance connection in OROC. Thus both of these categories can be interpreted to use some form of feature match in order to generate alternative uses of objects.

The Disassembly category refers to the ability of decomposing the object in specific parts and using those parts while thinking about alternative uses, or thinking of objects as having a potential role as an object part. This is reflected in OROC's compositional capacities. Note that the Disassembly strategy frequency has been shown to make an important contribution to novelty.[10]

The Context category reflects a use of context for the initial object in the process of coming up with alternative uses. Though not yet implemented in OROC, *CreaCogs* posits the use of context, defined implicitly by the templates in which objects are used. Objects' spatial neighbourhood in the real world might also determine associative links and context.

10.3.4 Human Alternative Uses Answers

To further understand the processes humans use when they come up with alternative use answers, the study in which human judges evaluated OROC's answers had a second part. In this part, we gave judges an opportunity to freely express their own alternative use answers. This free part was two-fold:

1. After rating each statement, the judges were asked *"What other objects would you use for this purpose?"* (with the purpose being implicit from the initial alternative use sentence they were rating);
2. At the end of the evaluation of the 30 uses, a page asked for each of the 5 objects *"What other uses would you find for this object?"*.

As not to discourage participants which were in a hurry, or felt uncreative, from finishing the evaluation, these parts of the form were made non-compulsory.

---

[10] This is further motivation to put together a type of evaluation which includes OROC's compositional capacities. It might be that the objects created using these processes, or both processes in tandem, would be rated as the highest in Novelty. Such a rating might reflect a higher appreciation for the cases in which two processes are used to make such a inference: (i) composition/decomposition, used to transgress object boundaries, and (ii) creative replacement.

Through the questions it asks, this part of the survey links (i) each of the 30 uses to other objects, and (ii) each of the five objects to other uses. The other uses our participants came up with for the five initial objects of the test are shown in Table B in Appendix B. These uses were grouped according to how unique or frequent they were. The most frequent and some of the most unique alternative uses proposed by the human participants are shown in a summary in Table 10.6. For example, for the Cup object, 9 of the alternative uses given by the participants involved putting stuff in the cup (pencils, brushes, pens, sauce for mixing), and 7 uses proposed involved amplifying sound (using the cup as a speaker, headphones, musical instrument, or to hear through a wall). One use of Cup referred to using it as a shovel (specifically to dig earth with) and another one to use it as a mace, in order to smash garlic using the basis of the cup.

Table 10.6: Frequent and rare alternative uses proposed by participants for the five given objects

Object	Frequent use	No. times proposed	Rare use	No. times proposed
Cup	to put things in	9	as a shovel	1
	to amplify sound	7	as a mace to smash garlic	1
Newspaper	to make shapes and origami	10	as oven gloves for protection	1
	to wrap something	8	wrapping a mommy - fancy dress	1
Toothbrush	to clean with	16	as a nail on a sundial	1
	to brush with	4	weapon	1
Dental floss	fishing line	4	macrame	1
	jewellery part	4	keyring	1
Carpet	damping noise/vibrations	2	to protect against wind	1
	keeping fire lit	2	make new shoe soles	1

This data, grouped by uses, was analysed in order to find out:
(a) what properties are relevant for humans when connecting an object to a possible affordance, and
(b) whether feature similarity, a principle which OROC's processes use, is relevant when coming up with creative answers.

The results of this analysis are as follows. First, we had a look at how often properties of *shape* and *material* were important when humans came up with a new affordance for the given 5 objects. For that, we compressed the proposed alternative uses to unique uses. Then, we explored whether the proposed alternative use referred to an object that was similar in shape and material to the given object. For example, for the given object Dental floss, some participants proposed a use as a fishing line. This was classified as similar in shape. Table 10.7 shows how often participants proposed an alternative use which refers to an object similar in shape or material. On average, shape and/or material properties were relevant for 85.67% of the new uses human participants came up with.

Table 10.7: Relevance of shape and material properties when coming up with new uses

Object	Total unique no. of other uses	Total unique no. of uses with shape and material relevance	Percentage of uses with shape and material relevance
Cup	26	21	80.77%
Newspaper	25	24	96%
Toothbrush	18	17	94.45%
Dental floss	28	20	71.43%
Carpet	28	24	85.71%
Total	125	106	84.8%
Average per obj.	25	21.2	85.67%

Out of these instances in which shape and material were relevant, shape was sometimes relevant on its own, material relevant on its own or both properties were relevant together. As Table 10.8 shows, for the unique alternative uses for which shape and material mattered, shape and material were relevant together in 51.15% of the cases, shape was relevant on its own in 19.32% of the cases and material for 29.53% of the cases.

Table 10.8: Shape and material relevance itemized

Object	Total shape &material	Shape	Shape %	Material	Material %	Shape & Material	Shape & Material %
Cup	21	9	42.86%	4	19.05%	8	38.1%
Newspaper	24	0	0	14	58.33%	10	41.67%
Toothbrush	17	2	11.76%	5	29.41%	10	58.82%
Dental floss	20	5	25%	1	5%	14	70%
Carpet	24	18	16.98%	38	35.85%	50	47.17%
Average			19.32%		29.53%		51.15%

10.4 Discussion

OROC shows a good comparability to humans in both results and process when answering the Alternative Uses Test. However, OROC has not been purposefully designed to answer the AUT, and its abilities encompass a larger area than answering this one creativity test. OROC can further be investigated using the Wallach-Kogan test on object similarity or object composition tests (which need designing).

An interesting knowledge organization property of OROC is that each object in the knowledge base is anchored in a set of features. To recognize an object uniquely, a determinant set of features is needed, otherwise a set of objects are retrieved as possible answers. Unless a name is given, the answers retrieved depend on the features provided, thus on the upwards mapping of various features in certain concepts. For example, to recognize object O_{14}, the name of the object can be given to the system, in order to retrieve the existing knowledge about the object unambiguously. However, when a general description of the shape is given, this maps to 6 possible objects. When material is given, this maps to 10 objects. When material and shape are given, this maps to 2 possible objects, etc.

This set up lends itself to the future modeling of the shortest discriminant description of an object. Such a description would depend on the other objects in the KB, and the way ambiguity grows or diminishes when adding more objects and features to this knowledge base (cognitive economy would indicate that it is mostly discriminants that are retained). Furthermore, in the context of OROC, changes in the shortest discriminant description could be calculated as a function of learning. This would provide a good setting for experiments on various measures of information entering the KB, for example (a) how coherent that information is with the pre-existing information; (b) how informative that information is to the system and (c) how the ability of the system to generate new information changes as a function of the new information (Olteţeanu, 2015).

It is important to note that the hypothesis of creative processes modelled by OROC is clear enough to be falsifiable, as its computational underpinnings transform into the following empirically testable assumptions.
We can increase people's ability to be creative by:

1. increasing their ability to see the way objects are structured;
2. enhancing their ability to notice similarities between objects or object parts;
3. increasing their ability to notice similarities between structures;
4. generally giving them a larger number of object templates and types to know/choose from (this would be like learning more items in the KB, thus growing the generative capacity);
5. encouraging them to destroy and construct objects, or to generally cross over what the gestalt of an object is perceived to be;
6. encouraging fluidity of transfer between different parts and templates.

These assumptions could be proven or disproven using specifically designed alternatives of the AUT and Wallach-Kogan object similarity tests. A simple form of such a design could involve splitting the participants in two groups, training one group on the ability mentioned by the assumption, and then checking whether that group improves.

The Likability–Usefulness correlation which we observed also provides an interesting point of further investigation. This can have interesting implications for usability in design, and for the more complex investigation of aesthetic appreciation of creativity in the domain of objects.

We have thus seen that a prototype system based on CreaCogs principles is capable of both object replacement and object composition. The system was shown to offer results comparable to the Alternative Uses Test. We have explored ways of evaluating such systems in terms of both results and process, in a manner comparable to human evaluation. However, how about more complex problems, like creative insight problems? Could we close the gap between such complex problems and the types of problems we have already shown solvable via CreaCogs principles?

Daily Eurekas About Candles and Strings. Approaching Insight with Practical Insight Problems

To have this account of creative problem solving be complete, the mechanisms of the proposed CreaCogs framework needed to be tested on some insight problems. If you remember from Sect. 5.1, cognitive scientists cannot study insights such as discovering the benzene molecule or coming up with the structure of the DNA, in the wild. Mostly because such events are historical creativity events, therefore by their definition rare and surprising (to study such events, a scientist would need to know where and when in the world they would occur). Cognitive scientists can however study personal creativity insight events, that is they can give human participants, in the lab, problems the solving of which has been shown to, at most times, require or bring about insight. Empirical insight problems are thus the equivalent of extraordinary h-creativity feats, which the cognitive scientist can reliably study and grasp by bringing them in the lab. However, as insight is such a unique phenomenon, the study of such problems brings with it a few issues.

One such issue is that problems are unrepeatable. Imagine you were given the same insight problem over and over again. How many times do you think you will manifest insight when managing to "see" the problem solution? You might continue to enjoy the problem and its cleverness after you know the solution, and perhaps even thest the mental prowess of some of your friends with it, a well known act of amiable torture. However, it is likely that insight will happen for your personally in relation to that problem exactly once: that is, the first time when you managed to solve it. Insight problems are thus like shiny rocks you find under the water and bring home. They are insight problems only before solving them, and then lose their status. Asking a participant to solve again a problem the answer of which they can conjure up from the pits of their memory is most likely not going to showcase any insight connected process, unless the participant truly forgot the solution, and is solving it anew again. This is hard to account for, so it is safer to assume that once a person has acquired insight about how to solve a particular problem, the same problem becomes useless in studying insight with that person.

As such problems are a one-shot deal, work with such problems requires taking into account whether or not the participants have seen each particular insight problem before. It also means that empirical insight problems are each different from each other: different insights are required to solve each problem. Because of this, studying the insight process with insight problems also requires the sometimes unspoken assumption, that different problems will address similar problem solving processes, though the knowledge required to solve such problems, some of the processes required by the problem steps and the solution itself might differ between them.

The set of processes and knowledge that such problems engage is thus quite complex. Administering such problems also takes a while, as you will see in the next sections. This is why think aloud methodologies are adopted in order to analyse the data provided, rather than gathering large amounts of datapoints and only running statistics on response times and accuracy. Think aloud protocols involve asking the participants to vocalize their thinking process as they are solving the problem. Their spoken data is recorded, transcribed as a written manuscript and then encoded in ways which will be explained later. Thus, the process of problem solving is analysed using the think aloud protocols of the participants.

We might want to model the solving of such problems computationally at some point in the future. From this perspective, another question is what kind of insight problems to address. As we have seen in Sect. 5.1, multiple types of empirical insight problems exist, including mathematical, spatial and verbal insight problems. Abstract problems involving abstract concepts might be interesting to observe, but hard to model. Also, problems requiring large amounts of specialist knowledge, for example knowledge about benzene or about engine designs, would require an expert population of solvers to administer. Even if we could gather such a population, this would mean that each cognitive scientist looking to check whether our results hold or not will need to find a similar population of experts. This might make our results harder to replicate.

We thus opted for studying insight with problems which require the kind of knowledge everyone has – that is knowledge about objects we use or see around us on a daily basis. A few such problems were well known problems in the literature, with classical status. We call these practical object insight problems. The number of such problems in the literature is quite small. Thus by adopting this practical object problems domain, we have assumed that different problems in the same domain could be created, as long as we observe existing classical problems.

In the rest of this chapter, these classical problems will be described and analysed (Sect. 11.1). The insights coming from these problems will be put together to form a strategy for creating new insight problems. We will aim for this strategy to be so clear, as to make possible the computational creation of new insight problems in the future. A think aloud protocol with human participants will then be run with these problems.

How could one make sense of all the things participants say during such problem solving? An encoding strategy will be set up, and the codes deployed to analyze the data will be described and explained (Sect. 11.2) with examples of what the participants actually say when being encoded in the various categories.

How can such codes come together, to analyse and explore the problem solving process? Two case studies of the highest performing human participants will be analysed in depth (Sect. 11.3), as to provide a window into how insightful problem solving looks like, in different flavours, when the participants rely on multiple, different strategies.

Are CreaCogs mechanisms comparable to the observed process? A comparison between CreaCogs processes and observed results will be performed (Sect. 11.4). To enable the future computational modeling of insight problem solving, in the context of the object domain, we will also have a look at the order in which processes take place during such creative problem solving – that is at the possibility of process flow (Sect. 11.5).

Could the principles in CreaCogs be similar to the ones used by humans when performing insightful creative problem solving? First, let us see how the classical insight problems look like in the practical object domain, and what methodology we could put in place to create new such problems.

11.1 Setting up the Practical Insight Problems

Five classical empirical insight problems have been selected from the literature as belonging to the practical object domain. These are:
1. The Candle Problem by (Duncker, 1945)
2. The Two Strings problem by (Maier, 1931)
3. The Hat Rack problem by (Maier, 1931)
4. The Loop problem or the Paperclip problem by (Duncker, 1945)
5. Attach the pendulum problem or The Weight problem by (Duncker, 1945)

Some of these problems came with classical illustrations, some required the author to recreate the visual stimuli using the verbal description of the problem in the literature. Whenever a verbal description of a problem was provided without the illustration in the literature, there was a possibility that the verbal description focused on the solution and the general setting, rather than mentioning all the objects which were provided in the inaccessible original image. The creation of the scenes of such problems thus also required the addition of various other objects, as will be described in the context of each problem below.

In order to propose a strategy for coming up with new insight problems, the classical problems will be taken as case studies and analysed. This analysis will start from the assumptions that:
1. there is a simple, non-creative (or much less creative) version of the problem which does not require insight;

2. that by observing the steps and possible stumbling blocks of the solvers, while they receive the version of the problem which does require creative skill, we can extrapolate some processes which make a problem require creativity;

3. that by using a variety of such interpolated processes and knowledge about cognitive problem solving, we can begin to create more such problems, even if we do not yet cover the entire variety of skills which can be tested through them.

Next we will have a look at these problems and try to extrapolate the potential principles which go into creating an insight problem.

11.1.1 Classic Practical Object Insight Problems

The Candle Problem by (Duncker, 1945) is stated as follows: *You are given a candle, a box of thumbtacks and a book of matches (see Fig. 11.1). You are supposed to fix the lit candle unto the wall in a way that doesn't allow the wax to drip below.*

Some formulations of the problem include a table next to the wall, onto which the wax is not supposed to drip. Others include a box of nails rather than a box of thumbtacks.

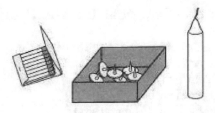

Fig. 11.1: The Candle Problem

The solutions that human participants come up with for this problem are varied in the literature. Some participants melt some of the candle to then use wax as a gluing agent. Some use the thumbtacks to pin the candle to the wall. Obviously, this is not enough to make the wax not fall below, which is why some participants attempt to make a small bridge or support under the table from thumbtacks. This bridge is sometimes made of nails, in the problem variant which includes nails rather than thumbtacks. A nail might be a better tool for pinning a thick object (like the candle) to a wall, thus leading the participants on a wrong representation path.

However, the solution considered as "correct" for this problem is to use the thumbtack (or nail) box as a support, to pin it to the wall with thumbtacks (or nails), put the candle in it and light it. It has been shown that human participants are better able to come to this solution if the thumbtack box is already empty, and the thumbtacks are presented outside of it. It might very well be that, while the thumbtack box is being used as a container (and full), human participants do not consider its other possible uses or affordances. The solved Candle Problem is shown in Fig. 11.2.

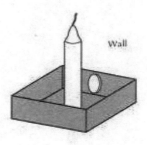

Fig. 11.2: The Candle Problem solved

Let us now assume a version of the problem which would not require creativity. For example, you are asked to fix the lit candle unto the wall, without the wax dripping below, but you are already given a candle holder. What are the strategies that turn this problem, which does not require creativity, into a problem which requires it? Two aspects can be observed:

- Hiding an object which is necessary for a (non-creative) solution of the problem within a different other object. A candle holder, which would have made the problem straightforward, is not present. Such a candle holder needs to be created via the re-representation of existing problem objects – the thumbtack box for containment and thumbtacks for fixing, in this case. From the perspective of the problem creator, one can look at this process as one of hiding the candle holder in a different object (or set of objects) with a similar affordance. Such a similar affordance however needs to be inferred creatively, perhaps in a process similar to that used when solving the Alternative Uses Test (Guilford, 1956).
- Hiding the affordance of an object by emphasizing a different affordance and (optionally) having that affordance already taken up or in use. This aspect shows up in the candle problem by the act of adding the thumbtacks inside the thumbtack box. Adding them near the box would have been a case for emphasizing the affordance of the box as a container. Adding them within the box is a case for having the affordance already in use. The purpose of the latter is, of course, to trigger and thus help study the functional fixedness bias.

The Two Strings Problem by (Maier, 1931) is stated as follows: *A person is put in a room that has two strings hanging from the ceiling. The task is to tie the two strings together, but it is impossible to reach one string while holding the other. What can the person do to tie the two strings together?* A depiction of this problem is shown in Fig. 11.3.

Fig. 11.3: The Two Strings problem

The participants make various attempts at tying the two strings, including getting on the chair, thinking this might enable them to pull one of the strings further, and thus enable them to reach the other.

The correct solution to this problem involves creating a pendulum, by using one of the strings and a heavy object from the pile of objects scattered on the floor (like the pliers). The creation of the pendulum allows the solver to set one of the strings in motion, so that the string comes towards the solver. This allows the solver to hold onto one of the strings, and also catch the other which was set in pendular motion.

Some participants struggling to solve the two strings problem are helped to come to this solution by the investigator, which brushes past one of the strings, setting it in motion. The idea behind this intervention is that the affordance for motion of the string might thus be triggered in the mind of the solver. After this intervention, solvers which were previously struggling are generally more successful at coming up with the solution. However, most of them report post solving not being aware that the investigator has helped them, nor even that they have seen the string set in motion by him (Maier, 1931).

The insight in this problem is about switching the representation template from trying to reach the other string to trying to make the string come to the participant. The second creative step is the construction of a pendulum out of the given objects (see Fig. 11.4). This is were both object composition and object replacement procedures can help.

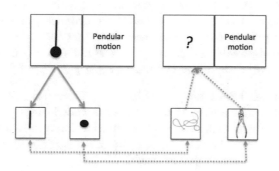

Fig. 11.4: Composing a Pendulum, a subpart of the String problem

Starting from a version of the problem which would not require creativity, one can assume the process of making such a problem creative involves the following aspects:

- As a general strategy, make objects which need to be used for the solution lose part of their affordances. A specific technique, observed in this problem, is to enable the loss of affordance by removing affordance related parts of the object. The object, in this case the pendulum, will thus need reconstruction, while the parts themselves are less likely to trigger the same affordance. The affordance of the pendulum to be mobile is removed, through splitting the pendulum in two parts. Also, the attention of the solver might be diverted from the insight that objects can be made to move on their own through emphasizing the (potential) movement of the person. For example, the verbal description of this problem specifies that "it is impossible to reach a string while holding the other", focusing the attention of the solver on a self-based motion frame of reference. This might direct the participant to think of themselves as mobile, rather than of other objects.

- Split a key object that you are aiming to remove affordances from into parts and scatter the parts across the problem scene. This strategy is somewhat overlapping in the context of this problem with the principle above. However, the principle above can also involve removing solution-leading affordances of an object in different ways, by, for example, changing the frame of reference, representing the object in a space which makes the affordance less salient and constrains thinking about the object.

- Hide the object required to solve the problem (or object parts) within other objects. This principle is shared with the candle problem, with the added bonus that, here, not just objects but also parts of objects are exchanged for similarly affording objects. Whereas in the candle problem the candle holder was *"hidden"* in the thumbtack box, here the weight of the pendulum is hidden in (multiple possible replacement) heavy objects across the floor, and the pendulum string is already attached to the ceiling.
- Add objects that lead to other possible affordances, and thus other possible constructions, in this case the chair (getting up on the chair gets triggered as a possible solution path), the nails (fixing one of the strings closer to the other by using the nails gets triggered, etc.).

The Cardboard and loop problem was taken from Duncker's treatise *On problem-solving* (Duncker, 1945), where it is called *the paperclip problem*[1],. The cardboard problem came without an illustration and is stated as follows: *You are asked to help the experimenter attach this piece of cardboard to the loop in the ceiling. How do you proceed?*

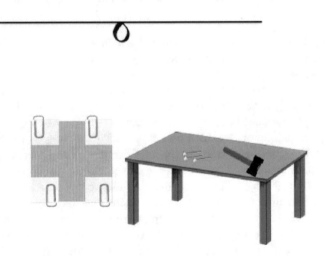

Fig. 11.5: Author's depiction of the cardboard problem

In order to present the problem to solving participants, we represented it as in Fig. 11.5, adding as other objects in the room a hammer and some nails on a table. The cardboard to be attached to the loop has four pieces of paper attached to the four corners with four paperclips – as per Duncker's formulation. The solution to this problem is to get one of the paperclips out

---

[1] We have not used the original name here because the name contains the object used for the solution.

of its position in holding the piece of paper, bend it and turn it into a two way hook (an S); then use one side of the hook to attach to the loop, and the other to pierce through the cardboard. This second pierce can also be done in a corner, to hold the piece of paper in place, if necessary.

The difficulty in solving this problem comes from two different sources:

a) switching between seeing the paperclips in two different functions; that is between seeing them as *holding* one of the pieces of paper attached to the cardboard, to seeing them as *bendable* objects which can be *detached* and used for hooking and piercing

b) the necessity to pierce through the cardboard, an action which might be perceived by the participants as destroying the cardboard, and thus yield resistance.

There is perhaps an added amount of difficulty in our visual presentation because of the addition of the nails. The similarity of affordance between the task of attaching something to the loop and nail related affordances of fixing things to wall might get in the way of constructing the desired solution, which uses the paperclips (not the nails) for *"attaching"*. In fact, an interesting second condition here would be to present this problem to a second group of participants with different objects in the visual scene (not including nails), the affordance of which would have less of a chance in interfering with the one of the request. This would probably make the solvers much less likely to perceive objects like the nails as salient, and fixate on them as useful for the solution. It would thus lower the chance for an imperfect mapping between the goal of the problem and problem objects with affordances which appear similar to the goal, that however do not afford the solution.

Creating problems like the cardboard problem could include the following strategies:

- Hiding part of the solving objects as parts of other objects. In this case, the paperclips are attached to the cardboard, and thus can be perceived as being part of it, thus part of the object which needs attaching to the loop, rather than of the tools which the attaching can be done with.

- Using one of the actions people would refrain from doing as part of the solution – i.e. destroying an existing object, disobeying rules or norms or arrangements perceived as implicit or unbreakable. In this case, not only the paperclips are used to hold together the white piece of paper at the corner of the cardboard (using them thus having the possible consequence of disassembling that part of the object), but also piercing the cardboard can be viewed as a way of damaging the cardboard irreversibly (in other problems, parts of objects can be pulled away by disassembling the object to pieces, however the object can also be reassembled).

- Have other objects with a similar affordance in the scene, to see if they interfere with finding the objects which would truly provide the solution. In the case of this problem, the affordance that nails and hammer have to fix something to a wall or a ceiling can interfere with seeing the less salient affordance of the paperclip, setting the nails and hammer center stage as red herrings.

At this point, the main types of strategies used to turn a problem which does not require a creative solution into a problem requiring one are becoming clearer. Before summarizing these strategies, here are the other two classical problems used.

The Hat Rack problem by (Maier, 1931) is stated as follows: *You need to make a hat rack (a rack to put your hat) in the room shown below; on the floor they are two planks and a G-clamp. What do you do?* The hat rack problem is depicted in Fig. 11.6 – with measurements adapted from the original (in inches), to cm[2] – as to be suitable for participants more familiar to the metric system. The hat rack problem seems to be amongst the hardest practical insight problems in the literature.

Fig. 11.6: Depiction of the Hat Rack problem with metric measurements

The solution to this problem is to use the two planks laying on the floor vertically. The planks can be overlapped for 20 cm of their length, and then clamped with the G-clamp. The overlap is necessary in order to match the maximum height possible here, that is the height of the room. After the planks have been secured vertically between the floor and ceiling, with the G-clamp

---

[2] This was an adaptation, not a direct translation of original measurements, as measurements which were not rounded might have encumbered the solver with more information to consider than necessary in the metric measurements variant.

holding them together, the handle of the G-clamp can also be used as a hook for a hat, because of its shape. Thus the planks together form something like a tree hat rack with the handle of the clamp being the only hook.

In our opinion, two main difficulties are presented by this problem. The first one is the lack of resources. In other problems, the main difficulty might be selecting the best suited object or set of objects amongst many, and the memory of the solver might be overloaded as a function of considering all these options. By contrast, very few objects are present in the hat rack problem,: two planks and the G clamp, together with two boards that are attached to the ceiling (and which serve no purpose in reaching the correct solution, however they might be considered red herring objects).

The second difficulty of this problem is the ambiguity of the goal. Having the goal of forming a hat rack begs the question which kind of hat rack, and what the hat rack looks like. Depending on which kind of knowledge is brought to the fore by the solver, the hat rack goal can be horizontal (shelf-like), or vertical (tree-like). The latter template obviously has more chances in triggering the right solution.

Besides needing to bring the right kind of template to the foreground, the hat rack problem involves two elements of solving which might require or trigger insight: a composition element and a double use element. The composition element of insight requires that the two planks on the floor, despite of being longer together than the height of the room, be thought of in terms of adjustable height. The solver thus needs to realize that, despite an initial mismatch, the height of the two planks can be made to match the height of the room ,depending on where one overlaps the planks and puts the G-clamp. This insight can probably be triggered by noticing the measurement of 4 cm on the opening of the G-clamp, which is equal to the sum of the widths of the two planks. However, the G-clamp in itself is a tool the width of which can be altered (to a certain extent). This might make solvers miss the cue of the measurement of the clamp opening, while seeing the tool under its adaptive nature rather then as a fixed point to start building the problem solution from. In a way, this makes insightful and creative problem solving be a game of *understanding which parts of the problem should be kept fixed, and which parts should be looked at as if they were mobile or adaptive*. The second insightful part of the solution consists in realizing that the G-clamp can be used not only for its clamping affordances, but also, because of its shape, as a hook. This double use part might be hard because solvers might tend to assign no use or one use to each problem object. Thus when looking for what objects might provide the next affordances they need, solvers might look at objects with unassigned uses, while discarding the others as already fulfilling a purpose.

Attach the pendulum problem

This problem was taken from Duncker's *On problem-solving* (Duncker, 1945), where it is called *the weight problem*[3] – and came without an illustration. The problem is stated as follows: *You are to help the observer set up the room for an experiment. You need to attach the pendulum to the ceiling. What do you do?* We represented the problem for empirical investigation as depicted in Fig. 11.7, adding as other objects the red sock, the glasses, the table and the ladder.

Fig. 11.7: Author's depiction of the pendulum problem

The solution to this problem is to use the pendulum head as a hammer to put the nails in the ceiling, before attaching the pendulum. The difficulty in this problem resides in seeing the pendulum in two functions – the object to be attached to the ceiling, and the hammer replacement. The nature of the problem, or the stumbling point in attempting to solve it, might not be clear to the participants initially. Participants might thus take a while to realize that the inherent problem – making a hammer – is not formulated in the problem description, but comes as a consequence of one of the solving steps.

11.1.2 Strategies for Creating New Problems

Five cases of classical insight problems in the practical object domain have been observed. We analysed, in the case of the first three such problems, what strategies can be used to turn the simpler, no creativity required version of the problem, into a problem requiring creativity and insight problem solving. We can now collate these observations together in order to formulate a strategy.

---

[3] The original name of the problem was not used here in order not to confuse this problem with another one which we created and which will be described shortly – the Jack and Jill problem.

A non-exhaustive list of some of the techniques that can be used in problem creation, in light of the previous case studies, includes:

(i) Diminishing the saliency of the objects required for the solution, by (a) putting them in a different context of affordances and possibly (b) having those affordances already allocated or used;

(ii) Hiding objects in a different form by re-representing them as other objects which have similar properties and affordances (but for which said affordances might not be as salient as for the initial objects);

(iii) Decomposing the solution in different parts, and re-representing the parts in different structures or objects;

(iv) Representing needed parts as integrated parts of other objects;

(v) Using an object twice in the solution, with two different contexts of affordances. In this case, participants need to look at both sets of affordance contexts, to perceive the object in both of its potential roles, similar to being able to look at two ambiguous figures, the perception of which can emerge from the same set of elements;

(vi) Adding to the problem other salient objects, the affordances of which might interfere with the solution;

(vii) Making use of natural or learned biases against breaking objects, crossing commonsense, common practice norms or aesthetic values.

This set of strategies also lends itself to being implemented using the CreaCogs principles, for example by:

(a) replacing objects of a given problem with other objects which have the same particular affordance, but for which that affordance is less salient using OROC and

(b) decomposing the solution into various objects and putting such objects in a non-salient context in the environment, by using different problem templates which emphasize different courses of action and solutions.

Using these strategies, a set of problems were created by the author. In the following we will describe three of them:

1. Dusting the Clock;
2. Lost Teddy and
3. The Jack and Jill Weight problem

Some of these problems, like the Dusting the Clock problem, were meant to provide multiple solutions, and thus allow the experimenter to explore how multiple solutions are formed, and how the solvers "move" between such solutions. Others, like the Jack and Jill Weight problem, were meant to require "insight" in the classical sense. Here are the three problems, with the application of the strategies to Lost Teddy and Jack and Jill explicitly discussed.

Dusting the Clock is a problem meant to elicit multiple solutions. The problem is stated as follows: *Johnny is cleaning a room. How can he reach to dust the clock?* Fig. 11.8 is provided, depicting the room which Johnny is cleaning and the various objects in it.

Fig. 11.8: Dusting the Clock problem

A large amount of constructions and solutions are possible in this problem, due to the large amount of objects presented. For example, the solver can attempt to make Johnny go up on the table, build higher constructions involving the chairs, use the tennis racket to elongate Johnny's arm, etc.

The goal of this problem is thus to observe the process of construction of various solutions. An interesting part of this problem is that some solutions or constructions can be perceived as unstable, and therefore dangerous to Johnny.

One possible solution for this problem was using the surfboard on the table as a seesaw and putting the globe on the other side, as a weight, in order to keep the wall facing side of the seesaw up. This involved bringing knowledge about a new object (the seesaw and how weights modify its position) to structure some of the objects in the given environment.

The difficulty in this problem thus consists in considering each of the multiple objects present and in the multiplicity of possible solutions. This richness of objects makes it hard to keep track which solution paths were followed and which were not. This could make the solvers stuck, by making them unable to see new possible ways of structuring the problem. This difficulty is coupled with another one: it is ambiguous from the problem and hard to assess which solutions present stability and safety.

Blown Away Teddy is another problem created using the strategies above. The problem is stated as follows: *The wind blew your son's teddy bear from the clothesline into your neighbour's garden. The neighbour is in holidays*

and the fence is too high to climb. How can you retrieve the teddy? Fig. 11.9
depicts the problem.

Fig. 11.9: Blown Away Teddy problem

The solution to this problem is to construct a fishing rod, using the mop,
the clothesline and the bended clothes hangers.

The difficulty in this problem can reside in having to see objects outside of
the normal context of affordances in which they are shown: a) seeing the mop
out of it's cleaning context (which is why the mop was put in this context
using a bucket and water) and b) seeing the clothesline and clothes hangers
out of their context of being used for drying clothes.

However, this might not be as big a difficulty as when an object has two
uses, in two different contexts of affordances, which both are required for
the problem at hand. In terms of insight, this problem requires the solver to
realize a fishing template would be useful to *"catch"* and drag the teddy over
the fence. In terms of object composition, this problem requires the solver to
map various objects as parts of a fishing rod.

The exact distance to the teddy is ambiguous in the depiction. Thus the
observing experimenter can intervene at various solution construction points,
and state that the object constructed might not be long enough to reach the
teddy, or that the solution provided is not appropriate because of the distance
to the teddy being larger. Such interventions would require the solver to come
up with another solution, and sometimes a new way to see the problem.

In terms of applying the strategies previously proposed in order to construct such a problem, here is a description of problem construction:

1. Start from a problem and an existing solution. The problem is that you need to obtain an object that is far away. The solution is to reach for the object.
2. Make the solution creative. A fishing rod is used for fishing, but can have the alternative use of hooking something that is far away. The object replacement part of a system like OROC A.1v can be used to generate such alternative uses.
3. Decompose the solution object into parts. The parts of the fishing rod used here are the pole, the string and the hook.
4. Hide the parts of the solution in other objects (with different salient affordances), or in parts of other objects. The string is presented as a clothesline (one to one object mapping). The hook is presented as part of the clothes hanger (part of object). The pole is presented as part of the mop (part of object). The participant can also attempt to use the pole that is part of the umbrella, if the participant perceives this as movable.
5. Embed the replacement (or re-represented) objects in different contexts of affordances. The clothesline is presented holding clothes to dry, attached to the umbrella pole. The hangers have clothes on them, and are also partially visually obscured by the clothes (the part which provides the affordance conducive to the solution is, however, visible). The mop is presented next to the bucket and a water puddle, which emphasize its cleaning affordances.

The Jack and Jill Weight problem is another new problem created using the above set of strategies. The problem is stated as follows: *Jack and Jill are arguing about who weighs more. What could they do to find out for certain?* Fig. 11.10 shows the problem.

The solution to this problem is to create a seesaw out of a borrowed surfboard and the bucket in order to weigh Jack and Jill comparatively.

We consider this problem as the closest to a classical insight problem. The surfboard, an object which exists in the picture in a different context, is already in use and is not salient, is (re)used for the construction of another object, the seesaw. The solver has to retrieve the seesaw from their knowledge base as an useful object, which provides a productive way to restructure the problem. The second object used in the construction of the seesaw is the bucket (as a pivot). The bucket, like the surfboard, exists in a different affordance context (playing with sand), with such an affordance already used: the bucket is full of sand (in a similar way in which the thumbtack box is full of thumbtacks in the candle problem).

These alternate contexts of affordances can constitute sources of difficulty, together with the fact that the problem only allows one correct solution. Furthermore, the inflatable swimming pool can be taken as a red herring, leading to Archimedes's principle for measuring mass rather then weight being deployed. Similarly, the appearance of the two people can be taken as a red herring.

Fig. 11.10: Jack and Jill Weight problem

How are the strategies observed in the previous classical problems applied to create this problem? Here is a description of creating this problem:

1. Start from a problem and an existing solution. The initial problem-solution pair was that balancing scales are used to measure weight.
2. Change the problem, so that the solution would be creative – e.g. use a seesaw instead of scales; put the problem in the beach setting to provide a change of context to one which less affords thinking about weights and balancing scales, like a kitchen; and use of a different object than the seesaw, with similar properties.
3. Split the object in various parts – the seesaw was split into a pivot and a support plank.
4. Hide the objects which form the solution by re-representing them as other objects or object parts – the plank was turned into a surfboard (this also involved an adaptation to the current beach context) and the pivot into a bucket (similar adaptation). Through the adaptation to context, both objects thus can be envisaged as belonging to a normal beach scene, rather than triggering the attention of the participant as objects that have especially been added to the beach context because they are part of the solution.
5. Hide the objects in different contexts of affordances and possibly have those affordances be already in use – the bucket is turned with its side up, and presented in its container affordance (full of sand); the surfboard is being surfed on, and quite far away, which makes it less salient visually. Some participants might also have social qualms with solution steps that involve asking for an object which is being currently used by and belongs to someone else.

6. Add objects which act as red herrings, providing a similar affordance as the ones necessary for solving the problem, thus getting the participant started on a different path – the small plastic swimming pool can get the participant started in this case on an Archimede's principle solution path.

The strategies above are clear enough to allow for computational descriptions (Olteţeanu, 2016), and perhaps for the future computational creation of insight problems in the practical objects domain.

While designing problem stimuli, an interesting difficulty encountered was that adding virtually any object to a scene can introduce multiple possibilities of interaction between that objects and existing other objects of the problem. For example, in the Blown away teddy problem, adding a table with an umbrella seemed necessary, in order to have something to attach the string, as a clothesline, less conspicuously. However, this adds the umbrella pole, which can then be used as a different fishing rod, and the pole+umbrella combination, which can be used to grab and drag things with. New objects thus introduce new affordances, new possibilities of affordance through combinations with existing objects, multiple new possible problem solving paths, problem representations, and sometimes new solution paths. As the intention was to explore the complexity of restructuring and re-representation, salient objects that could lead the solver on different paths and multiple solution paths have been added in some problems.

Some of the strategies for problem creation summarized here were also taken into account when a classical problem lacked the accompanying image and required us making an illustration for it. As mentioned before, some classical insight problems are depicted in the literature by describing the main objects that are necessary to solve the problem, with no mention of what the *"filler"* objects originally were. Making a choice for what other objects to add to the problem automatically implies considering whether one is making the problem harder or easier by the objects one adds, the way their affordances interfere with the known solution path and by the contexts (of affordances) one depicts these objects in.

While exploring these strategies, several other problems were created, on the same principles as the problems above. However, these eight problems (5 classical and 3 new) were the ones employed in an empirical investigation of the creative problem-solving process, as explained in the next section.

11.2 Encoding Strategy and Codes

The problems we described above were used in a think aloud experiment. In this, participants were meant to attempt to vocalize as much as they could of what went through their mind, when attempting to solve these problems. In accordance to the procedure of think aloud protocols, in order to analyze the answers and the problem solving process of the participants, the recorded verbal data needed to be transcribed and the transcription segments needed to be coded. For this, a set of codes needed to be created which corresponded to categories of problem solving process the participants were engaging in. These codes were then to be attached to the transcript segments, thus being used to classify and analyse them.

In order to usefully analyse to what extent the processes posited by the theoretical CreaCogs framework are present in the solving of such problems by human participants, a relation between the transcript and the theoretical model of processes needed to be established.

For this, we first run a pilot version of this study, inspected the pilot answers and constructed a set of codes. Some such codes pertain directly to the CreaCogs framework and formalization, while others are parts of the general process of problem solving.

In the following, we explore these codes, together with examples of how they may look like in think aloud protocols. The pilot protocol on which these codes where established will from now on be referred to as P0. Some of the initially posited codes did not have a suitable example in P0, but we established them as they referred to relevant parts of the CreaCogs framework. Segments corresponding to these posited codes were later found in the protocols of the other participants. In this case, examples of the code application are shown from the other participant. For each example, the anonymous participant code is mentioned (e.g. P0, mb8, fb6), together with the name of the problem. Wherever possible, we grouped codes in sets or categories, like *Problem solving general process codes*, *Affordance related segments*, *Problem template use codes*, etc. Let us delve into the codes and see how they look like.

*Problem solving general process codes (**PSP**)*

<PSP – Reading the problem> – This code refers to both initial reads and complete re-reads of the problem. In the case in which only the key requirements are read again, the more specific code <PSP – Defining key requirements of the problem> is used.

<PSP – Comprehending> – A process of attempting comprehension of the problem can appear in transcripts through moments of re-reading the problem, pauses at various points when reading, and verbal cues like *"So let me understand this ..."*.

<PSP – Defining key requirements of the problem> – In these segments, the participants focus on extracting the main problem requirements and constraints; thus they scan through the problem statement to synthesize them. Future search strategies might be based on requirements which were defined as key at this stage. Furthermore, these requirements might be later used in evaluation. Transcript segments in which the solver reiterates key parts of the problem statement could be encoded under this, for example P0 reiterating in *Attach the pendulum*: *"It needs to be attached to the ceiling"*. This code can also correspond to more explicit attempts at discovering the key requirements and constraints, like P0 in *Blown away teddy*: *"So, let's redo*

the... the logical assumptions here, and these are that the fence is too high ...
Yeah, that is actually the only one that is to be taken into consideration."

<PSP – Mapping problem formulation to objects> – This code describes the attempt of the solver to anchor the verbal formulation of the problem into visuospatial input, or visuospatial representation. The two presentations of the problem – visual depiction and problem formulation – present complementary information. Looking at objects to map them to the problem formulation has either been encoded by the experimenter that was observing the solver, or is reflected in speech segments of the transcript. An example of mapping the problem formulation to the visual depiction of the objects in the *Blown Away Teddy* is: *"I have to get teddy ... so that's the teddy over there"*.

<PSP – Taking stock of problem objects> – This code reflects statements in which the participant seems to run an inventory of the objects in the room. P0 in the *Two strings problem* takes stock of the problem objects as follows: *"So, what do we have? There, we have a chair and some... some bowl. And we also have some... some old objects that could look like some pieces of paper, and some things on the ground [...] Maybe some... some very, very small nails."* At times, such an inventory is run in conjunction with the mentioned objects' affordances (or might trigger such affordances). In some cases, this strategy of listing objects appears later in the process of solving (after at least a way of solving the problem has been already tried). This might help the solver which is not satisfied with the initial solving path to switch their focus on other objects, and to build solutions around them. Thus we assume this is used to both *select* useful objects in a fast and broad manner, and to *trigger* associations of uses, which might be unconscious or not vocalized.

<PSP – Proceeding on path> – Once a direction or a path to attempt solving has been set (starting with some objects or a problem template which will be used intuitively as a heuristic), the participant then proceeds on this path. This is a complementary code to <PT – Template Switch>.

<PSP – Backtracking> – This code refers to going backwards on a solution path, and picking things up from an earlier state. Backtracking can involve reverting to a *"crossroads"* decision point. This is sometimes done explicitly, like in P0 does it in *Dusting the clock*: *"Okay, sorry, wait, let me... let me come back on that"*. At other times, such backtracking is done implicitly, by turning back fast from a hypothesis that was being considered; this can sometimes be followed by a return to <PSP – Defining key requirements>, for example: *"And we... we will tie that left end of the rope to the fence... No, we will not do that. So, you... you cannot climb the fence"* (P0, *Blown away teddy*).

<PSP – Evaluation> – In these segments, participants evaluate a particular solution to the problem. This evaluation can involve comparing solution states to constraints, or can be more general than that. Here is P0 evaluating his solution in *Attach the pendulum*: *"so I would have to go with this solution, although [...] maybe five percent certain that this solution would work"*. Evaluation might also involve expressing satisfaction or dissatisfaction with a produced solution, in objective but also in emotional, intuitive and aesthetic terms.

<**PSP** – **Running through consequences**> – This code describes segments in which the participant thinks about the consequences of moving objects, or the consequences of deploying various actions on the problem objects. For example: Here is P0 running through consequences of his actions in the *Two Strings* problem: *"And we will have, after this action will be performed ... so we will have that piece of paper nailed to the ceiling by three or four nails, and will have that piece of rope left and on top of that piece of paper, and right under the ceiling ..."*

*Affordance related segments (**Aff**)*

<**Aff** – **Determining object affordance**> – This can range from listing the traditional affordances of the problem objects, to listing more creative affordances for these objects – that is affordances for which the objects are not generally used (like in the Alternative Uses Test). In the latter case, we generally also use code <OU - Object used in novel way>. Here is P0 determining object affordances in the *Candle problem*: *"The matches could be there just to [...] light the candle ... and maybe to melt the candle"*. It is useful to remark that determining affordances in the context of a problem is not just related to the object in question, but can be related to another object, upon which the affordance of the affording object will be deployed. Affordances thus act as links in the process of building higher compositions of solution chains; these solution chains can sometimes be matched to various existing or known problem templates.

<**Aff** – **Inferring more affordances**> – This refers to a process of inferring new affordances that are not initially explicit to the solver from the given problem context, as well as to developing upon direct object affordances, in order to infer what other affordances might be present. Such inferences of extra affordances generally make use of common sense knowledge, and can prepare the object for use within a specific template. For example, here is P0 inferring width from the height and shape of the two wooden beams in the *Hat rack* problem: *"so those two wooden objects out there seem to be of the same width and length [...] it looks like a square. So that means that actually the lower width ... width is also 30 centimetres as the vertical width there."* However, such inferences are to be differentiated the mentioning of unusual or creative affordances with existing objects.

<**Aff** – **Determining lack of affordance**> – This code stands for stating or determining that a certain object cannot be used in a certain way. Determining a certain lack of affordance may begin with the initial statement

of an affordance, followed by its negation or retraction. This is a form of affordance rejection in which the solver prompts herself to stop considering an affordance as being enabled by the object. Here is P0 doing just that in the *Candle problem*: *"The thumbtacks would .... couldn't possibly be used for nailing the candle to the wall"*.

<Aff – Determining template affordance> – If a certain template is being used consciously, or if the participant has access to meta-reasoning tools about which template is being used, this code marks segments in which affordances of templates are being considered. Here is an example of determining whether a platform template would afford the solution: *"I could construct a platform but that's not going to be any good, what I need is [...]"*.

*Problem template use codes (**PT**)*

<PT – Requirement-based search of template> – This code refers to segments in which the solver is searching for an appropriate template in which to cast the problem, and this search for a template is started from the problem constraints and requirements. Here is P0 searching using the requirements of the *Candle problem* to search for a problem solving template: *"So, how can you... how can you fix something up near something [...] Oh yes, you can provide some sort of stable platform for... for it."* Sometimes this code overlaps with <Determining PT to use>, at other times determining PT to use is simply a less specific code, as it is not clear how the template to be used was reached. This code is also part of the <Search> codes.

<PT – Determining PT to use> – This code describes segments in which the participant is choosing what template could be suitable for the problem, and is starting to use a specific template. Here is P0, determining what PT to use in *Dusting the clock*: *"So, of course, there is no way for him to reach that clock, yes, which is on the left wall. Okay, so once again we would have to provide some steady platform for... for Johnny to be able to dust that watch."* Here is P0 determining what PT to use in the *Jack and Jill weight problem*: *"by looking at it... by looking at it... It seems to be a very straightforward application for the Archimedes' principle"*. These segments correspond to determining the use of a PT, which will guide the following steps of the solver until either a solution is found, or an impasse is reached. If an impasse is reached, or other problems in adapting the template appear, the participant might decide to let go of the template. A new template could also appear in an insightful, "pop out" manner, intersecting the current solving and providing a more productive alternative to the currently used template. Such a new more suitable PT could appear as a consequence of the associations being made during the solving process, which converge to form a new template, or which point to a new way of solving things.

<PT – Adaptation of PT to problem> – A chosen problem template is adapted to fit the constraints of the problem (or is adapted to work with other templates). Sometimes this adaptation can occur when determining a PT to be used. Here is P0, attempting to adapt a PT to the objects of the *Candle problem*: *"So, how can you... how can you fix something up near something, or in this case, to the wall?"* (P0, Candle problem). This is also a <Creative Adaptation> code.

<PT use to search for suitable objects> – An abstract template that would be suitable has been found, in the estimation of the solver. Now this template is used to select objects that could participate in realizing it in the given problem environment. For example, here is P0, using a platform template to search for suitable objects to instantiate it with, in the context of the *Candle problem*: *"So, the only thing that could be provided as a stable platform in which to place the candle is of course that box, that it couldn't be something else."* This code is also part of the <Search> category.

<PT – Adaptation of problem template to objects> – An existing problem template is adapted to properties of the objects. Here is P0, adapting their platform template to the objects in the *Candle problem*: *"If you put it [...] on a horizontal position, then you would need just two thumbtacks on each end of ... it to nail them to the wall, and in this case to really fix, to link the box to the wall by using thumbtacks, which would provide a stable horizontal platform for the candle, in which you could place the candle"*. In this example, after the platform template is applied to the objects, a modification is observed: the candle is not *on top of* the platform, but *in* the box that has initially been used to fill the platform template, which is actually upon inspection also a container. This code also belongs to the <Creative Adaptation> category.

<PT – Use of PT construct> – This code marks segments in which a previously determined PT is being used to organize objects in an attempt to solve the problem. This code is also used when the same PT is being reused immediately or when a solver comes back to this PT after trying out different solving paths. However, the objects used to populate the template might differ on each try or use. The Use of a PT construct is also a <Composition> code.

<PT – Use of PT construct with reaching solution path> – This code marks segments in which a problem template has been used successfully to reach a plausible solution for the problem.

<PT – Rejecting template> – In the segments encoded under this category, the participant decides against using a specific template, or makes statements about how a certain template would be inappropriate to use in a problem. Sometimes, such a PT is rejected "out of hand", without running through the consequences of using it. Such rejections might be made on the fly because a certain template "does not seem to fit", as some of its affordances or requirements come in conflict with the requirements of the problem, or because it seems the template cannot be enabled by the objects of the problem. A PT could also be rejected because it appears that, affordance-wise, it comes somewhat short of getting the job done. Here is P0 rejecting, with some regret, the use of the Archimedes's principle as a template in the *Jack and Jill weight problem*: *"but unfortunately, here we have to... to establish if some.. some sort of differentiation can be obtained from weighing, and not from... not from just calculated... calculating volume"*.

<**PT – Template Switch**> – This reflects segments in which the solver switches from a PT which she was using to a new one. Such template switches might ensue during, or after the process of restructuring the problem elements. Here is P0 switching from a *fixing object to wall* to a *providing support* template in the *Candle problem*: *"So, instead of ... instead of fixing the candle to the wall in the most regular way, you could just provide a platform for it on which it could stand."*.

*Assessment category (**A**)*

The Assessment category generally refers to partial assessments during the solving process, rather than to Evaluation segments which occur after a problem solution has been reached.

<**A – Checking joints in plan**> – This code reflects segments in which the participant considers how the various objects or groups of objects, actions or parts of the plan fit in the overall attempt at solving the problem. References may be made to particular parts of objects fitting with other objects, in the general context of the plan.

<**A – Checking object against constraints**> – This code pertains to checking whether a particular object fits the given problem constraints, or whether the object fits the constraints of the PT which is currently being used. Subsequent to this check, the object could be integrated in the solution plan, or found to be lacking. If the object is found lacking, the participant could discard it, or adapt the PT to this limitation, by adding other objects to the problem space. Here is P0 checking whether Johnny fits their current *"climb on platform to reach further up"* solving path in *Dusting the clock*: *"Okay, but right now Johnny is... Johnny is still very small to be able to get on that... that platform"*.

<**A – Comparing solving state to constraints**> – In these segments, the participant directly compares some state reached in solving with the constraints or requirements of the problem. For example, here is P0 comparing the solving state to the requirements in *Dusting the clock*: *"... which will make him a little bit higher and maybe able to place himself and... and now climb on [...] that platform, from which he ... he can easily dust that clock."*

Focus changes

<**F – Focusing on object**> – This reflects segments in which the solver focuses on a particular object (or objects) and builds solutions around it, or

tries to use to use this object in every solution for a while. Here is P0 focusing on the rope in *Blown away teddy*: *"So, obviously, we ... we would have to use that rope in some way to reach the... the teddy"*.

<F – Switching focus to new object> – This reflects segments in which the focus of the solver switches from an object or a set of objects (and implicitly their affordances), to another object or set of objects. This switch allows for new types of solutions to be built, to emerge or to be considered – that is solutions centered around the new objects in focus, and their affordances. Sometimes this provides a fresh start in solving the problem, and it leads to restructuring the problem. At different times, such switches are the consequence of the solver noticing a new object, which then can be integrated in the solving process. Here is P0 switching focus to a new object in the *Candle problem*: *"[...] and the box would be fixed to the wall by using thumbtacks. But why that box of matches there?"*

The equivalent of these processes of focus and switch of focus in problem template (rather than object) terms are codes <PSP – Proceeding on path> and <PT – Template switch>.

Creative problem solving specific

These are codes specific to the creative problem solving process.

<Composing fuller results based on previous exploration> – This code corresponds to segments in which the solver assembles more completely and with more details a solution, which might be based on previously noticed affordances, earlier inferences of creative uses of objects, previous "hunches" of what might or might not work in the problem, and on other forms of preceding problem exploration. It is sensible to consider that, after making previous fast and wide searches of objects and templates which might afford the solution, the solver takes, at this stage, more time to deploy in detail and explore a solving path which seemed plausible.

<Insight marker expressions> – This code is assigned to segments or expressions which may reflect insight. For example, it is used to mark utterances like: *"Ah!", "I see!", "I know!", "Aha!", "I got it", "I have a new crazy idea which might just work"*. These utterances are especially interesting when they come after a long break in verbalizing, or after long break in coming up with new ideas; they can also be telling when they seem to come out of nowhere, or when they intersect a previous (coherent) line of thought. These segments may or may not be indicative of actual insight. In our analysis, they act as a marker, and further proof of new restructuring of the problem is necessary, in order to deem such expressions as actually reflecting an insightful moment.

<Making assumptions> – With insight problems and problems which require creative problem solving, a decent amount of ambiguity comes naturally. Participants seem to contend with this by setting up assumptions of their own. Such segments may (but must not necessarily) start with *"I'm gonna assume that.."* or *"Can I assume that..?"*. Here is P0 making assumptions in *Dusting the clock*: *Okay, assuming that Johnny can... can easily move on... on top of the table.* Here is P0 making assumptions in *Blown away teddy*: *"So, assuming that you... you in no way are able to disembowel that... that table"*. These assumptions may or may not be valid or even helpful.

<Stuck or Functional fixedness> – This code reflects segments in which the solver cannot come up with anything new, and is either silent, voices that no new idea is being found, or keeps on iterating previous ideas.

<Forcing the solution> – This code is allocated to segments in which the solver is trying to force a certain solution to work, despite evidence to the contrary, or their already declared assessments that it would not work. Some such forced solutions can be far fetched, and can be seen as a way of trying to close the gap between the current solving state and the solution or goal state. Such segments of forcing the solution might impose very low limit thresholds on what can be done with the problem objects, and might also showcase extra complicated attempts at solving the problem. For example, P0 forces the solution to the *Cardboard and loop* problem by attempting to nail the table to the wall vertically, in such a way that a table leg is placed under the loop, in order to be used as support for the cardboard which also now touches the loop. Such forced solutions might appear after being stuck in functional fixedness for a long while, and possibly being frustrated with the inability to solve the problem in any simple and straightforward way.

*Object (**O**), Object templates (**OT**) and Object Use (**OU**)*

<O – Disassembles or breaks object> – An object is split in pieces or broken, possibly to extract parts which can be used for their affordances. For example, Mb8, when solving *Dusting the clock*, proposes to *"take the shoelace or the lace of one of the skates there"* or to *" pull the legs off the table"*. The code is also part of the <Disassembly> category.

<O – Property-based search of object> – This code stands for segments in which a solver has already decided or identified what kind of property is essential for an object, in order for that object to help produce the solution, or to fit into a particular problem template which is being used to currently solve the problem. The solver is thus using a certain property or its corresponding affordance to search through the objects in the problem. For example, Fb6, when solving *Blown away teddy*, shows such evident of property-based search of object when saying: *"so wow now I can take the clothesline because it's a long wire"*. This code is also part of the <Search> category.

<O – Adaptation of objects to template> – An object is fitted into a problem template by changing its main properties or uses. This sometimes comes as a consequence of the object being seen through a certain object

template. Thus certain properties of the object might be required by the template, but such properties might not initially be salient in the object. For example, properties of the object "paperclip" need to be changed for the object to become a hook. Physically, the object needs to be unbent. Similarly, paper sheets can be folded to use their length and bendability properties, when operating under a Chain template and trying to use them as the chain loops, etc. This code is also part of the <Creative Adaptation> category.

<O – Object used to search for template> – This code applies to the segments in which, starting from a given object, the solver is trying to extrapolate what template the object could be part of, or find a template that is suitable for both the object and the problem. The constraints of the problem can thus simultaneously be used in this search, overtly or covertly. This process of using objects to search for templates might be why sometimes object affordances are initially explicitly stated, or later developed. Here is P0 using the rope to search for a template in *Attach the pendulum*: *"(I am thinking of) different sorts of construct, but all of them would imply that... that rope some...somehow, because we need to ... to make that pendulum moving, and we can do that by only...by only linking... tying that one end of that rope to the upper side of the pendulum"*. This code is also part of the <Search> category.

<OT – Object template use> – An object template is used to re-create the object out of parts or out of other objects. Thus, parts of other objects or full other objects are adapted to an object template. Here is P0 using a pendulum template, which is recreated out of objects at hand, in the *Two strings problem*: *"Okay, to use the right rope for tying down the neck of that bowl right there, then swing it and the weight of the bowl will just make the rope act like a pendulum."*. Here is P0 using a ladder and steps template in *Dusting the clock*: *"So, that means we will actually use... we will actually use that table as some sort of prerequisite step for him to be able to gradually move... move up the... the ladder up on.... on that platform"*. This is also a <Composition> code.

<OT – Object template adaptation> – An object template is adapted to the parts at hand. For example, Mb8, in the *Jack and Jill weighing problem* considers how to: *build a scale of sorts [...] But you don't have anything to support it on except for the bucket*. This code is also part of the <Creative adaptation> category.

<OT – Object template rejection> – This code marks segments in which an object template is rejected, after its use has been considered for a brief or a long period of time. Mb8 rejects an object template in the *Jack and Jill Weighting problem*: *"It's not like you can build a scale"*.

<OU – Object used in novel way> – This is used to label segments in which an object with a set of familiar affordances is used in a novel way. This is similar to coming up with new and creative uses for the Alternative

Uses Test. P0 uses matches in a novel way in the *Candle Problem*: *"maybe we will use some of the matches to further prevent the candle from dripping down"*. In this example the matches are used as a miniature dam, or a drip stopper.

Meta-cognitive

<**Meta-remark on problem nature**> – This code marks segments in which the solvers make meta-cognitive comments, or reason at a meta-cognitive level about the nature of the problem they are confronting, and sometimes about the nature of such problems in general. P0 in the *Two strings problem* makes the following meta-remark on the nature of the problem: *"so those objects put there in the right side of the room, obviously we will have to... I will have to give them some purpose in order to help me to make this person able to reach both strings"*.

<**Meta-remark on own process**> – This code reflects segments in which the solvers make comments about their own process of solving the problem. Mb8, in *Blown away teddy*, makes the following meta-remark on his own process: *"I have a few solutions that come to mind quickly. I can't really iterate them or I can't really verbalize them that quickly. I got a couple of different ones coming. You could [...]"* Fb6 in *Dusting the clock* makes the following meta-remark on her own process: *"Okay, right now I'm just looking at all these different things, trying to figure out how... which combination can be of any help."*

Other codes

<**Other – affective state**> – The solver expresses an affective state about the problem or about their own solving process. Such comments about affective states can be made directly, by telling the observing experimenter about them: e.g. *"I am getting frustrated with this now"* or *"That's interesting!"*. Affective states like joy, interest or frustration can also be expressed indirectly through tone of voice, giggles, gestures, etc.

<**Other – talking to audience or observer**> – These are statements in which the solver addresses the observer directly or talks as if having an audience.

<**Other – talking about self action**> – The participant describes an action she has done, like moving to the next slide, or picking up the glass of water, etc.

<**Other – talking about previous experience**> – The solver relates the current way of solving the problem to a previous experience or a memory. For example: *This would work, as I have done this once, when [...]*

<**Other – distraction**> – The participant distracts themselves from the problem. Such a self-distraction can be an indication of encountering a difficulty, or of the need for rest and refocus.

<Other – talking to self> – This might show up in the form of boosting one's own solving process by attempting to direct it in a certain way or another. It can also be linked to the participant's self-evaluation of how they are proceeding and performing. Fb6, in *Attach to loop*, tells herself: *"Okay, not forget, don't forget"*. She also reminds herself in the same problem: *"Okay, keep talking"*.

Finally, some of the already described codes can be groups in other interesting categories, like for example:

Creative adaptation processes (CA)

Codes corresponding to creative adaptation are:
    <PT – Adaptation of PT to problem>
    <PT – Adaptation of problem template to objects>
    <O – Adaptation of objects to template>
    <OT – Object template adaptation>

Composition and disassembly

Codes in which composition and disassembly are likely to be observed are:
    <PT – use of PT construct>
    <O – Disassembles object>
    <OT – Object template use>

Search

Codes relevant to search processes are:
    <O – Property-based search of object>
    <PT – use to search for suitable objects>
    <O – Object used to search for template>
    <PT – Requirement-based search of template>

Insight relevant

This includes insight moments, as expressed in insight marker expressions, sudden moments of attempting a new strategy and restructuring the problem.

11.3 Two Cases Studies

How would a problem solving session of the eight problems described above look like, and which ones of the previous codes will it engage?

A think aloud study was performed using the eight problems previously described. In this study, the 32 participants (16 male and 16 female), were given 10 minutes solving time for seven out of the eight insight problems presented above, that is for all but the Hat Rack problem. Looking at answer times of other participants for the Hat Rack in the literature, we suspected this problem might be harder than the others, and allocated 15 minutes of solving time for it.

Each participant was asked to rate their problem solving skills and creativity skills before and after solving, and their performance after finishing the solving session. Participants were also asked to assess whether the given time was enough or not to solve the problems.

Voice recordings were made from the think aloud sessions of each of the participants. In the following, we will have a look at two case studies, involving the best participants in each of the groups. For anonymity reasons, codes will be used to refer to each of the solvers. In what follows, mb8 is the best solver of the male group, and fb6 is the best solver of the female group.

11.3.1 The Case of Mb8

Participant mb8 is a male Entomologist graduate student, with native level English skills. He rated his problem-solving and creativity skills at 5 on a 1 to 7 Likert scale (with 7 being excellent), both before and after the solving session. The participant solved in the expected correct way 7 out of the 8 problems, and provided multiple plausible solutions to the eight, Dusting the clock problem. He rated, on good grounds, his performance at a 7 (excellent) and considered he had plenty of time.

Here is a summary of mb8's tackling of each of the eight problems, run as a narrative through the codes he engaged. D stands for the difficulty rating the participant provided for that problem.

P1 – Attach to the loop – solved in 4m 25s, D=1-2

The participant read the problem and took stock of the problem objects. He then aimed to determine the key requirements of the problem which he refined as attaching the cardboard to the ceiling. He tried to determine what template to use by asking the experimenter how the solution would look:

> "How do you want to attach it to the ceiling? Do you want to attach it flat like the broadest surface to the ceiling like that or do you want to hang it?"

The experimenter did not give more information. The participant then focused on the paperclips objects, and started building solutions around them and the nails. In this process, the *bendable* property of the paperclips was used multiple times, to bend paperclips around the nails. The nails were then used to attach the cardboard to the ceiling.

The observer prompted the participant to the initial requirements of attaching the cardboard to the loop. The participant adapted his initial solution to using a nail to hold the paperclip in place on the cardboard. He then used the paperclip to make the connection to the loop. While talking about these solutions, the participant mentioned object properties (*"paperclips are light"*) and object parts (*"the round end of the paperclip"*).

The participant kept on applying the same template even when confronted with the constraint that the cardboard might be too heavy to be supported by one paperclip hanging from the loop. He attempted to get around this by adapting the same template to multiple paperclips, and making more complex constructions with nail supports. After using multiple times the nails to pierce the cardboard, he realized that the nail could be skipped (Discarded object), and the paperclip used more directly:

> *"You could always just skip the nail and stab the paperclip through the cardboard. [...] Oh yeah. If you – yeah, you could just punch the paperclips through the cardboard and then hook that onto the loop"*

He motivated this template switch, which afforded him the correct solution, with noticing the parts of the paperclip distinctly: *"because the paperclips have two open ends"*. However, his evaluation of the solution, at the aesthetic level, was not positive: *"I think that would look pretty ugly"*.

P2 – Candle problem – *solved in 7 s, D=1-2*

Participant mb8 solved this problem immediately. He also added to the known correct solution the refinement of previously dripping wax into the thumbtack box. He then proposed to use this wax to better fix the candle.

P3 – Attach the Pendulum – *solved in 2m, D=2-3*

After reading the problem, mb8 took stock of some of the problem objects – the pendulum, string and nails. He then focused on properties of the pendulum, looking for parts of it to attach it from, and observed the hole at the top of it which he could used for this purpose. He proceeded to compose a fuller result based on the string and the pendulum, by looping string through the hole. He then moved his focus on securing the pendulum to the ceiling. For this, he asked about the weight property of the pendulum, checking the object against constraints of what could be hanging from a string nailed to the ceiling. After detailing on joints of the plan – how to tie the string to both the nail and the pendulum, he was asked by the experimenter how exactly he would nail the string to the ceiling. At this, mb8 finally noticed the lack of the hammer.

Mentioning he has previous experience with such situations, mb8 proposed using either the pendulum or one of the legs of the table to replace the hammer. Thus, in this context, both objects received an alternative use. The participant however worried about damage to the pendulum, and the ability of the table to be disassembled.

P4 – The Two Strings problem – *solved in 1m 15s, D=2-3*

Mb8 read the problem and proceeded to take stock of the some of the objects: the pliers, the pieces of paper, the nails, the stool. He then focused on the nails and the chair and re-iterated the problem goal. He made the assumption that collateral damage was not an issue. He then proposed as a first solution to climb the chair, nail a string to the ceiling, then grab the other string and bring it to the previous fixed one. Running through consequences, he verbalized the damage he was initially describing: *But then you have a hole in your ceiling.*

Told by the experimenter that he might be unable to reach the ceiling, even while standing on the chair, mb8 then asked about the strength property of the string and about the parts of the jar (whether it has a lid or not). He proceeded to empty some of the nails out of the jar to make it lighter (still worried about the strength of the string), then tied the string to the jar, and used the pendulum principle to solve the problem:

> *"Okay, so you can empty some of them (n.a. nails) out so it doesn't weigh very much, and then you could screw... screw the string so that it's – you know – kind of on the jar. Then you stand on the stool, grab your one string, hop on the stool. Then if you tied the jar of the nails to the other string, you could let it swing... And then you could grab it when it comes back to you, just kind of get your string out and tie them together."*

P5 – The Jack and Jill Weight problem – *solved in 6m 36s, D=2-3*

After reading the problem, mb8 recommended that, due to social politeness norms and etiquette, Jack could declare his weight as higher than Jill's. He then started taking stock of the problem objects. He checked for access to the seawater, and depth properties of the pool, looking like he was already applying a certain unvocalized template and checking if objects would be in place to apply it. He then indeed proceeded to apply an Archimedes's principle template, on the path of which he stayed and added details for a while. This involved getting rid of the sand in the bucket and using the bucket to bring water from the sea. Then, in his solving, the two kids took turns filling the pool and displacing water. He proposed to measure the water remaining in the pool after each kid's immersion. He correctly evaluated this solution path to lead to a volume determination, rather than weight. This made him discard the template for a while.

Mb8 then focused on the other people in the visual depiction of the problem, asking whether they can help. After the experimenter answered positively, mb8 still discarded such a possible path due to subjectivity of the measurement, which might be affected, in his opinion, by social politeness. After discarding a path which involved the other people weighing both Jack and Jill, mb8 returned to his previous Archimedes's principle template, and tried to realize it using different objects, specifically sand rather than water:

> *"You can do the same thing in the pool with sand. You could set one of them in the pool and fill it up with sand and then have them get out and see how much is left, but ..."*

Mb8 then started making a template switch, based on considering the requirements of the template. The certainty required by the weight assessment made him try to search for a form of a scale. He then attempted to obtain a scale in various ways, by filling in the template of a scale with initial unlikely objects. He oscillated between keeping and rejecting the scale template for a while:

> "Huh! The only way to say for certain would be to put each of them on the opposite ends of the scale and there is no way to construct a scale here... or is there? ... You can't build anything out of sand because it's not like it's going to hold up... or maybe you could. I don't know... [...] I was just thinking about what kind of options you would have if you have a bucket of sand and the shovel in play when you could build different things but I mean that wouldn't really be useful. It's not like you can build a scale."

Despite the initial unlikely thoughts of building a scale out of sand, considering the scale template did proved useful, because mb8 then found more likely objects to fill it with – the bar of the umbrella and the bucket:

> "so I initially thought about taking the poles from the umbrella and using that as ... as something to help build a scale of sorts because you have two ends of it that could hold... (and show you) which one is heavier. But you don't have anything to support it on except for the bucket [...] like if you put the bucket upside down and you put the bar over it"

Mb8 then proceeded to compose the solution in more detail. He ran through its consequences and evaluated it. He then switched back to argumenting for his Archimedes's principle's solution, and evaluated that solution again. However, he noticed a new object all of a sudden "Uh! Surfboard!" and then integrated this object in the "scale" template (which by now became a seesaw as scale template):

> "You can do the same thing. So you could scrap the pole idea and then ... and then just use the surfboard on the bucket."

P6 – Hat Rack – solved in 2m 30s, D=3-4

After reading the problem, mb8 made some assumptions: "So it doesn't matter how it looks, as long as it holds the hat(s)". He then jokingly proposed to "Put the hat on your head. The very first hat rack!"

Mb8 then inspected the measurements in the scene, focusing on the width property. From that, he put the width of the two planks together, and inferred affordances, like "That's probably big enough to stand on". Mb8 then proceeded on a path of constructing a vertical hat rack made by the two planks held together by the G-clamp, fitted in a corner of the room. He then asked the experimenter about more problem requirements, specifically on whether the rack should fit one or multiple hats. He evaluated this construction, then proceeded to develop it. Noticing one of the parts of the G-clamp, he then determined it's affordance in terms of holding the hat, thus achieving the first part of insight required to solve the problem in the classical way. He returned to aesthetic evaluation:

> "I mean it's not going to look pretty. You're not going to want your guests to see that. You want a hat rack that looks nice."

Mb8 then switched template, to a new type of vertical construction: posting the planks between the floor and the ceiling, with a small overlap. This meant he was now providing the second part of the classical solution of the problem. He then composed the fuller solving path and described it, proposing to put the hat on the part of the construction where the boards overlapped.

Mb8 then switched his attention back to the G-clamp. While integrating the G-clamp in the new type of vertical template, he noticed its uses as a hook and achieved the full solution.

P7 – Blown Away Teddy – solved in 3m 58s, D=2-3

Mb8 read the problem, then proceeded to take stock of the problem objects, by now already regarding them as tools: *"What kind of tools do we have?"* He then inquired about object properties – whether the clothesline is a long solid or non-solid object. Mb8 asked about the distance between the fence and the teddy bear, which the experimenter cannot provide, as it is part of the ambiguities of the problem. Mb8 then made meta remarks on his own process:

> "..so I have a few solutions that come to mind quickly. I can't really iterate them or I can't really verbalize them that quickly. I got a couple of different ones coming."

The participant then proceeded to describe one such solution path, under the assumption that *"collateral damage is not an issue"*. This solution, based on the fence and an ability to disassemble it, was evaluated as *"probably not the best way to do it"*. Mb8 then looked closer at the assembly properties of the fence, and decided to use the mop handle in a novel way (as a lever) to *"Pop off the boards"*. He then proceeded to compose further on this path. Next he proposed alternative fence-centered paths, like *"walking around the fence to see if there is a door"*.

The participant then focused on another object, the umbrella, and used an object template, a *rake*, to cast the umbrella. Immediately after, he recast the same rake object template to another filler object – the mop.

> "You could try using the umbrella like a rake in reaching over the fence to grab the teddy bear. You could do that with the mop, too."

Mb8 then switched template again, proposing to climb on the table and jump over the fence. At the experimenter's prompting that he may not break or dismantle the fence, nor set foot in the neighbour's garden, he restated the previous path. The casting of the umbrella as a rake was so strong, that later he referred to the umbrella with the name *"rake"*, despite being a native English speaker:

"The rake or the mop over the fence, trying to rake the teddy bear back would be the best thing to try"

Determining a lack of the *long enough* affordance for these previous constructions, mb8 then started focusing on other objects that could be used to lengthen the last one. Thus, the coat hangers where considered, adapted to the "lengthening" template, and unbent. The mop was also considered for its length properties. After searching for suitable objects to lengthen the construction, mb8 composed a fuller path based on previous exploration of affordances. Thus he proposed making a straight line out of the coat hangers, the length of which he estimated. Analysing the properties of the coat hangers, the bendability property became suddenly apparent, and mb8 adjusted his construction to better suit the goals of the problem: *"You can put a hook at the end of it"*. Considering this construction further under the *length* lack of affordance, mb8 added to it the sunglasses, appearing to search for long objects (property search), or objects that could be adapted as to become long (e.g. by straightening them). The bucket handle was also considered.

With markers of surprise and possibly insight (*"Huh! (laugh to self)"*), mb8 used the already fashioned hook at the end of his construction to switch to a new template. Thus the hook alone was kept, disassembled, and attached to the clothesline. Soon enough, this construction, using a *grappling hook* template, turned to a *fishing rod* template:

"Huh! (laugh to self) It's a little bit cliché ... but you could take the clothesline, and you could fashion a pronged hook out of the coat hanger. You could attach that to the clothesline, and then you could throw it over like a grappling hook until you get the bear. So that would be longer, but then you could tie the end of that line to the end of the mop, so you get the mop then the end of the clothesline, then some coat hanger construction whatever you want. Then you could throw it like a fishing rod."

P8 – Dust the Clock – *multiple plausible solutions given in 10 m. D=3*

After reading P8, mb8 got quiet. Upon prompting he said he was *"thinking about the objects we have available"*. He proceeded to initially focus on the duster, and to re-state the key requirements of the problem. He then asked about the height property of Johnny, which the experimenter was not allowed to provide in a quantitative manner. Without this data, mb8 proceeded to make a height estimation comparing Johnny to the depiction of the wall.

"He looks like he's about there (points to wall), so that's like what? ... That is that plus his height, so that puts him here, then his little arm will reach up and he can dust the face."

Mb8 then proposed a variety of constructions to put Johnny on top of. First, he proposed to put Johnny on the table. However, this construction was evaluated to still lack in height, thus precluding the reaching the clock affordance. He then switched to an *elongating arm* approach, adapting objects to this template. Thus, the duster was tied with the shoelaces (which were disassembled from the skates) to the tennis racket, in order to elongate Johnny's reach.

Mb8 then switched back to considering what objects he could use to fill the *construction* template. He considered stacking the chairs and discarded that option, because of the lack of stability (lack of affordance) of said chairs, estimated based on experience: *"I've stood on chairs like that before and they've just broken"*. He considered using the globe as a filler for his construction and then discarded this object. He then proceeded on a new path, adapting the construction template to a *platform* template. This template was then refined to include another object (the table), which has already been considered:

> *"You could put these two chairs on each end of the room, put the surfboard over the arms of them and stand on that or put the table on top of the surfboard and then stand on that."*

After integrating the standing on table construction into the platform template, Mb8 also integrated the extending arm construction into this new solution path.

When asked by the experimenter whether he could consider other solutions, mb8 focused on the clock and asked whether it could be moved. He then proceeded on an affordance based search for objects suited to moving the clock. Objects considered were the globe, the chessboard (being thrown at the clock) and the surfboard. The skates were also considered and discarded, because of running through the possible consequence of throwing them and having them stick in the wall. The participant then returned to the former template, and voiced it in terms of a *table* object template rather then a *platform* template; this hints at him seeing the surfboard as a table surface: *"Putting the surfboard over two arms of the chair so that the arms of the chair are basically formed legs of the surfboard table, then you could stand on that..."*

Mb8 then proceeded to go through his previous strategies, re-iterating them, evaluating them, and sometimes modifying them. For example, he considered the *arm elongation* template with a new object in it – the surfboard; the surfboard was however discarded in favour of the tennis racket, because of an analysis of its properties, in the context of previous experience:

> *"I woud've suggested tying the duster to the end of the surfboard, but I don't think that would work, because the end of the surfboard is round like that, not like a cone but it's kind of rounded, so I don't know if you've ever tried tying a string around an end like that. It just doesn't work, like the tie just slips off. But the tennis... the tennis racket would be perfect. I mean I have tied shoelaces around – I have – the end of tennis rackets before because the grip is squish, it just tightens right there."*

Mb8 then considered disassembling the table and using the legs of the table to build something long, at the end of which the duster could be attached (this using the elongate arm template). However, this variant of the *elongate arm* template is dependent in his assessment upon Johnny's *strength* property, and will have as a consequence the destruction of the table.

The participant then switched focus between different other objects. This switch may be an attempt to trigger new solving templates, or check whether some objects have other meaningful affordances which can be used in finding new solutions:

> *"I was just thinking about the chandelier, and whether or not it's possible bringing that into play, but I don't think so. It's not possible to bring it into play in an effective way".*

Mb8 also attempted to integrate the new objects of focus with the previously used templates. The participant then got stuck in functional fixedness, iterating only through already proposed strategies, without producing any new ones. The only novel improvement produced at this stage was his realization that surfboards have a ventral fin, on which the duster could be attached in a more stable manner.

11.3.2 The Case of Fb6

Participant Fb6 is a female Business Psychology graduate student, with advanced English skills. Her rating of her own skills was: pre-test – 6 (problem solving) and 5 (creativity); post-test – 5 (problem solving) and 4 (creativity). She rated her performance as 4 and considered she had enough time. Fb6 solved correctly 5 problems, provided a partial solution to a sixth (the hat rack) problem, and multiple solutions to the Dusting the Clock problem.

P1 – The Jack and Jill Weight problem – solved in 2m 40s, D=4.

Fb6 read the problem, then proceeded directly to a solving path which focused around the small swimming pool, involving implicitly Archimedes's principle. The solution state was then compared to constraints: *"Then they would know how much the <u>volume</u> is there ..."* (underlining reflects intonation emphasis) *"I don't know if that helps for the weight, but it should, kind of...".*

After switching attention to other objects, Fb6 reiterated the key requirements of the problem. She then compared the affordance of the Archimedes's principle template to the requirements of the problem: *"If I have a certain amount or volume of water, will it weigh as much as a certain amount of human? I'm not entirely sure".*

The participant then searched for suitable objects with the same template. Still, a gap remained between the affordance of the template and the requirements of the problem:

> *"Same you could do with the little shovel and the bucket like (laughs)... bury yourself in the sand an see how much sand is coming out and then weigh the ... they don't have a scale to weigh the sand, but they can see how much sand there is..."*

After comparing the solution state of the current template with problem requirements and constraints again, Fb6 continued to determine template affordance: *"But still, it doesn't mean... that just helps me to see who's... who's bigger. That doesn't help me see who's heavier"*. Discarding the template for the moment, Fb6 started switching her focus to another object – the surfboard.

The participant then used this object to search for a template. The initial template she found was a traditional one - standing on the surfboard. Fb6 attempted to adapt this to the context of the problem: *"Stand on the surfboard and see how far it... yeah... it goes down in the water"*. Fb6 then compared the solution state to the goals of the problem, she evaluated and aimed to further determine template affordance. She tried to adapt the template to the goals of the problem by putting both Jack and Jill on the surfboard. After this, using the surfboard as a focus object for a template search and to build a solution around yielded the solution:

> *"Or... I don't know if that works but like... switch the bucket around, put a surfboard on it, they both stand on a side. It might work as the – how is that called – like on a play slide?"*

P2 – Attach the pendulum – solved in 8m 5s, D=6

After reading the problem, Fb6 started taking stock of the problem objects and also determining some object affordances: *"I got a sock, this is the pendulum, I got nails. I got ... umm... glasses and what's that? A string. So I got a ladder so I can reach the ceiling. That is good already"*. She noticed the need for the hammer straight away, while checking the joints in her plan.

Fb6 proceeded to construct a partial solution, using the objects she already knew were part of the solution. She then started to search for a hammer replacement based on properties. She called a property "stability", but this can be inferred to represent solidity or hardness of the object (the participant is not a native English speaker). The participant focused on various objects, trying to use them as a hammer replacement, and showing a particular fixation with the sock. Fb6 attempted to improve/adapt replacement objects as to fit her property criteria:

> *"Maybe if ... I mean I could wrap them (the sunglasses) in this sock like help for stability, and then use that if I like fold them together and wrap it in the sock, use that to hammer in the... the nail [...] what is this sock doing there? [...] or if I ... wrap the sock around the... the ball of wire, will that be hard enough to use it as a kind of hammer thing?"*

Fb 6 continued to use the object template of a hammer – *"So let's go on with my idea to try to build a ... a hammer"*. She then attempted to let go of the red-herring sock object, while making meta-comments about the nature of the problem: *"I just don't understand what the sock will help me for, it's..."*

*or maybe not every object is important for me. That could be, too. I just...
They're just there to confuse me, so... "*

Fb6 returned to checking the other parts of her template construct (of attaching the pendulum to the wall), and re-determined the affordance of the objects within the current plan. She then showed all the signs of being stuck for a while, with statements like: *"I feel like I can't really figure it out in another way. Or if I just... I don't know ... I don't know. I don't see another way."* and *"I am ... kind a... at a dead-end here I feel".*

Fb6 attempted to exit this state by focusing on different objects, and checking whether the objects which she was already using were necessary in her solution construct, or could indeed have different affordances. This helped her see the double use of the pendulum, as a consequence of the property of its material: *"I can use the pendulum if it's hard enough to hammer the nails in the ceiling. I mean it looks like it's (giggle) made of metal."*

P3 – Blown Away Teddy – solved in 4m 40s, D=3

Fb6 read the problem, mapped the problem formulation to some objects (bear, garden), then focused directly on the handle of the broom and started constructing solutions around it, along it's length property. When prompted that this handle (stick) might not be long enough to reach the bear, Fb6 continued searching for objects with the length property: *So wow now I can take the clothesline because it's a long wire.* Fb6 then decided to attach the clothes hanger at the end of her construction, and considered this handle+clothesline+clothes hanger similar to a lasso in its uses. Then, the object template was adapted to the hook of the clothes hanger: *"throw it and hope that with the hook of the cloth hanger might grab one of his arms or legs or his head and then pull it to me".*

After being further prompted that this construction might not be long enough, Fb6 proceeded to make other constructions. One of these involved using the clothesline and the broom, and proposing to using the broom end for "shovelling" the teddy with. While dragging or gathering an object with the end of a shovel is definitely not the traditional use for this object, this use was either part of the participant's *shovel* template, or the participant meant a *rake*.

Fb6 then switched focus to other objects, by taking again stock of the objects presented in the problem scene, including the umbrella, the sunglasses and the bucket. The same shovel/rake object template was used with other objects, like the clothesline and the umbrella. Next, the participant investigated the properties of the clothes, and discarded the possibility of using them. She then proceeded to determine the affordances of other objects, which she deemed more suitable:

"I got this clothes hanger(s) which I really like where I think I would like to do something with them. So if I maybe... open up, I mean they like like they're just made from wire like metal wire. Can I open them

up, tie them together somehow they're a long line, and just make a hook at the end and then grab it like this."

This idea, together with a comparison to the goal state, allowed further construction, until something like a fishing rod template solution was built from the umbrella stick, the clothesline and a clothes hanger (cast as a hook).

P4 – Attach to the loop – *not solved, D=5*

After reading the problem and taking stock of the problem objects, Fb6 proceeded on a solution path which involved putting a paperclip around the loop. She then persisted in this template, attempting to improve it with various nail constructions and then manifesting functional fixedness. She attempted to force the solution by nailing the cardboard to the ceiling.

Fb6 then exited the state of functional fixedness, and had two other template switches: she attempted to build a short paperclip chain, and to use the hammer itself as a connector for attaching to the loop. Fb6 then tried to force the solution again: she proposed folding the cardboard and putting the cardboard on the loop (pushing the limits of what it means for something to be attached to the loop).

Finally, Fb6 admitted to being stuck. She made remarks on her own process and the limits she was experiencing in coming up with ways of attaching things to the loop: *"Everything that comes to my mind are almost the same things that I've already said, like just a different... where I'm framing them... to the loop in the ceiling"*. She proceeded to reiterate through the solving paths she could think of, until the time allocated for the problem run out.

P5 – Dusting the Clock – *multiple plausible solutions provided, D=6*

Fb6 read the problem. She defined its key requirements as being centered around Johnny's height property, which was the cause of his lack of affordance in reaching the clock, and she focused on compensating for this property. She then took stock of part of the objects in the scene. She determined the chairs' lack of affordance in "stacking them on top of each other", from what she later revealed to be personal experience. Fb6 then made a first attempt at solving the problem, by attaching the dust cleaner to the tennis racket. This attempt seemed to be based on the length property of the tennis racket, which translated into an arm elongation affordance. Fb6 however did not find any object suitable to attach the dust cleaner to the tennis racket.

She then focused on searching for objects to construct a platform or a high construction to put Johnny on, alternating this with searching for objects to elongate his arm. She thus realized that she could disassemble a part of the ice skates and use them for this purpose:

"Okay, I can use the laces of the... ice skating shoes to attach the duster to the tennis rack. Should be possible, so I've got a longer duster, and... so that is already a little bit of... that is already closer."

She constructed in parallel a platform made of a chair and the table, in order to make Johnny taller. Fb6 then started taking stock of the problem objects again, switching between observing them and determining their affordance in the context of the constraints. She thus discarded the surfboard because she was *"not sure you can really climb on it"*, the globe and the chessboard. Fb6 then made meta-remarks on her own process: *"Okay, right now I'm just looking at all these different things, trying to figure out how... which combination can be of any help."*. Fb6 then focused again on the surfboard, using it in the context of a platform template, with the two chairs arm rests as support. She commented on the new straight surface property thus obtained. Then, she proceeded on inferring more affordances, and considering what other objects she could put on top of her platform in order to increase its height.

After focusing on different objects, Fb6 started object-based searches of a productive template. Focusing on the different objects, some of the templates thus yielded included leaning the surfboard on the wall under the clock, and swinging on the lamp on the ceiling using the shoelaces, which she evaluated as very dangerous and *"not good for little Johnny"*.

Fb6 then got in a functional fixedness state. She continued by reiterating previously voiced solving paths and slightly improving on some of them. For example, she expanded her platform construction, which initially involved using the surfboard as a platform on top of the two chairs, by putting the table on top of it, and then the globe, which she fixed by using the shoelaces.

After attempting this problem, Fb6 showed some signs of tiredness, which generally manifested in her stating the goals or key requirements of the problem at hand much more often than before. This reiteration of the key requirements was possibly an attempt to refresh her own working memory, and keep her attention processes directed on the goal.

P6 – Candle problem – solved in 3m 10s, D=3

After reading the problem, Fb6 defined its key requirements. She then built her solution directly on the path of using the box of thumbtacks some space under the candle, in order to protect the floor from drips. She was thus seeing the box as a possible container for the wax drips, or as a stopper of wax falling down. She was however not seeing it simultaneously as a container for the candle itself, or as a solution for fixing the candle to the wall.

Fb6 then went on finding a way to attach the candle to the wall, which she reiterated as a key requirement of the problem. For attaching the candle to the wall she first considered using the wax, which she discarded. She then considered using the thumbtacks, with their affordance of piercing on the candle; this affordance she then also discarded. After searching for more objects to fit the requirement of fixing the candle to the wall, she focused on the matches as a possible candidate. She then composed a fuller solving path using the matches:

> *"So there's the candle... and with the tacks and the matches I feel like
> I want to build a little holder to the wall, so take four of these so that
> they make a ... a little thing that I can put the candle in, so that the
> matches are around it [...]" etc.*

Fb6 then proceeded to evaluate her construction, comparing it to the key
requirements of the problem: *"Will that hold or will it fall out? Or would it
even be too big! I don't know. It should not drip on the floor".*

Fb6 then returned to the mechanism which she had previously set up for
wax dripping: the thumbtacks box, which she called the *cardboard* in this
case, possibly by appeal to a familiar cardboard stopper, floor protector or
cardboard box template. Her return to this part of the construction triggered
her full realization of the solution:

> *"Yeah, there's a cardboard for that. But maybe that's not the solution.
> Ah! Can I attach it to the wall? Yeah, can attach the cardboard to
> the wall with the tacks, so that is it attached to the wall on one side,
> then just stand the candle in there after dripping some wax so that it
> stands."*

P7 – **Hat Rack** – *not solved (partial solution)*, D=6

Participant Fb6 read the problem, then defined the key requirements of the
problem. She went on to take stock of the measurements offered. Returning
to the requirements of building a hat rack, Fb6 seemed to start looking for
the visual instantiation of an object template: *"Okay, hat rack... So how is
that supposed to look like?".*

The solver then focused on the beams in the ceiling as a pre-existing construction, and aimed to use the planks on the floor to reconstruct a shelf object
template around these beams. She proceeded on this solving path, considering
using the walls as part of the shelf sides. She examined the assumption that
the planks on the floor were long enough to fit between the beams on the ceiling. She then searched for an object which had the affordance of attaching the
two planks to the beams. This search revealed the G-clamp as a possibility.

Fb6 determined that the G-clamp would lack the affordance of attaching
the plank to the ceiling beams, because of the size of the beams. She then
inferred from the measurement of the G-clamp opening and the size of the
planks, that the G-clamp could be used for attaching the planks to each other.
However, this lead to the further inference that only attaching the planks in
certain ways was possible, which acted as a constraint for further templates:
*"If I just put them like a T together (the planks on the floor), that won't work
because I can't use the G-clamp then, so they kind of have to be both horizontal
or vertical".*

Switching back to the previously used template, she reconsidered her assumption over the length of the planks: *"This time I can't just assume they
are very long".* Fb6 then assumed that she might be able to infer the length of

the gap between the ceiling beams, and then fit her already made floor plank construction between them, bridging the gap between them.

Prompted to try to solve the problem in a different way, Fb6 switched the template and considered using the planks upright, but evaluated this as not working. She then got stuck on considering solutions involving the beams in the ceiling. She tried refocusing on the measurements, however this did not take her out of the bridging template: *"Let's assume it all comes down to just slamming planks between one of the spaces for me. I don't see another way of doing it."* She then persisted in this template, attempting to create a bridge under various places around and under the beams, and in the corners of the room. She considered and then discarded making a hat rack that laid on the floor: *"My hat rack can't just be laying on the ground because it's a hat rack. I have to have it somewhere up...".*

Backtracking into meta-reasoning seemed to help break this fixation. First, Fb6 made the following meta-remark on her own process:

> *"I'm just staring at the plank, some of the measurements, adding them altogether and trying to search for something that fits to it because I hope that that might help me to find the perfect spot for the planks..."*

This brought about a new assessment of the key requirements of the problem. Fb6 retreated this time from some of the already made assumptions of what type of template to use, producing a template switch and showing the markers of an insight moment:

> *"A hat rack. A hat <u>rack</u>, so that is not really a hat shelf... And if I just... a hat rack is something where it hangs on. I know! If I just.... put one of those, lean it up the wall, put the clamp on it or both of them if I can so that it's fixed. Then use the end of the clamp to hang my hat on it."*

Fb6 then had just enough time left do detail this solution. She thus had part of the insight required to solve the hat rack problem - using the G-clamp to hang things on. However, she did not provide the full solution of an upright hat rack between the floor and the ceiling, making the hat rack lean against a wall instead.

P8 – The Two Strings problem – *solved in 8m 30s, D=5*

After reading the problem, Fb6 started on a solving path which involved using the chair to stand on, in order to attempt to hold both ropes. When this solution was rejected, she backtracked into taking stock of the problem objects. She then switched to attempting to attach the two strings by having one fixed in the middle of the ceiling. Fb6 thought of creatively using the pliers as a hammer to fix a string in the ceiling, with one of the nails on the floor. This creative use of the pliers as a hammer could show an influence of her previous solving: in the Attach the pendulum problem, she previously created a hammer out of the pendulum.

When the constraint that she could not reach the ceiling was made explicit, Fb6 switched to a template of elongating the strings, as a prerequisite for reaching both of them: *"Then I have to make the string somehow longer, so that I have more .... that I have at the end the opportunity to reach them both with my hands while standing on the ground"*. For this purpose she decided to use the paper sheets to make a tube and the nails to attach the tube to one of the strings.

Fb6 then reflected that this improvised tube or string extension might not constitute a long enough construction. She then focused on the pliers, specifically on their affordance of elongating one's arm when grabbing one of the strings. Fb6 then got stuck: she reiterated through the solving paths visited before, and she attempted combinations of them which would use their various affordances. She even tried to force a solution by ripping the strings of the ceiling.

She then attempted to exit functional fixedness via a template switch, which involved attaching the chair to a string. Subsequently, she started reconsidering the various problem objects, and tried to find other ways in which she could use them (object based search of template). Then, a new remark on her own process and on the nature of the problem seemed to bring her close to switching from the elongating the strings and reaching the strings templates to something new:

> *"I really just feel like attaching different things that I got here to the wire to make wires longer. Maybe that's not the problem. Maybe I'm (not) supposed to make the wires... the strings longer, but... to find the possibility to reach them both, or do I even have to reach them both? Is that even necessary?..."*

Another round of functional fixedness and considering previous solutions followed. Fb6 the finally switched template and came by the correct solution, in which the pliers were used for their weight property as part of the pendulum: *"Put something heavy like attached to the pliers with a knot to the wire ... to string to make it swing like this [...] Then when it swings, it should at some point ... the pliers should reach my hand"*.

11.4 Analysis of Process and Codes in the Context of CreaCogs

How do the codes which we set up before and used in analysing and constructing the narrative of the various case studies reflect the CreaCogs framework and processes? Are the processes supported by CreaCogs reflective of the human problem solving, and could they be used for the future computational modeling or implementation of such solving? In the following, we have a look at each code in turn and assess how it relates to CreaCogs.

Problem solving general process codes:

<PSP – Reading the problem> – In CreaCogs, this code would correspond to a read-out of the problem, which is given as input.

The input would be a mix involving the main objects and requirements of the problem statement, supplemented by the objects and relations in the picture representation of the problem. Both are necessary, as not all objects nor all object relations are given in the problem text.

The problem also states a goal, or makes a request to the solver. All this needs to be interpreted in terms of the knowledge the agent already has. For example, the textual statement of the Two Strings problem could be translated for CreaCogs as follows:

Objects (or concepts): $(Person, String_1, String_2)$
Relations: $Attached(String_1, ceiling)$, $Attached(String_2, ceiling)$, $Hanging(String_1, ceiling)$, $Hanging(String_2, ceiling)$
Goal: $Tied(String1, String2)$

The problem also provides the constraint that if $Hold(Person, String1)$, then $\neg Reach(Person, String2)$.

<PSP – Comprehending> – This might correspond to building a mental model of the given problem: of the relations the various objects are in, and of the problem goals. Various stages of comprehending the problem might unfold, as the relationships are understood at a deeper level. In a model of human cognition, this would correspond to a process of mapping the problem statement and the problem requirements to items in the knowledge base of the solver, then loading this knowledge in the working memory.

<PSP – Defining key requirements of the problem> – In a model of human cognition, this would mean parsing out of the given text the goals and constraints to focus on. These goal and constraints will later be used in evaluation – to know whether the solving process can be deemed successful. Such goals and constraints can also be used to define an initial strategy to approach the problem. This is the equivalent of a search for a problem template using the solution in CreaCogs.

<PSP – Mapping problem formulation to objects> – In CreaCogs this might imply mapping concept names to positions in the image representation given as a scene of the problem. Also, at this point, some of the other objects which are not mentioned in the problem statement, but are present in the picture, might be implicitly integrated in the comprehension of the problem statement. In the context of the two Strings problem, some new concepts and relations obtained from the picture could be:

Objects or concepts: $Jar\ of\ nails, Chair, Pliers, Sheets\ of\ Paper$
Relations: $Contains(jar, nails)$
Spatial relations: $onFloor(Sheets\ of\ Paper), onFloor(Jar\ of\ nails)$

New information can also be gained by observing details about objects or parts of objects from inspecting the picture. An example of such a detail is that the person in the depiction of the two strings problem is clothed. This observation yields new objects, like *Shoes, Shirt, Pants*. Observing new objects can also mean observing new relations, like *clothedIn(Shirt, Person)*. Such relations may require an explicit move on the part of the solver to *remove(Shirt, Person)* in order to gain access to said objects, and use their affordances. The model of the problem can then be expanded to contain the *Shirt* object, and it's affordances.

<PSP – Taking stock of problem objects> – This is a strategy easy to implement computationally, which involves the iteration through the objects observed in the depiction of the problem. During this iteration, these objects come into the solver's focus and activate knowledge from the KB of the solver. This iteration may proceed to cover all the objects, but most likely it will ensue until the solving agent makes note of an interesting affordance. How could an interesting affordance be defined, computationally? An interesting affordance is probably an affordance which triggers a solving template, leading to a possible solution path.

This taking stock of some of the problem objects might yield *explicit* affordances, that is the kind of affordances which are consciously noticed and verbalized in think aloud protocols. It might also yield covert activation of affordances which is not strong enough to make these affordances explicit. However, it is sensible to assume that once an object has been noticed and talked about, it has been mapped to a representation of the concept in the KB of the agent. Thus it is possible that affordances of the object can be activated with much more ease after taking stock of the object, and that such an activation process might start covertly the moment the objects are noticed. In the context of CreaCogs, this would mean activating the concepts corresponding to the problem in the KB, their most salient properties and the most salient templates they are part of.

Search and comparison processes between the affordance of the objects, the affordance of the templates which the objects trigger and the requirements and goals of the problem might already be running at this stage in the background. At later solving stages, taking sock of the problem objects might kick in as a strategy to get out of functional fixedness. This strategy would rely on the assumption that noticing something which has not been noticed before will lead to new inferences.

<PSP – Proceeding on path> – In CreaCogs, this would be the equivalent of having already selected a PT to build the solution around, and then trying to build this solution, with the given objects, until either the solution is built in full or a more complex impasse is reached.

<Proceeding on path> can happen immediately after receiving the problem as an input. In CreaCogs this would mean focusing on and building solutions around specific salient objects, their affordances, or the most

salient templates yielded by the problem statement from the knowledge base. <Proceeding on path> can also happen after having selected such objects through cycles of <Taking stock of objects>, <Focus>, <Determining Affordance>, <Determining template>, <Searching for template>. In this case, the codes <PT-Use> and <Composing fuller results based on previous exploration> and the processes they describe are a more suitable characterization.

<PSP – Backtracking> – In CreaCogs, backtracking can happen on two levels. One is the classical problem solving level, on which a previous state of the problem is revisited, and an attempt at solving the problem proceeds forward from that place again. In the creative problem-solving paradigm, backtracking can also be seen as corresponding to abandoning a problem template, which has been deemed unproductive. In this case, backtracking leads to a state in which the problem objects and the problem statement are considered free from a particular interpretation, and a PT can still be chosen.

In the context of CreaCogs, backtracking through abandoning a PT can happen through a fast assessment that it will lead nowhere (because the template does not fit problem objects for example), or because of noticing that a very good possibility of solving the problem is afforded by a certain other template.

Backtracking, in the creative definition sense, would correspond to changing the state of an agent's working memory to a state in which restructuring, or a <Template Switch> is possible with more ease. Being stuck in a problem template for a while or seeing no possible solutions can also yield such a working memory state. In CreaCogs this could be simulated through the decline of activation of a specific template after multiple tries of solving through it, or through attention shifts meant to take the creative solving agent out of a cognitively frustrating state. The binding of template roles to various sets of objects can also be abandoned; backtracking to the state of deciding what to fill a selected problem template with would thus ensue.

For example, let us say the PT used for solving the Dusting the clock problem is that of building a construction of a certain height. Thus a CreaCogs agent can attempt to solve the Goal: $reach(Johnny, clock)$ and overcoming the Constraint: $height(Johnny) = small$ by increasing Johnny's $height$ using PT: $on(construction, Johnny)$, until the $height$ attribute of Johnny's arm is deemed suitable to fulfil the $reach$ goal. The $construction$ object automatically inherits the requirement of matching in height the difference between Johnny's height and the clock's height ($height_x = height_{clock} - height_{Johnny}$), or the difference between Johnny's imagined point of reach and and the clock's height. Objects which would help match that height are required to fill in such a template. Besides inheriting height requirements, the template $on(construction, Johnny)$ also brings with it implicit stability constraints for the $construction$ object.

Let us envision a scenario in which a CreaCogs agent which attempts to fill the *construction* template with a *chair* object. Upon evaluation, the *height* requirement is not matched. Backtracking in this case means retreating from previous objects used for *construction*, and choosing other objects to make part of it, or another object arrangement. For example, the agent might make an attempt at filling the construction with the two chairs, the second reversed and on top of each other – *construction* = $on(chair_a, reverse(chair_b))$. However, this fill in of the construction template does not match the *stability* constraint. This requires the solving agent to further backtrack to the abstract level and consider anew the other possible objects is required.

<PSP – Evaluation> – In CreaCogs, evaluation could correspond to mapping the constructed solution to other known templates or situations, to check if, at the end of deploying a solution path, the key requirements of the problem are satisfied. Also, implicit requirements might be checked for. As we've seen, in the case of the Dusting the Clock problem, an implicit requirement might be that the construction has a property of being *stable*. Evaluation can thus include an analysis of whether the created solution respects this *stability* requirement, because of the possible consequences of people falling when attempting to climb unstable constructions. This stability requirement become contextually important, because Johnny is a person. If the same template was accessed in a different problem context, stability might not have been an important factor. For example, imagine that the problem required pressing a certain button on the ceiling. And that the solver approached this by attempting to use a construction template: build a construction of objects to reach, with the top object, the button on the ceiling. It is unlikely that the solver would have cared as much about stability if she did not have to place a person on the construction.

Whether the right *height* was achieved in order for Johnny to reach the clock, a problem requirement, will also be analysed in the evaluation phase. This will of course involve comparing the sum of the heights of Johnny, his reaching span and the construction to the height of the clock.

The analysed human data shows that some participants also assess the solution they came up with against aesthetical criteria. Aesthetical evaluation could be translated in a computational version in various ways. A hypothesis that could be tested is that the adaptation of the problem template to the problem objects must be done without damaging the aesthetical components of the object that first inspired that template. For example, the constructed *hat rack* can be compared to some template known by the agent of how a traditional or fashionable *hat rack* looks like. Aesthetic appraisal will of course not depend only on how close the construction using the problem objects matches the initial template, but also on both subjective and objective aesthetical preferences. Other aesthetical properties can be taken into account when modelling aesthetic preferences computationally, like for example the cleanliness of the object countour lines, the simplicity of the solution, personal tastes in object design, etc.

<PSP – Running through consequences> – In the course of building a solution, or part of it, various problem elements are put together. After this, a sequence of affordances can be examined in its totality. Both consequences and side effects of this partial solution composition can be inferred. In computational terms, in the Candle problem, a CreaCogs agent can for example need something with *gluing* properties. The agent can aim to get *hot wax*, to obtain access to the *gluing* property. Various ways of obtaining *hot wax* are possible. The agent could light the candle (PT *light(matches, candle)* → *lit candle*), or could melt the candle (PT *melt(candle, fire)* → *slimmer candle*).

Running through the consequences of these actions though, the agent can realize that they are not equivalent. The second course of action will also, as a consequence, adjust the width property of candle. This adjustment allows for the candle to be fixed to the wall using the pins – that is the candle object can now fit the PT *pin(thumbtacks, o_x)*, were object o_x needs to be smaller than the thumbtack pin to fit this template. The second course of action though could also have the side effect *melted candle*. With the candle getting soft, implicit requirements of the problem, like the candle holding upright while it is attached to the wall, might become unachievable.

Affordance related segments (Aff)

<Aff – Determining object affordance> – In CreaCogs, this code corresponds to explicitly retrieving an object affordance from the knowledge base of the solver, iterating through the affordances of various problem objects, or applying an object affordance to another object. For example, a CreaCogs agent which has activated the object *Pliers* could retrieve *aff(Pliers, to hold objects with)*. As we see from the case studies of human participants retrieving such affordances, these are not always retrieved in their abstract form – that is solver might not just state affordances of a particular object. Sometimes, affordances of an object that has gained focus are already projected on other objects – that is the solver states what she can do with the object to another specific object, rather than just stating the affordances on its own.

In CreaCogs, this would involve linking an affordance to another object directly, thus already creating mini compositions of two object interactions, or compositions of the action of an object upon the other. For example, instead of retrieving the affordance *aff(Pliers, to hold objects with)*, the agent can instantiate this affordance as the mini composition *holdWith(Pliers, Sheets of Paper)*. An affordance can thus be seen as a mini-template for a tuple of objects: instead of looking at the affordance *to hold objects with* as a property of the *Pliers* focus object, the agent instantiates *holdWith(Pliers, o_x)*, in which o_x has to correspond to some size/weight constraints to fit the template. Such instantiations can constitute a natural link between objects (and the concept level), their affordances, and the problem template level.

<**Aff – Inferring more affordances**> – In CreaCogs, more affordances can inferred by interpreting the current context of objects through existing knowledge, and by seeing if other affordances have applied to such contexts in the past. For example, given that in the Two Strings Problem the relation $hangingFrom(ceiling, String_1)$ is provided, affordances like $attachedTo(ceiling, String_1)$ can be inferred. Upon consulting other properties of templates including strings (or string-like) objects attached to the ceiling from one's knowledge base, a CreaCogs agent should ideally provide further inferences, like $nailedTo(ceiling, String_1)$ or $attachedTo(ceiling, String_1, nail)$. It is easy to see how in this case consulting such templates plays the role of making commonsense assumptions. Retrieval of new affordances allows for further or different problem solving constructions to take place.

Inferring more affordances can also involve building longer affordance sequences. For example $aff(Pliers, remove\ nails)$ can be used to interact with the previous stated assumption $attachedTo(ceiling, String_1, nail)$. Thus, if the aforementioned $Pliers$ affordance is developed to its action template form of $remove(hard\ surface, nail, Pliers)$ by applying $remove(ceiling, nail, Pliers)$, the new state would be $onFloor(String_1)$, and the problem environment can then be updated to include $String_1$ as a non-attached, freely usable object.

<**Aff – Determining template affordance**> is generally done in the context of the goals and key requirements of the problem. In this process, the agent might determine that a PT's affordance shows promise in matching the goal. For example, a template of putting something in a container might be determined to have an affordance which matches the *non-spilling* of wax requirement of the candle problem.

It might be the case that a problem template the affordance of which produces the goal has already been found, however this PT cannot yet be applied. This is the case for solvers which infer that a container can be used in the candle problem, but do not see the box of thumbtacks as a possible container. Using means-end reasoning, the agent might determine another template's affordance to enable the application of the goal-producing one. As seen in the case studies, constructing a support, a stopper or a container out of matches can be determined as a template which produces such an enabling affordance.

Problem templates can also be discarded after they have been applied for a while. This can happen after the agent has unsuccessfully attempted to bridge the gap between a template, its known affordance(s) and the problem goal. Even if their affordance matches the problem goal, templates might be discarded if the solver finds it very hard to adapt them to the objects of the problem. Productive problem templates may also be mistakenly discarded at a shallow glance, though in fact they might have enabled the solution.

<Aff – Determining lack of affordance> – This code generally refers to assessing that a particular object does not possess a particular affordance – for example that a piece of *paper* cannot be used to *nail* things to the *wall*. It also can refer to assessing that the affordance of a particular object cannot be applied to a specific other object. For example, in the case of the Candle problem, a CreaCogs agent might focus on the *thumbtacks* objects and initially retrieve from memory the affordance $aff(thumbtacks, to\ pin\ with)$ related to them. Let us say o_x stands for an object to be pinned, in the action template of this affordance – $pinWith(thumbtacks, o_x, medium\ hard\ surface)$. Constraints on the size of the object to be pinned will depend upon the size of the provided *thumbtacks*. In the Candle problem, o_x, the object to be pinned, is the candle. Because the diameter of a prototypical candle is greater than the size of a *thumbtack pin*, affordance $aff(thumbtacks, to\ pin\ with)$ would be rejected in this context.

Problem template use category (PT)

<PT – Requirement-based search of template> – An initial search of useful problem templates can be triggered by a CreaCogs agent using already determined key problem requirements. For example, if the requirement of a problem is to reach a particularly high object, this requirement might be used to search for PTs which offer this as an affordance or as a side effect. A template which details that extending one's arm will enable one to reach further might be selected as a result of this requirement-based search.

<PT – Determining PT to use> can be done in a variety of ways in CreaCogs. An object the agent is focusing can be used to search for templates. The requirements of the problem can be used to determine what problem template to use. Properties of the solution or of the objects at hand can be used to search for templates, and determine one which looks promising. Also, the most salient objects of the problem might simply trigger their most salient associated templates in the mind of the solving agent. One of these templates might then be pursued.

<PT – Adaptation of PT to problem > – Let us say that a problem template PT_x was brought from the memory of the agent as being similar in affordance to the requirements of the problem. For example, the problem requires the agent to water a plant. The agent's most salient memory or knowledge pertaining to watering plants might be a template of using a watering can to water a plant. However, the problem environment might not provide any water can. The agent might still use this template to find a solution, or at least the parts of it where there is a water container which drips water into the plant pot. However, pot which is tilted to allow for water to drip might become the watering can, or the shower head, or a sprinkler.

Some such solutions, like using a pot instead of a watering can, refer to adapting the problem template to the objects of the problem (this is discussed in one of the next codes). However, other solutions, like using a sprinkler rather than a watering can, require deep changes and flexibility in the way in which the template itself is being used. In CreaCogs, an adaptation of the template to the problem means modifying the pre-existing PT_x. This can be done either by changing parts of PT_x, or by linking/expanding or combining PT_x with another template PT_y as to afford the problem goal. For example, the only sprinkler that the agent has access to might not be a garden one, but one for fire fighting. In this case, a template PT_y about how to make such a sprinkler turn on might need to be integrated in the plan to make the original PT_x reach its purpose.

<PT – use to search for suitable objects> – When a promising problem template has been discovered, its application must be determined in relation to the problem context at hand. The template and knowledge about its adjacent objects, object properties and affordances can be used in CreaCogs to search for similar objects in the problem space. If suitable objects have been found, the template can then be applied. If some suitable objects have been found, and one is missing, the missing one can be used as an object template. That is, a further search can ensue based on this object, in the hope that it can be created from other objects or parts in the problem environment. For example, let's say that the solver decided the template of a fishing rod has the suitable affordance to reach for the teddy bear. A search with this template for suitable objects might yield the clothesline and the mop as a potential fishing line and rod. A further search with the hook as an object template might ensue – for example a paperclip or a bit of wire might be selected as suitable objects to be cast in the *hook* object template. The search for suitable objects for the PT can thus involve as further refinement searches in which some of these objects are used as object templates (OT).

<PT – Adaptation of problem template to objects> – A PT can be adapted intrinsically when various non-traditional objects are cast in it, because of the differences between the new objects and the objects specified by the template. However, these differences can be so large that, after adapting a PT, the agent becomes aware its realization is closer to other PTs than the PT which was adapted, or that the PT resulting after the adaptation is different enough that it can be encoded as a new example in the knowledge base. For example, using a *platform* PT with the box and the candle (in the candle problem) results in creating a construction which is closer to a partial container template. In CreaCogs, the very cast of a PT on new objects might involve adaptation. Mechanisms which would remark upon useful adaptations, consolidating new successful cases, can also be built, thus increasing the KB of the agent.

<PT – use of PT construct> – In CreaCogs this means applying or re-applying a problem template to the set of problem objects. Thus, given the template PT_x, problem objects set $\{c_1, c_2...c_n\} \in C_P$, and problem goals G, try to apply PT_x in various ways to problem objects C_P so that G becomes possible. Various constructs can be used on various subsets of the problem objects in a solving session.

<PT – use of PT construct with reaching solution path> – In CreaCogs this reflects the case when a problem template has been used with the result that the solving state now matches the goal state of the problem.

<PT – Rejecting template> – In CreaCogs, rejecting a template may happen in various situations. The agent might infer that not enough objects from the given problem environment can be matched to the currently used template; it might determine that the currently used template only had a similar affordance, and upon closer inspection, it does not have the desired one. The agent might attempt to use a template in various ways without reaching the goal, and have a frustration threshold which ensure it will not get stuck in trying the same things over and over in such cases.

<PT – Template Switch> – A problem template switch in CreaCogs might happen through abandoning a previous PT, which is considered unproductive. A chain of previous affordance inferences or of new object constructions might also lead to a PT which seems more promising than the currently used one, thus warranting a switch. The agent might produce a template switch by considering a new set of objects as the main focus, or by noticing a new object. This change in object focus might trigger new templates.

Template switches can also be triggered by considering a different context for what the goal is or what required properties mean. It can also come about by noticing new affordances or properties of the given objects, or by discovering different ways in which these affordances can be linked. A template switch means projecting a new PT on a subset of objects in the problem environment. The new template might require the use of certain objects, and it might be applied only partially to start with. Further work might be necessary in order to discover or create other objects or actions which can be used to fully apply the new template.

Assessment category

<A – Checking joints in plan> – In CreaCogs, checking the joints in a problem solving plan can easily be exemplified with the simple machines analogy. Remember how, in the simple machines domain, motion is being passed between the different machines. One can check whether a certain simple machine like a cog (sm_4) can take said motion from another machine, like a pulley (sm_1), and pass it further to a lever (sm_5). Basically, whether the chain of simple machines $\{sm_1, sm_4, sm_5\}$ is properly connected and transmits the motion in the desired way.

Returning to problem solving, the joints between the various objects and the chain of actions are checked. For example, let us say that the problem requires reaching an object on the ceiling, and templates of making the agent taller by climbing on something and elongating their arm to reach further have been selected. Long objects, or object parts that can create long objects and act as good arm elongators are selected too. Tall objects are selected as well. Checking the joints in this plan would mean putting it all together. This means seeing whether the objects which can make the arm elongator fit together, and whether the objects meant to make the agent taller fit together, It also involves checking whether the actions chain well into a plan. For example, the agent might need to put a plank on the arm rests of the chair first, then the table on top of it, then put the various objects which will elongate one's hand together, than push these on top of the table, and only then climb.

At various points, the plan might be spoiled if the joints between actions and objects do not hold – for example, if the plank is too small to fit the table, or if the agent cannot push the arm elongator on top of the table, but it cannot climb while holding it either, etc. Checking for such joints might at times be the only way to reveal object which are missing, and which the agent took for granted – like revealing the lack of a hammer in the Attach the pendulum problem.

<**A – Checking object against constraints**> – In CreaCogs, knowledge of objects in the problem environment can be used to check whether their properties correspond to the constraints of the problem, or to various subgoals and templates. Upon checking, knowledge of whether c_{14} (*cardboard*) can be pierced and whether object c_{10} (*a paperclip*) is sharp enough to pierce it, satisfy constraints which enable the agent to apply a piercing template, and thus solve the Cardboard and loop problem.

<**A – Comparing solving state to constraints**> – In CreaCogs, this means comparing the current progress in solving to the problem goal. This might involve checking whether the affordances yielded by the current template used respect the problem requirements or not.

Focus changes

<**F – Focusing on object**> – In CreaCogs, focusing on an object when solving a problem means starting the search or construction processes based on this object, its properties or affordances. This can lead to creating chains of affordances starting from the object in question. Focus on an object can happen because the affordances of the object, and the associate problem templates it triggers are very salient to the agent. Thus such properties and templates might be the strongest associates to the environment objects. Focus on an object can also happen due to a perceive match between the required goals and the object and its associate PTs. This perceived match might happen as an initial result of shallow search, before deeper and better matches have been found.

<**F – Switching to new object as focus**> means iterating the focusing process with a new object and its associated affordances, templates and properties as the centerpoint of a new attempt of deriving a solution.

Creative problem solving process specific

<Composing fuller results based on previous exploration> – Let us say that a CreaCogs agent has already triggered some of its own knowledge about affordances of various objects. It has also superficially checked that a certain affordance chain might get it closer to the problem goal. In the process of composing fuller results, the entire solving path can be deployed in more detail, and its ensuing inferences explored.

For example, when looking at objects with the template of *elongating* one of the strings, the agent might be able to take advantage of previous knowledge and observations. Even if there is no other string in the room to *elongate* the string in the classical way the template of the agent might hold, a *string* can be easily substituted with a *tube* in this case, which holds a useful *has length* property. The agent might have already triggered the property (*paper*, *foldable*), and realize it could apply the object template of a tube to the paper. It might have also already noticed that multiple pieces of paper exist, and that other objects, like the *nails* have *fixing together* affordances. Composing fuller results based on this previous exploration, the agent will attempt to elongate the string by folding various pieces of paper, turning them into tubes, and fixing them to each other and to the string with nails.

<Insight marker expressions> – An insight marker could be triggered in CreaCogs when a new template which matches the goal has been discovered, in order to check for consistency with human data.

<Making assumptions> – If the application of a problem template is being explored, this requires not only matching objects to fill in this template, but also matching certain relations and properties. The agent might have no knowledge whether these properties and relations truly hold in the problem environment, so it might need to make the assumption that they do hold. Thus in CreaCogs, making assumptions can be a matter of considering some needed properties and relations to be in place in order to apply a certain template. Such assumptions would thus be transferred from the requirements of the template, if no contradictory knowledge can be established given the problem environment.

<Stuck or functional fixedness> – In CreaCogs, this would apply to moments in which a template or a set of templates are applied over and over with different objects, and there is no actual progress in bringing the affordance of those templates closer to the goal of the problem. This reflects spans of time in which no new solutions or solving paths are proposed, either.

<Forcing the solution> in CreaCogs could manifest itself in various ways. Applying a PT even if it is not entirely suitable, when it is the only solution path the agent perceives, or when the agent perceives this to be the most salient solving path, despite its inadequacies, might be a way of forcing the solution. Another is breaking some of the key requirements, constraints or givens of the problem, or modifying them in such ways as to fit a template that is being used, rather than the other way around.

Making constructions which are too complicated and too far removed from the initial templates, or from the actual properties of the objects, is a third possible way of forcing the solution. A fourth is applying various objects in object or problem templates, despite their lack of needed properties, or despite them having other properties which interfere with the smooth creation of the template.

Object (O), Object Templates (OT) and Object Use (OU)

<O – Disassembles object> – In OROC, object templates are disassembled in the knowledge base when attempting to make new objects which are composed of parts. CreaCogs thus holds a property for disassembly. However, to keep in tune with the human counterpart, objects in the environment should only be disassembled in CreaCogs when only a subset of their particular parts is considered useful for the problem at hand. Disassembly can happen even if the other resulting parts of the disassembly are not used, and the object is broken – thus unavailable for its previous affordances.

However, cognitive biases seem to be in place for many people against pointless disassembly. This could be reflected in a model by tracking the cost of disassembly, and setting biases against deleting existing object affordances. A decision to disassemble an object can follow the search of a certain property, deployed over the parts of the object in the problem environment. To which extent the affordances of the parts of an object get triggered at the same time as the affordances of an object get triggered is an interesting question, which requires specific cognitive investigation.

<O – Property-based search of object> – In OROC, this is one of the mechanisms which powers object replacement. Property-based searches can be done on both simple and composed objects, or on composed object parts, if knowledge of those parts is available to the agent. Properties are searched for in objects generally because it is assumed such properties would provide a certain affordance. Thus a property-based search can also be a form of implicit affordance search.

<O – Adaptation of objects to template> – This code might require changing an object to fit a particular object or problem template, by either modifying properties – like length, orientation – or by simply using the object for its non-traditional affordances. For example, a *matchstick* object could be used not for its direct affordance of *setting on fire*, but for it's length, width, solidity. Objects can also be modified: the matchstick can be broken, a string cut, a paperclip bent, etc. Some such physical modifications can be done with an agents' hands or body, some require the use of other objects. In CreaCogs, this requires knowledge about possible object transformations. Such knowledge could in principle be projected from templates of what has been done with thin metal wires, ceramic objects, thin wooden objects, etc.

<O – Object used to search for template> – In CreaCogs, this corresponds to the process of triggering the problem templates associated of a given object in the knowledge base. If this search yields no good template, it can be expanded to include the problem templates associated with similar objects.

<OT – Object template use> – The use of an object template is similar to OROC's process of object composition: different new objects are cast as the parts of a more complex object, that the agent has an object template for. This cast is done based on object similarity, that is similarity of properties. For example, if the template of a rake is being used, the solver might try to find a rake handle and a rake head by replacing them with similar objects in the environment of the problem.

In this process of applying an object template, <OT – Object template adaptation>, might also happen. This depends on what parts are being used to recreate the object. Using different parts can of course have the consequence that the new object composed under the object template is somewhat different from the object that inspired or got stored as that template to start with.

For example, let us say that the object template of a rake is elicited because the solver needs something to shallowly pierce the ground with. This will put more weight on recreating parts of the rake that are produce this affordance. Recreating the handle and one of the rake's teeth will be enough to do the job – so the head of the rake could be replaced with a big hook for example. If, on the other hand, the object template of the rake is triggered because the solver needs something to gather leaves or crumpled pieces of paper with, at a distance from one's body, the width of the head of the rake might be more important to instantiate in the new object creation than the rake's teeth. Using a flat mop with a wide head might be more useful for the task at hand, which is to grab and move multiple objects at a distance at once, rather than instantiating the teeth with a hook to pierce one object at a time.

A newly created object might thus maintain the initial affordance of the object template; it might instantiate only the most important parts of it; it might also bring about new affordances which were not part of the initial template, but are inherited from the parts used. For example, let us say that the solver is trying to deal with a situation in which he has to clean a floor on which a bottle got broken. Both liquid spills and big glass pieces are scattered on the floor. The rake object template gets invoked, and a flat mop is used as a replacement. Unlike a rake, a flat mop will not be able to pierce the ground. However, besides gathering the big pieces of glass, the flat mop could also absorb some of the liquid spills, thus containing an extra affordance than the object template which was initially invoked and which it is currently replacing.

It is possible that, in the process of creating such an object, the resulting construction, with the inherent ensuing adaptations, might be evaluated as being more similar to another known object altogether. It is also sensible to assume that the use of object templates and the adaptation of such templates might sometimes produce completely new objects, with new affordances, which could then be learned as new object templates.

<**OT – Object template rejection**> – In the context of CreaCogs, rejecting an object template can be done for various reasons: a) because the object parts cannot be found; b) because the affordance of the object template, though initially salient, has proven not to lead to a productive path; c) because the object template does not fit well into the context of the larger problem template applied.

If other parts of the problem are solved first, the object parts which were originally used to instantiate a specific object template might now be also required in different constructions. In this case, if the other constructions are prioritised as more important, the object template could get rejected because it cannot be applied anymore.

<**OU – Object used in novel way**> – A part of CreaCogs which makes objects be used in novel ways has already been implemented in the OROC prototype. The parts of protocol classified under this category can be considered similar to OROC's object replacement processes, and to answering the Alternative Uses Test. The process of using an object in a novel way can computationally be produced, like in OROC, by searching for objects with similar properties and then exploring the option that such objects might have some similar affordances.

When an object template is applied to new objects, object are also implicitly used in novel ways. Similarly, when fitting in objects to a specific problem template, and using an object which is not traditionally used in that role, that object might also implicitly be used in a novel way.

Meta-cognitive

<**Meta – remark on own process**> – Meta-cognition seems a type of functionality close to awareness, thus very human in nature. However, initial steps towards a functionality of meta-remarks on its own process can be made available with CreaCogs. This requires implementing functionality which allows the various systems to report on the processes they are using, and on the state of problem solving per se. A meta-system which kicks in at times to observe the existing processes, perhaps when a deadlock of functional fixedness has been reached, could direct the other systems with strategies in an attempt to break this deadlock. Such strategies could be, for example, refocusing on different objects, trying to find new, previously unobserved affordances and trigger new templates.

Other codes

<**Other – affective state**> – CreaCogs does not include a model of human interest or pleasure in dealing with a challenge. However, such a model could be implemented based on assumptions of what a challenge can be translated

to, in computational terms. For example, the use of multiple objects in a way which is far removed from their initial use, but aligns well in a problem template, might yield excitement, joy, playfulness, or a sense of freedom.

Requirements to come up with multiple solutions, or the necessity of recasting the same problem through multiple problem templates, until a productive one is found, might yield a sense of challenge through mental stimulation.

Reaching a possible solution may computationally be reached by finding and applying a problem template which can provide the problem requirements. Managing to successfully fit the problem objects in such a problem template might yield contentment, joy at one's success, excitement. Failing to find a suitable PT even after multiple manipulations, or generally being stuck in one PT and following the same path to no avail for a long time, without the ability to switch to a more productive one, might yield frustration, or a desire to abandon the problem altogether.

Agents with different personalities might have varied reactions to different levels of challenge. Such reactions could depend on their different endowments in terms abilities such as perseverance, flexibility in switching between templates, fluency in proposing new applications of a template. Different such abilities could be implemented and act as a foundation for modeling such affective states. The implementation of various such abilities would also allow us to model individual problem solving courses in a more diverse manner.

<Other – talking about previous experience> – If the problem templates of CreaCogs would not be implemented directly, but would be a function of abstracting over a number of problem situations, then a CreaCogs agent could talk about these situations as "previous experience". Also, if such an agent would keep on learning templates from its solving interactions, including extrapolating new templates from new problems it has solved, it could refer to these cases as a form of episodic memory when retrieving knowledge to use in new problems.

11.5 Order of Process for Modeling in CreaCogs

As it could be seen from the two case studies we analysed, different solvers might have different strengths, or different preferred processes. For example, mb8 showed a strong propensity to break objects, and a high fluency in switching between various templates. Meanwhile, Fb6 showed a high use of refocusing strategies – she kept on focusing and refocusing on new objects and different object affordances, in order to to get herself on a new, more productive path. Variations of the order in which the different processes happen in creative problem solving is also quite likely.

Observations about the order in which humans apply such processes are important. They help us understand the possible order or flow in running such processes, for the modelling of future computational solvers. Thus, the running of certain processes in CreaCogs should make possible the application of other processes, in accord with the empirical observations made in such think aloud protocols.

Though many of the processes explained in relation to CreaCogs and defined as codes seem important for creative problem solving, various paths can be taken when applying these processes. Such paths can depend on the individual cognitive agent and their propensity to rely more on a process or another, the content of their knowledge base, the objects they focus on initially (or that seem more salient to them), the OT and PT they associate to various objects.

In the following we will present some of these possibilities of process flow, by sketching various types of process order. This process order will be exemplified using the predefined codes and the sign →, which should be interpreted as *"can lead to"*. Fig. 11.11 represents a non-exhaustive summary chart of these many possibilities of process. We detail some part of this process flow below.

The problem solving starts with reading the problem, can lead to one or several of four different processes:

<PSP – Reading the problem>
    → **<PSP – Comprehending>**
    <PSP – Defining key requirements of the problem>
    <PSP – Mapping problem formulation to objects>
    <PSP – Taking stock of objects>

These four processes are all related to making an initial model of the problem.

Let us take the code **<PSP – sol>** to stand for the moment when a solution has been reached. Various codes correspond to starting to build a possible solution. This can be done by (a) using initial salient templates and objects, (b) building a solution from the object level or (c) attempting to determine which template to use.

a) using initial salient templates and objects - this might lead to the solution, or to other processes:

<PSP – Proceed on path>
    → **<PSP – sol>**
    <PSP – Running through consequences>
    <PT – Rejecting template>
    <PT – template switch>

If the initial salient template was rejected, or the problem path abandoned, the agent can try to build a new solution from the object level (b) or determine a new problem template to use (c).

b) building from the object level, by determining and inferring affordances is represented by the following cluster of codes:

<PSP – Mapping problem formulation to objects>
<PSP – Taking stock of problem objects>
    → **<F – Focusing on object>**
    <Aff – determine object affordance>

<Aff – determine lack of affordance>
<Aff – inferring more affordances>

c) attempting to determine a PT to use is represented by the following flow between codes:

<PSP – Taking stock of problem objects>
<Defining key requirements>
→ **<PT – requirement-based search>**
<O – object search for template>
<Aff – Determine PT affordance>

An initial selection of a PT can lead to attempts to apply it or adapt it:

<PT – Determining PT to use>
→ **<PT – adapt PT to objects or problem>**
<PT – use PT search for objects>

This leads to further filling in the template with objects, via:

→ **<Disassembles object>**
<O – property-based search of object>
<A – checking object against constraints>
<O – Adapt object to template>
<OU – object used in a new way>

and to processes of partial construction and evaluation:

→ **<PSP – Running through consequences>**
<A – comparing solution state to constraints>

If the so constructed path does not lead to a solution, either functional fixedness or an attempt at restructuring the problem ensues. The attempt at restructuring can be performed by going back to previous processes. For example, by applying to focus on new objects, and trying to build a new solution, or trying to determine a new template to use from there on.

In the cases in which the previous processes have led to a promising solution sketch, this yields attempts at fuller descriptions of the solution.

→ **<PSP – Proceed on path>**
<PSP – Composing fuller solution>

When such developments are satisfactory, a solution has been obtained. If time is left, an evaluation follows. If such developments are not satisfactory, functional fixedness or new attempts at restructuring occur.

This summarizes the main possibilities of solving flow between the various processes described with the codes. It also reflects the solving flow variations we have seen the human participants manifest.

A computational model implementing these processes should thus be able to traverse them during problem solving in such a variety of ways.

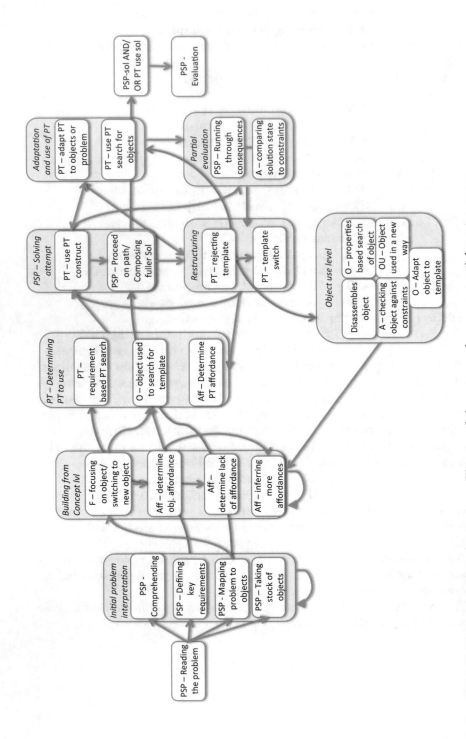

Fig. 11.11: Summary of flow of processes. The tip of the arrows shows a potential next process. The colour of the arrows is only meant to help readability

11.6 Towards Modeling Practical Object Insight Problems in CreaCogs

In order to be able to model insight problems, knowledge pertaining to insight problems needs to be formalized as to be given to the system. A strategy for doing this is to define each practical insight problem as a scene. Each scene contains a set of objects and some particular relations between these objects. Here is how the modeling of two such problems could be prepared : the candle problem and the two strings problem.

11.6.1 Modeling the Candle Problem

The initial state of the candle problem (Duncker, 1945) contains a set of objects and relations. These could be recognized as concepts and relations by the solver, upon inspection of the problem:
- C_1 – matchbook
- C_2 – candle
- C_3 – box of thumbtacks OR box of nails
- C_4 – wall
- C_5 – table
- C_6 – thumbtacks OR nails
- R_1 contains(matchbook, matches)
- R_2 – contains(Box_of_Thumbtacks, Thumbtacks) OR
   contains(Box_of_Nails, nails)

Each problem has a goal – which is about achieving a certain composed object, a certain set of relations, or successfully performing some action. For example, the candle problem (Duncker, 1945) has as a goal obtaining an object within a certain state C_x = candle_lit, a relation R_x = on(wall, candle), and making sure another relation is prevented $\neg R_y$ = on(table, wax).

As next steps in problem modeling, the object in each insight problem can be described in terms of its properties. If the object is a composed object, it can also be described in terms of relations between its parts, as done by the OROC prototype. A set of known problem and action templates can be defined for the KB of a CreaCogs agent. These templates consist of commonsense knowledge about actions which could be performed using the objects in the problem, and the results of such actions. The formalization of these problem templates can thus be done in terms of participating concepts or objects, relations, actions and solution states or consequences of action. This has been described in chapter 8, and could be applied to the candle problem by developing templates like the following:

PT_1 – *how to take matches out of a matchbook:*
   $PT_1 = \{$c=\{matchbook\},
      r = \{contains(matchbook, matches)\},
      h=take_out(matchbook, matches),
      sol = \{c= matches\}\}

PT_2 – *how to light a match:*
$$PT_2 = \{c=\{\text{match, lighting strip}\},$$
$$r=\{\text{brushes(match, striking strip)}\},$$
$$h=\{\text{swipe(matches, striking strip)}\},$$
$$\text{sol}=\{c=\text{match on fire}\}\}$$

PT_3 – *how to light a candle:*
$$PT_3 = \{c=\{\text{candle, fire}\},$$
$$r=\{\text{touches(candle\_tip, fire)}\},$$
$$h=\{\text{light(candle, fire)},$$
$$\text{sol} = \{c=\text{candle\_lit}\}\}$$

PT_4 – *how to attach poster with thumbtack to wall:*
$$PT_4 = \{c=\{\text{poster, pin, wall}\},$$
$$r=\{\text{touches(poster,wall)}\},$$
$$h=\{\text{push(thumbtack,(poster,wall))}\},$$
$$\text{sol} = \{r=\text{attached(poster,wall)}\}\}$$

PT_5 – *using a container to catch drips:*
$$PT_5 = \{c=\{\text{leaky radiator, water, container}\},$$
$$h=\{\text{put(on floor(container)},$$
$$\text{under(leaky radiator, container))}\},$$
$$\text{sol} = \{r=\text{catch drips(container,water)}\}\}$$

PT_6 – *shelf with vase on wall:*
$$PT_6 = \{c=\{\text{shelf, nails, wall, vase}\},$$
$$h=\{\text{attach (on nails(shelf, wall)), put(vase,shelf)}\},$$
$$\text{sol} = \{r=\text{on(wall,shelf), on(shelf,vase), on(wall,vase)}\}\}$$

Of course, the examples above are not meant to present a precise formalization, but rather point the way towards how such templates could be modelled.

CreaCogs will then use the problem objects and the goals to search in its KB for the most suitable templates which could be used to reach the problem goal. Parts of the goal can be reached with various affordance chains. For example, PT_1–PT_3 can be chained: PT_1 provides the matches required for PT_2, which provides the match on fire required for PT_3. After applying PT_1–PT_3, the goal C_x=candle_lit is reached.

If a search starting from problem requirements on how to attach something to a wall finds the PT_4 template, the *candle* object can be replaced in the *poster* slot. PT_4 is thus adapted, yielding an attempt to attach the *candle* directly to the *wall*. However, a property search would show that a candle is too thick for the use of this template.

PT_5 – *using a container to catch drips* – could be used by replacing the *container* slot with the *box* object (as it was the case with participant Fb6), and *water* drips with *wax* drips. The requirements of the problem to not have wax on the table trigger the catching drips PT_5. PT_5 could then lead to the search for a *container* or a similar object. This might make the *box* object salient, despite its initial lack of salience because of being part of the composed object C_3 (box of thumbtacks). This solves the $\neg R_y =$ on(table, wax) part of the problem goal.

PT_6 – *shelf with vase on the wall* – could be triggered as a response to the relationship goal of having the candle attached to the wall $R_x =$ on(wall, candle). PT_6 is a less direct way of attaching something to the wall then PT_4, however it still brings about the relationship required by the goal of the problem.

When using PT_6, the object *shelf* could be created out of *matchstick* parts, which could be found as suitable based on their material (wood) property. Their size would of course prove unsuitable for creating a shelf. However, the application of PT_6 would allow the agent to understand the entire goal $R_x =$ on(wall, candle) in a different light, thus restructure the problem under a new set of templates. While creating a shelf out of matchsticks might be unsuccessful, thinking in the direction of creating a platform for the candle rather than attaching the candle to the wall directly will prove profitable.

Viewing the problem through the template of finding a *platform* allows for the lax use of the *box* object. This might require a new adaptation of the general template of using a platform, as *box* would provide a mixed platform-container affordance.

If the *box* was already used to stop drips (by e.g. being set on the floor at some distance under the candle), a reuse of the *box* as a platform or a container might become cognitively harder to produce. A reuse requires re-parsing already applied templates down to the elements they contain – in this case disentangling the *box* from its projected role in the template in which it lays on the floor. Such a reuse also requires backtracking from already achieved problem goals. Such operations of reparsing the problem elements, disentangling elements from already assigned roles in templates and backtracking from already achieved goals are most likely cognitively expensive. An understanding that the *box* would provide in this case both container and platform affordances, thus answer both the second and third problem requirements, would make the use of PT_5 – *using a container to catch drips* – unnecessary.

11.6.2 Modeling the Two Strings Problem

The initial state of the Two Strings problem contains the following objects and relations; part of them are offered in the problem statement and part in the problem depiction:

- C_1 – String1, C_2 – String2
- C_3 – Person
- C_4 – Chair
- C_5 – Pliers
- C_6 – Jar of nails
- C_7 – Sheets of paper
- C_8 – Nails

- R_1 – hanging(String1,ceiling), R_2 – hanging(String2,ceiling)
- R_3 – onFloor(Chair), R_4 – onFloor(Sheets of paper), R_5 – onFloor(Jar of nails), R_6 – onFloor(nails), R_7 – onFloor(Pliers)
- R_8 – holds(Person,String)

The goal of the problem is H_x=tie(String1, String2), and the constraint that, if R_x=holds(Person,String1), then $\neg R_y$=reach(Person,String2).

Upon a closer inspection of the problem, C_3 can be inferred to contain other objects, which may only become salient when a search for objects to elongate strings with is performed: dressed(Person(Pants, Shoes, T-shirt). Also, the opposite of the constraint will be inferred, thus if the person holds the second string – R_y =holds(Person,String2), then it cannot reach the other – $\neg R_x$= reach(Person,String2). The agent might also inspect the components of C_6 - Jar of nails. These are not just the nails, but the jar itself, and its lid.

At the beginning of solving such a problem, various objects can be taken as a focus. A focus on the *Chair* object would trigger its affordance to be climbed upon, which is generally associated with templates for *reaching higher*. The activation of such templates might also be primed by having previously used it in solving a problem, like Dusting the clock.

The goal action H_x=tie(String1, String2) can trigger different templates. The more general template of tying two things together out of which one is a string might look like the following:

$$PT_1 = \{c = \{o_1, \text{String}\},$$
$$r = \{\text{overlap}(o_1, \text{String2})\},$$
$$h = \{\text{tie}(o_1,\text{String})\},$$
$$\text{sol} = \{r=\text{tied}(o_1,\text{String})\} \}$$

At this point, at least two paths may be taken. If the agent focuses on the fact that the objects are not long enough, and perceives this as a lack of affordance preventing the tying of the objects together, then templates of elongating the string might be triggered. On the other hand, if the focus is on having the objects close or in overlap as a prerequisite for applying the tying affordance, then the template of bringing the objects closer together will be triggered. These two paths can be expressed as follows:

$$Goal(tie(S1, S2)) \rightarrow close(String1, String2) \rightarrow PT_2 \text{ bring objects closer}$$
$$Goal(tie(S1, S2)) \rightarrow tooShort(String1, String2) \rightarrow PT_3 \text{ elongate}(String1)$$

Templates like the following might thus be triggered by the two paths:

PT_2 - *bring objects closer:*
$$PT_2 = \{c = \{obj_x, obj_y)\},$$
$$r = \{\text{far}(obj_x, obj_y)\},$$
$$h = \{\text{move}(obj_x, point_x), \text{move}(obj_y, point_x)\},$$
$$sol_2 = \{r = close(obj_x, obj_y)\}\}$$

PT_3 - *elongate string:*
$$PT_3 = \{c=\{\text{String}, obj_z\},$$
$$r = \{\text{close}(\text{String}, obj_z)\},$$

$$h = \{attach(String, obj_z)\},$$
$$sol_3 = \{c=longer\ String\}\}$$

If an elongation template is applied, then a search on objects which can be used to elongate the String will ensue. For this purpose, various objects might be used in alternative ways:

- the clothes of the person;
- the sheets of paper on the floor, folded as to resemble a string in width and fixed together;
- pulling one of the strings away from its fixed place (though this action could also be triggered by a bringing objects together template);
- the pliers, jar and even chair could be used for elongation.

When using the pliers or the jar, the insight that the object thus obtained would move like a pendulum can emerge from the agent's commonsense knowledge.

Another template which could be used is reflective of the problem constraint: the lack of ability to reach the other object. The pliers' affordance to be held in one's hand and to grab onto objects with might yield the special case of elongating one's hand, and thus using the pliers in order to reach further. A possible development of the template in the direction of elongating one's reach could be to attach the open pliers to the chair, thus constructing a longer arm. We have not seen this strategy in human participants yet, and it is useful to point out that the end of that arm has to be maneuverable and have the ability to grab the string. Thus one's own fingers and the pliers have a much better chance than a chair's feet.

Bringing objects together can in itself be done in various ways:

(a) by moving both obj_x, obj_y at once, which in this context is made impossible by the constraint of not reaching a string when holding the other;

(b) moving one object at a time, but only if that object remains fixed in place after movement; trying to apply this strategy would trigger *fix object to point$_x$* templates, which are visible in the human participants' attempts to fix one of the strings to the ceiling or to one of the walls;

(c) more generally, through personal motion in cases (a) and (b);

(d) through the motion of a second agent that accomplishes the task, or the part of the task which is unreachable by the initial agent (sometimes human participants ask if they have someone else that can help them), or

(e) through the motion of the object itself – a reframing which generally triggers a productive template, if a suitable way to make the object move by itself is found.

11.7 Discussion and Future Work

In this chapter, we have seen that new practical object insight or creative problems with one or multiple solutions can be created following a strategy.

Three new practical object problems were designed, and a think aloud protocol study on five classical insight problems + three newly created problems was run.

We derived a set of codes corresponding to the CreaCogs framework in order to analyze the think aloud protocol data. Two case studies of highly performant human participants solving these problems were presented. The codes and their correspondence to processes which already exist or can be implemented in CreaCogs were explored. We have seen that the CreaCogs framework shows promise in modeling the processes used by human participants when solving such problems.

An initial question we had was whether the newly created problems would be similar to classical ones, and whether they would require insight and/or creativity on the part of the participants. In terms of these problems requiring insight, perhaps fMRI methods could issue a stronger answer on this matter. With the methodology currently available to us, we can say that the various codes which we used showed that participants manifested both restructuring and insight in the context of the newly created problems. The Jack and Jill Weighting problem comes perhaps the closest to classical insight problems, in terms of requiring one specific type of restructuring to solve.

The Dusting the Clock and Blown Away Teddy problems were built to allow for multiple solutions, and thus prompt the participants to deploy a variety of composition and restructuring processes in a rich problem environment which allowed it. In order to turn these two problems to a form closer to that of classical insight problems, we would probably need to remove many objects and allow for only one possible (and reliable) solution.

In future work, these problems could be given to participants in a variant which allows for only one reliable solution; they could also be in various conditions, in which more or less functional fixedness is triggered, and different ways of (unproductively) structuring the problem are activated.

A strong control over such variables in the design of insight problems will allow for a more in depth study of structuring and restructuring costs. These costs might be different for different individuals. An interesting point of exploration is whether such restructuring costs can be measured via other creativity tests. Narrowing down re-representation and restructuring across multiple types of creative problem solving tasks will surely prove profitable in better understanding high level creative processes.

The approach set in place in this chapter can be used to create a larger battery of practical insight problems. Gathering normative data on this larger set of problems will be useful for cognitive psychologists, which could then compare the performance of their participants with this data. A larger set of problems could also be used for acquiring knowledge for artificial systems which have as a goal the computational modeling and solving of such problems, or general work with creative uses of object affordances.

The set of codes described in Sect. 11.2 shows that there are differences and overlaps between classical and creative problem solving. Classical problem solving is generally seen as the search for a path in a problem space, using operators or functions which move the solver from one state to another. Creative problem solving shares evaluation (looking at the goal to check if one is approaching the solution, or has reached it), backtracking and the exploration of one already framed problem space with classical problem solving.

However, the problem space can be restructured in creative problem solving, by producing a different interpretation of the "initial state". This interpretation depends on what objects are considered salient in the environment, and on what object templates, affordances and problem templates are activated in the KB of the solver. The problem goals can also be restructured in creative problem solving, as these goals are at times ambiguous and can be interpreted in a variety of ways by the solver.

During such creative solving, objects which did not exist in the given environment can be brought forward from the KB of the solver, and then created in the problem space. This changes the problem space, and the possible states to be reached from it. The concept of *operators* in classical problem solving corresponds loosely in practical object insight problems to: a) object moves; b) the projection of known or noticed object affordances on other objects; and c) the composition of new objects and templates by using object property and affordance chaining.

In the future, a computational prototype will be implemented to solve the set of practical object insight problems described in this chapter. Implementation is generally a good test for theory, and it opens up new possibilities for observation, potential issues which were not considered before and data on how a process works computationally.

This implementation requires the formalization of a set of problem templates, which could be acquired directly or indirectly from human data. A direct strategy would be to ask human participants to provide such templates regarding a set of objects. An indirect strategy would be to use part of the think aloud protocols produced by participants in order to to analyze, extract and formalize the templates used. The rest of the sessions could then be used as comparative data points to the prototype's solving process.

A computational system could be used to automatize the creation of practical object insight problems. This could be done, as shown in this chapter, by reversing the process of creative problem solving, by: (i) using object and problem templates to generate problems and solutions; (ii) creating the possibility for the solution to be found by placing objects with similar affordances as to fit the object and problem templates in the problem environment; and (iii) adding to the problem scene objects which would provide an interference effect by triggering different templates.

After having explored whether insight problems are amenable to solving through the principles proposed here, how does it all tally up? What have we learned and achieved, and what are the next questions and possibilities of exploration this has opened up for us?

The Journey Thus Far and the Journey Ahead

This book has offered the beginning of an answer to the question – how can we think of creative problem solving in a unified way.

Problem solving has been previously defined as searching in a problem space with a certain goal. However, when solving problems creatively, humans do more than search in well defined problem spaces, where they know for sure there is a solution to be found, with a specific goal in mind. Humans create new possible *solutions*, new ways of looking at the *problems*, new ways of looking at and using *tools and objects* which exist in the problem space. These objects can be practical (physical objects when solving object related problems) or abstract (concepts, heuristics).

Humans can also solve such problems when they do not know (or have ambiguous information) about how the goal should look like. This ability of creating new ways of seeing the problem, and creating new problem objects, changes the problem space in which the solver is operating. It also reflects the productive side of human cognition.

In the rest of this closing chapter, we will first overview the contributions of the explorations in this book. Then, the experimental contributions will then be discussed in the perspective of the larger framework. We will use the success of our comparative evaluations to propose a general approach for modeling cognitively comparable systems in the creative problem solving domain. Finally, conclusions and future work will wrap up the entire book.

12.1 The Journey Thus Far – Contributions Overview

After setting up the stage, clarifying some of our questions and reviewing existing work in Part I, on the different strands and guises under which parts of creative problem solving have been studied, our journey provided us with the following contributions:

1) A theoretical framework of the creative problem-solving process has been proposed in Chaps. 6 and 7. This cognitively-inspired framework aims

© Springer Nature Switzerland AG 2020
A.-M. Oltețeanu, *Cognition and the Creative Machine*,
https://doi.org/10.1007/978-3-030-30322-8_12

to enable AI agents with a wide scale of creative problem-solving capabilities. The framework proposes that certain types of knowledge organization might help enable creative processes.

2) A formalization of the representations and processes of this theoretical framework has been presented in Chap. 8, together with examples of how these processes can describe creative problem solving in various domains.

3) Prototype systems have been built on some of these processes, and experiments have been conducted in different problem domains:

(a) A Remote Associates Test computational solver was implemented in Chap. 9; comRAT offers correct and plausible results to the RAT creativity test, and has been compared to human data;

(b) A proof of concept expansion of the Remote Associates Test to the visual domain was performed in Sect. 9.9; the computational solver comRAT-C was extended to comRAT-V;

(c) A creative object replacement and object composition prototype was implemented in an everyday object domain (Chap. 10); OROC was evaluated with human judges and process categories from a think aloud experiment.

4) Empirical data has been gathered and analyzed on the human creative solving of various tasks, and on the comparability between human data and data from the prototype systems. This has taken different forms:

(a) Comparability data between the performance of the comRAT-C system and normative human data when solving compound RAT queries;

(b) An initial prototype of a visual variant of the human Remote Associates Test was set up, and related data on human performance was collected;

(c) Comparability data has been obtained between the object replacement system and human answers to the Alternative Uses test. Likability and Usefulness metrics of human judges on OROC's performance were gathered and analysed, together with the traditional Novelty metrics. Property related data on the new answers provided by the human participants to the Alternative Uses test has also been analyzed;

(d) A process for developing new practical insight problems in the object domain has been designed in Chap. 11; a think aloud study has been conducted, and think aloud protocols have been encoded in a model shown to correspond to processes in the CreaCogs framework.

12.2 Experimental Work and the CreaCogs Framework

The CreaCogs framework aims to provide knowledge organization support in order to enable creative problem solving processes across a variety of tasks. In the experimental and computational work performed, we have seen that the CreaCogs principles of knowledge organization can enable creative processes, and that the results of these processes are comparable to those of human participants in a variety of creativity tasks.

The prototype comRAT-C system has shown that associative convergent processes can be used by a computational solver to successfully match human performance in the compound Remote Associates Test. The probability of finding an answer, based on frequency of expressions, has correlated with human performance in such problems, thus providing further validation that the principles used here reflect some of the cognitive reality of solving such tasks by human participants. This also shows that comRAT-C can be further developed in the future as a predictive model for exploring various hypotheses on how humans solve the RAT. Furthermore, comRAT shows promise to become a generative system, to be used for the creation of large sets of RAT problems with controlled variables.

The construction of a prototype visual Remote Associates test for humans enables further comparison of the RAT solving process across modalities. This is now the only creativity test that we know of which can be administered in two different forms, corresponding to two different modalities. Such cross-domain investigation will enable further differentiation between modality specific proficiency and creative process proficiency when solving the RAT. The implementation of comRAT-V has shown that the same computational principles can be applied to both variants of the Remote Associates test. More data is needed to make a strong argument about a correlation between comRAT-V's probability of solving queries and human cognitive difficulty in solving the same queries; however, the analysis with current data shows that this correlation will be achieved with the visual test as well as the compound verbal one.

The prototype OROC system implements use of property similarity between concepts, in order to enable object replacement and object composition. OROC shows that such processes can yield creative answers similar to those given by humans. We have also seen that such answers can be evaluated with similar metrics as those used to evaluate human answers to the Alternative Uses Test. OROC's answers have been rated on Novelty, Usefulness and Likability by human judges.

A comparison was performed between OROC's processes and a think aloud protocol centered on human processes of solving the Alternative Uses Test. This has shown that some of the main strategies which enable humans to solve such problems, like property use and disassembly, can be accounted for in OROC. The alternative uses given by our participants to the same objects as OROC were also analysed. This indicated that shape and material are highly useful properties, when one makes creative inferences about the ability to use an object with a new affordance.

The practical object insight problems experiment has shown that there is a correspondence between human solving processes, as classified by think aloud codes, and the CreaCogs processes of object replacement, object composition, and restructuring using objects and templates.

The creation of a few new practical creative problems has helped us propose a set of strategies for building such problems. These strategies can be further used for building a larger set of problems. Normative data could thus be made available for a set of insight problems, something which does not exist in the literature, and would allow for useful comparisons and points a reference for the work of many researchers. The establishing of such a set would allow practical object insight problems to be studied in varied conditions: with various interfering objects, with one or multiple paths of solving, with the solution split over a smaller or larger set of objects, made more or less salient, etc. Furthermore, the set of strategies for creating practical object insight problems which we created open up, as a next step, the computational implementation of a system that can generate such problems.

The creation of a set of codes for analyzing these think aloud protocols has shown that human participants indeed apply many of the processes posited by CreaCogs when solving such problems, for example:

 (i) they focus on various sets of objects and object affordances when solving such problems;
 (ii) such affordances are linked into a constructive whole;
(iii) they use property-based search to select replacements for missing objects;
(iv) they search for objects with a problem template in mind;
 (v) problem templates are searched for based one problem requirements and problem objects, and adapted to these;
(vi) elements of the given problem can be restructured under various templates brought from the KB; this process sometimes entails the creation of new objects from the initial problem elements, etc.

Developing the domain of practical object insight problems brings higher order creative problem solving closer to existing capacities, which we previously implemented, on object replacement and object composition. The same processes for object replacement and object composition can be used for implementing a CreaCogs prototype computational solver of practical insight problems. Other CreaCogs posited processes will also be necessary, especially the ones related to problem template search and re-representation of the given problem objects under various templates.

This book has shown that a unified framework for modeling diverse creative tasks and processes is possible. The proposed theoretical framework and its processes have been shown to reflect interesting creative properties, and the implementation of various creativity tasks has further confirmed the validity and usefulness of the proposed framework.

Furthermore, the application of these principles has shown that computational cognitive systems which give answers similar to those given by humans in creativity tests can be built, and evaluated in the same way as human answers. Can a general approach towards comparability in creative computational cognition be put forward?

12.3 A Comparability Approach to Creative Computational Cognition

Our previous endeavors have shown that a comparative approach between natural and artificial cognitive systems is useful in the domain of creative problem solving. A general approach could be extrapolated to involve the following steps:

1. Choosing a general creative problem-solving skill that enables some adjacent empirical validation; choosing a human creativity test, the results of which are to be replicated via an artificial cognitive system[1].

2. Obtaining human normative data for comparison, or using such data from the literature, where available.

3. Finding a source of knowledge for cognitive knowledge acquisition (like the n-grams from a balanced language corpus used for the KB of comRAT-C), or establishing forms of knowledge acquisition and organization which are cognitively inspired. Cognitive knowledge acquisition and organization might yield further cognitive results, which would validate the framework. For example, the OROC solver demonstrates other cognitive effects, like shape bias (Landau et al., 1988; Imai et al., 1994), comRAT-C correlates to human difficulty, etc.

4. Implementing a system which uses cognitive processes, like association, use of similarity and structure, re-representation, etc.

5. Evaluating the results of the artificial cognitive system employing either or both of the following techniques: (a) comparisons to human normative data and (b) an application of the methods used for the evaluation of human participants when solving that creativity task.

6. Deploying data analysis measures to observe new possible relations of scientific interest.

7. Aiming to model such tasks in multiple sensory domains, if possible, as to gather unified data of the creative process. An example of this is the correlation observed between Usefulness and Novelty ratings. Others could involve the measurement of the minimum discriminant in OROC's knowledge base, or of how informativity changes when learning features of new objects.

8. Aiming to enable the artificial cognitive system with generative abilities for that particular test or task (if possible), as to allow for the creation of new datasets of problems, and new, more refined empirical testing of human participants with better controlled variables. This will lead to further refinements in the hypotheses we devise and test about cognitive creative processes. It will also empower us to build better systems in the future.

---

[1] In Chap. 10, the general creative problem-solving skill we focused on was creative object replacement. This led us to using the Alternative Uses test as evaluation for part of the implemented processes.

12.4 The Journey Ahead

The breadth of the investigations performed in this book opens up a wide array of avenues in which further work can be pursued. Here are the main directions of possible travel, a subset of which we will later elaborate on:

- developing and implementing more of the constructive creative processes posited by CreaCogs (like concept creation, PT creation, etc.)
- using qualitative and quantitative human data to inform and evaluate more parts of the already existing systems, turning them into models.
- improving the OROC model by adding a subsymbolic layer, learning directly from sensory data stimuli and producing similarity metrics;
- developing a practical insight problem solving system;
- using the generativity part of these systems to refine cognitive hypotheses;
- further work in the direction of classifying creative problem-solving types depending on the processes they employ;
- philosophy of information work on the impact of structured cognition on informativity measures (Olteţeanu, 2015);
- applying the principles deployed here to construct assistive systems for creative problem solving support.

The comRAT-V system shows promise in terms of extrapolating the same principles to a multimodal series of the Remote Associates Tests. However, only 20 queries have been designed so far, in comparison to the 144 queries for the linguistic compound RAT provided by the literature (Bowden & Jung-Beeman, 2003), together with normative data. A larger set of visual queries needs to be constructed. More visual associates need to be gathered either by (i) asking human participants to provide them, or by (ii) establishing a way to automatically extract visual associates from images of groups of objects or scenes. More such data will enable stronger conclusions to be drawn regarding the correlation between the processes employed by comRAT-V and human participants solving the RAT-V.

Within the realm of the language based RAT, it is useful to note that we have only experimented so far with the compound type of associates. Functional associates (between which a relationship can be established whether or not a language relationship exists) remain unexplored. The difference between compound and functional Remote Associates (e.g. *"black magic"* vs. *"egg and nest"*) can further be explored by implementing a comRAT-F system which organizes in its knowledge base a set of functional associates. The biggest challenge regarding this would be gathering a good set of functional associates data. However, part of this knowledge could be extracted from ontologies, and different relations could be obtained by scraping the web and by other means of knowledge acquisition.

The relationship between visual, semantic and linguistic items can further be explored through a paradigm which employs a mixed version of the test. The language and visual skills of participants can be assessed previously to employing this mixed version of the test. This will allow us to discern between creative ability related to bringing together remote associates, and specific fluency in a particular modality.

A strategy could be developed to enable comRAT to solve, on its part, visual and language mixed queries. The relation between processes using visual and language queries could then be modeled and studied computationally. Further comparison of performance and response times across compound and functional versions of the RAT will allow for a better understanding of the processes deployed in such a test.

The generativity properties of comRAT-C can be fruitfully employed to create well controlled Remote Associates Tests and investigate cognitive hypotheses over topics including:
- the human preference of response in queries with multiple answers;
- the influence of the order of query terms order on query difficulty;
- the influence of the frequency of items over human appraisals of queries as more or less creative or surprising;
- the influence of semantic domain on difficulty.

Adding different language knowledge bases to comRAT-C, in collaboration with linguists, might help generate Remote Associates Tests in languages in which the test does not exist.

A subsymbolic implementation of the proof of concept OROC system will add to its cognitive validity, and would permit further development of the system and the further investigation of the impact of property similarity on creative processes. The subsymbolic layer could be developed as to learn from given sensory data, in which case the similarity functions over feature spaces could be implemented at a subsymbolic level too. If such similarity functions are refined in a comparative approach to human performance, further models could be enabled, aimed at explaining why certain objects are triggered as answers in the Alternative Uses test more than others.

Deploying an Alternative Uses test on a larger set of everyday objects would be an important next step. Besides gathering normative data on various objects, such a study will provide a great starting ground for:
- understanding the role property similarity has on creative processes;
- finding out how often composition and decomposition strategies are used;
- performing knowledge acquisition for the development of more advanced creative problem solving systems in the everyday object domain.

A better understanding and more data on the issues above will permit us to model more refined hypotheses about the influence of property similarity and composition-decomposition strategies in object replacement and object composition.

Further increasing and refining the knowledge base of OROC with more objects and more fine-grained properties will enable OROC to perform object similarity tasks in a more precise cognitive manner. Such a general skill could be evaluated using the Wallach-Kogan similarities test, thus establishing a new comparison point with empirical normative data.

A very welcome addition to the existing battery of creativity tests would be an object composition test. This would guide the further evaluation and development of OROC's object composition module, by establishing normative points of reference for human performance in this task. Further advances for creative AI and cognitive robotics will be supported in this direction by:

– computational investigations of shape-based composition;
– computational use of object templates;
– adaptations and "fitting" of new objects to older templates; and
– investigation into what shapes seem more suitable than others for composition.

A very interesting next project would be the construction of a computational proof of concept system which can solve ampler object related creativity problems and practical insight problems. With the knowledge gathered in Chap. 11, this is now possible. However, a mechanism for reliably performing knowledge acquisition of problem templates from human participants needs to be designed.

Our theory of how insight problems can be created can and should also be tested. A possible way of doing this, would be to automatically generate such problems and empirically evaluate them with human participants. fMRI or EEG techniques can also be used to explore in which cases such problems come closer to the category of insight problems.

Various processes of the proposed theoretical framework have been implemented separately. The various parts of the framework need to be integrated in a larger system, adding all these processes together, and investigating their unified properties, benefits and power in solving the tasks detailed above.

A large amount of work is now possible on the wide foundations which we have established. Our journey has been rich and varied, blending the narratives of creativity and problem solving, the methods of computational and empirical cognitive science. We believe to have shown that thinking of creative problem solving in a unified manner, and acting in a comparative perspective can help provide a more integrative and interesting view on creative problem solving. We have pushed the boundaries of the state of the art and, in that, we consider the current work has fully reached its purpose.

The time we took to explore these matters was done for our own curiosity and pleasure. The time we took to describe them was also done in the hope of motivating and inspiring others to refine this and other cognitive frameworks for creative problem solving.

A

Appendix A – Human and System Answers to Variants of the Remote Associates Test

This appendix is structured as follows. Table A presents expected answers vs. answers provided by comRAT-C, for the 144 compound RAT queries of Bowden and Jung-Beeman. Tables A.2 and A.3 presents frequency and probability data on the results given by comRAT v2 solver. Table A.4 shows candidate query items when using comRAT-G for query generation.

Table A.1: List of comRAT-C's v.1.0 answers to the 144 compound Remote Associate Test Queries by Bowden and Jung-Beeman. The "comRAT-C" column reflects comRAT-C's answers. The "Expected" column reflects answers considered correct and expected from humans in the normative data.

No.	Query	comRAT-C	Expected	Correct	Plausible
1	Cottage Swiss Cake	Cheese	Cheese	Yes	-
2	Cream Skate Water	Ice	Ice	Yes	-
3	Loser Throat Spot	Sore	Sore	Yes	-
4	Show Life Row	Single	Boat	No	Yes
5	Night Wrist Stop	Surgery	Watch	No	Partial
6	Duck Fold Dollar	Fat	Bill	No	Yes
7	Rocking Wheel High	Chair	Chair	Yes	-
8	Dew Comb Bee	Honey	Honey	Yes	-
9	Fountain Baking Pop	Soda	Soda	Yes	-
10	Preserve Ranger Tropical	Forest	Forest	Yes	-
11	Aid Rubber Wagon	Station	Band	No	Partial
12	Flake Mobile Cone	Homes	Snow	No	No
13	Cracker Fly Fighter	Freedom	Fire	No	No
14	Safety Cushion Point	Road	Pin	No	Partial
15	Cane Daddy Plum	Sugar	Sugar	Yes	-
16	Dream Break Light	Bad	Day	No	Partial
17	Fish Mine Rush	Gold	Gold	Yes	-
18	Political Surprise Line	Party	Party	Yes	-
19	Measure Worm Video	Tape	Tape	Yes	-
20	High District House	School	School	Yes	-

Continued on next page

© Springer Nature Switzerland AG 2020
A.-M. Oltețeanu, *Cognition and the Creative Machine*,
https://doi.org/10.1007/978-3-030-30322-8

Table A.1 *Continued from previous page*

No.	Query	comRAT-C	Expected	Correct	Plausible
21	Sense Courtesy Place	Common	Common	Yes	-
22	Worm Shelf End	Short	Book	No	Yes
23	Piece Mind Dating	Brilliant	Game	No	Partial
24	Flower Friend Scout	Girl	Girl	Yes	-
25	River Note Account	Book	Bank	No	Partial
26	Print Berry Bird	Blue	Blue	Yes	-
27	Pie Luck Belly	Pot	Pot	Yes	-
28	Date Alley Fold	Blind	Blind	Yes	-
29	Opera Hand Dish	Soap	Soap	Yes	-
30	Cadet Capsule Ship	Space	Space	Yes	-
31	Fur Rack Tail	Coat	Coat	Yes	-
32	Stick Maker Point	Decision	Match	No	Partial
33	Hound Pressure Shot	Put	Blood	No	Partial
34	Fox Man Peep	Show	Hole	No	Partial
35	Sleeping Bean Trash	Bag	Bag	Yes	-
36	Dust Cereal Fish	Bowl	Bowl	Yes	-
37	Light Birthday Stick	Coming	Candle	No	No
38	Food Forward Break	Movement	Fast	No	Yes
39	Shine Beam Struck	Support	Moon	No	No
40	Peach Arm Tar	Muscles	Pit	No	No
41	Water Mine Shaker	Salt	Salt	Yes	-
42	Palm Shoe House	Tree	Tree	Yes	-
43	Basket Eight Snow	Ball	Ball	Yes	-
44	Wheel Hand Shopping	Going	Cart	No	Partial
45	Right Cat Carbon	House	Copy	No	Partial
46	Home Sea Bed	Water	Sick	No	Yes
47	Nuclear Feud Album	Family	Family	Yes	-
48	Sandwich House Golf	Playing	Club	No	Partial
49	Cross Rain Tie	Blue	Bow	No	Partial
50	Sage Paint Hair	Green	Brush	No	Yes
51	French Car Shoe	Company	Horn	No	Yes
52	Boot Summer Ground	Glass	Camp	No	No
53	Chamber Mask Natural	Death	Gas	No	Yes
54	Mill Tooth Dust	Fine	Saw	No	No
55	Main Sweeper Light	Street	Street	Yes	-
56	Pike Coat Signal	Green	Turn	Yes	No
57	Office Mail Hat	Box	Box	Yes	-
58	Fly Clip Wall	Art	Paper	No	No
59	Age Mile Sand	Stone	Stone	Yes	-
60	Catcher Food Hot	Dog	Dog	Yes	-
61	Wagon Break Radio	Station	Station	Yes	-
62	Tank Hill Secret	Top	Top	Yes	-
63	Health Taker Less	Risk	Care	No	Yes
64	Lift Card Mask	System	Face	No	No
65	Dress Dial Flower	Blue	Sun	No	Yes
66	Force Line Mail	Service	Air	No	Yes

Continued on next page

Table A.1 *Continued from previous page*

No.	Query	comRAT-C	Expected	Correct	Plausible
67	Guy Rain Down	Just	Fall	No	No
68	Eight Skate Stick	Shift	Figure	No	No
69	Down Question Check	Able	Mark	No	No
70	Animal Back Rat	House	Pack	No	Yes
71	Officer Cash Larceny	Petty	Petty	Yes	-
72	Pine Crab Sauce	Apple	Apple	Yes	-
73	House Thumb Pepper	Green	Green	Yes	-
74	Carpet Alert Ink	Red	Red	Yes	-
75	Master Toss Finger	Station	Ring	No	No
76	Hammer Gear Hunter	Box	Head	No	No
77	Knife Light Pal	Hot	Pen	No	No
78	Foul Ground Mate	Water	Play	No	No
79	Change Circuit Cake	Design	Short	No	Yes
80	Way Board Sleep	Deep	Walk	No	No
81	Blank List Mate	Check	Check	Yes	-
82	Tail Water Flood	Control	Gate	No	Yes
83	Marshal Child Piano	Grand	Grand	Yes	-
84	Cover Arm Wear	Political	Under	No	Partial
85	Rain Test Stomach	Acid	Acid	Yes	-
86	Time Blown Nelson	Glass	Full	No	No
87	Pile Market Room	Small	Stock	No	Yes
88	Mouse Bear Sand	Deep	Trap	No	No
89	Cat Number Phone	House	Call	No	Yes
90	Keg Puff Room	Powder	Powder	Yes	-
91	Trip House Goal	Field	Field	Yes	-
92	Fork Dark Man	Green	Pitch	No	Yes
93	Fence Card Master	Post	Post	Yes	-
94	Test Runner Map	Road	Road	Yes	-
95	Dive Light Rocket	Engine	Sky	No	Partial
96	Man Glue Star	power	Super	No	Yes
97	Tooth Potato Heart	Sweet	Sweet	Yes	-
98	Illness Bus Computer	Terminal	Terminal	Yes	-
99	Type Ghost Screen	Silent	Writer	No	Yes
100	Mail Board Lung	Service	Black	No	Partial
101	Teeth Arrest Start	False	False	Yes	-
102	Iron Shovel Engine	Old	Steam	No	Yes
103	Wet Law Business	Suit	Suit	Yes	-
104	Rope Truck Line	Tight	Tow	No	No
105	Off Military First	Duty	Base	No	Yes
106	Spoon Cloth Card	Table	Table	Yes	-
107	Cut Cream War	Cold	Cold	Yes	-
108	Note Chain Master	Key	Key	Yes	-
109	Shock Shave Taste	Treatment	After	No	Partial
110	Wise Work Tower	Clock	Clock	Yes	-
111	Grass King Meat	Dead	Crab	No	Yes
112	Baby Spring Cap	Blus	Shower	No	Partial

Continued on next page

Table A.1 *Continued from previous page*

No.	Query	comRAT-C	Expected	Correct	Plausible
113	Break Bean Cake	Coffee	Coffee	Yes	–
114	Cry Front Ship	War	Battle	No	Yes
115	Hold Print Stool	Silver	Foot	No	No
116	Roll Bean Fish	Sauce	Jelly	No	Partial
117	Horse Human Drag	Sense	Race	No	No
118	Oil Bar Tuna	Salad	Salad	Yes	–
119	Bottom Curve Hop	Level	Bell	No	No
120	Tomato Bomb Picker	Cherry	Cherry	Yes	–
121	Pea Shell Chest	Nuts	Nut	Yes	–
122	Line Fruit Drunk	Star	Punch	No	No
123	Bump Egg Step	Small	Goose	No	Yes
124	Fight Control Machine	Political	Gun	No	Yes
125	Home Arm Room	Free	Rest	No	Yes
126	Child Scan Wash	Body	Brain	No	Yes
127	Nose Stone Bear	Cold	Brown	No	Partial
128	End Line Lock	Dead	Dead	Yes	–
129	Control Place Rate	Actual	Birth	No	Yes
130	Lounge Hour Napkin	Cocktail	Cocktail	Yes	–
131	Artist Hatch Route	Escape	Escape	Yes	–
132	Pet Bottom Garden	Rock	Rock	Yes	–
133	Mate Shoes Total	Work	Running	No	Yes
134	Self Attorney Spending	Defense	Defense	Yes	–
135	Board Blade Back	Wall	Switch	No	Partial
136	Land Hand House	Just	Farm	No	Yes
137	Hungry Order Belt	Money	Money	Yes	–
138	Forward Flush Razor	Straight	Straight	Yes	–
139	Shadow Chart Drop	Eye	Eye	Yes	–
140	Way Ground Weather	Stations	Fair	No	Yes
141	Cast Side Jump	Different	Broad	No	Yes
142	Back Step Screen	Door	Door	Yes	–
143	Reading Service Stick	Man	Lip	No	Yes
144	Over Plant Horse	Dear	Power	No	No

Table A.2: Results of the comRAT v2 solver. w_a, w_b, w_c are the 3 query items and w_{ans} is the answer. The third column reflects how often each of the three query words appears in conjunction with all other expressions. The fourth column shows the frequency of the expression formed by each of the query words with the answer word.

ID	w_a	w_b	w_c	w_{ans}	$\sum w_a$	$\sum w_b$	$\sum w_c$	$fr(w_a, w_{ans})$	$fr(w_b, w_{ans})$	$fr(w_c, w_{ans})$
1	cottage	swiss	cake	cheese	1089	1109	4105	342	233	50
2	cream	skate	water	ice	14534	134	74199	6777	39	803
3	loser	throat	spot	sore	218	1237	9251	52	351	112
4	rocking	wheel	high	chair	1008	4459	143097	653	876	
5	fountain	baking	pop	soda	664	9129	4410	107	1329	127
6	preserve	ranger	tropical	forest	174	547	3520	28	55	193
7	cane	daddy	plum	sugar	1038	155	1088	514	60	40
8	fish	mine	rush	gold	18898	2299	5431	45	566	632
9	political	surprise	line	party	133666	2852	50904	1551	85	446
10	high	district	house	school	143097	14468	79427	47596	3192	149
11	sense	courtesy	place	common	19399	387	38640	3701	72	271
12	flower	friend	scout	girl	3517	16399	844	82	700	160
13	print	berry	bird	blue	4491	2197	4724	84	173	52
14	pie	luck	belly	pot	3622	6662	1415	126	69	47
15	opera	hand	dish	soap	7994	46110	4359	962	29	143
16	cadet	capsule	ship	space	24	124	55325	24	73	110
17	sleeping	bean	trash	bag	4432	2706	1356	1054	76	159
18	dust	cereal	fish	bowl	3297	669	18898	65	74	55
19	nuclear	feud	album	family	34776	218	3883	437	125	69
20	chamber	mask	natural	gas	2931	1558	36751	248	232	4233
21	main	sweeper	light	street	33428	69	34498	849	39	110
22	age	mile	sand	stone	71469	710	3077	448	124	170
23	catcher	food	hot	dog	141	44971	27313	28	366	930
24	wagon	break	radio	station	1883	38241	24380	1101	144	1937
25	officer	cash	larceny	petty	19472	7231	99	360	57	25
26	pine	crab	sauce	apple	4923	1255	10418	439	78	35
27	house	thumb	pepper	green	79427	681	11046	3206	69	305
28	carpet	alert	ink	red	1707	874	1256	799	48	451
29	marshal	child	piano	grand	360	35218	2277	75	26	311
30	rain	test	stomach	acid	7436	30341	1664	870	88	112
31	keg	puff	room	powder	81	363	91097	81	37	111
32	trip	house	goal	field	8420	79427	10348	682	87	1416
33	fence	card	master	post	2770	19369	4762	117	100	45
34	test	runner	map	road	30341	658	3132	46	72	916
35	tooth	potato	heart	sweet	1077	3865	28454	199	867	446
36	illness	bus	computer	terminal	4269	7851	27385	197	85	176
37	wet	law	business	suit	4717	64118	65799	115	1686	338
38	spoon	cloth	card	table	16137	4018	19369	3422	172	325
39	note	chain	master	key	10749	5882	4762	597	162	30
40	wise	work	tower	clock	4239	102110	3110	66	65	129
41	break	bean	cake	coffee	38241	2706	4105	119	27	99
42	oil	bar	tuna	salad	48522	20967	1075	68	170	122
43	tomato	bomb	picker	cherry	3472	7526	210	68	25	24
44	end	line	lock	dead	28869	50904	1463	662	645	25
45	control	place	rate	birth	44203	38640	32204	2145	96	294
46	artist	hatch	route	escape	6309	1137	2051	39	94	249
47	pet	bottom	garden	rock	4163	11488	8467	35	307	157
48	self	attorney	spending	defense	2471	19183	12439	144	2095	780
49	back	step	screen	door	59215	11411	11972	2906	27	1126

Table A.3: Continuation of results of the comRAT v2 solver. The second column shows the probability of the answer, given each of the query items. The third column shows the total probability of the answer, given equal influence from all three items. The fourth column shows the influence of each of the query words in obtaining this particular answer – this influence might be different for different possible answers.

ID	$P(w_{ans} \mid w_a)$	$P(w_{ans} \mid w_b)$	$P(w_{ans} \mid w_c)$	$P(w_{ans})$	$P(w_a \mid w_{ans})$	$P(w_b \mid w_{ans})$	$P(w_c \mid w_{ans})$
1	0.314	0.2101	0.0122	0.1788	0.59	0.39	0.02
2	0.4663	0.291	0.0108	0.2561	0.61	0.38	0.01
3	0.2385	0.2838	0.0121	0.1781	0.45	0.53	0.02
4	0.6478	0.1965	0.0013	0.2819	0.77	0.23	0.0
5	0.1611	0.1456	0.0288	0.1118	0.48	0.43	0.09
6	0.1609	0.1005	0.0548	0.1054	0.51	0.32	0.17
7	0.4952	0.3871	0.0368	0.3063	0.54	0.42	0.04
8	0.0024	0.2462	0.1164	0.1216	0.01	0.67	0.32
9	0.0116	0.0298	0.0088	0.0167	0.23	0.59	0.17
10	0.3326	0.2206	0.0019	0.185	0.6	0.4	0.0
11	0.1908	0.186	0.007	0.1279	0.5	0.48	0.02
12	0.0233	0.0427	0.1896	0.0852	0.09	0.17	0.74
13	0.0187	0.0787	0.011	0.0362	0.17	0.73	0.1
14	0.0348	0.0104	0.0332	0.0261	0.44	0.13	0.42
15	0.1203	6.0E-4	0.0328	0.0513	0.78	0.0	0.21
16	1.0	0.5887	0.002	0.5302	0.63	0.37	0.0
17	0.2378	0.0281	0.1173	0.1277	0.62	0.07	0.31
18	0.0197	0.1106	0.0029	0.0444	0.15	0.83	0.02
19	0.0126	0.5734	0.0178	0.2012	0.02	0.95	0.03
20	0.0846	0.1489	0.1152	0.1162	0.24	0.43	0.33
21	0.0254	0.5652	0.0032	0.1979	0.04	0.95	0.01
22	0.0063	0.1746	0.0552	0.0787	0.03	0.74	0.23
23	0.1986	0.0081	0.034	0.0803	0.82	0.03	0.14
24	0.5847	0.0038	0.0795	0.2226	0.88	0.01	0.12
25	0.0185	0.0079	0.2525	0.093	0.07	0.03	0.91
26	0.0892	0.0622	0.0034	0.0516	0.58	0.4	0.02
27	0.0404	0.1013	0.0276	0.0564	0.24	0.6	0.16
28	0.4681	0.0549	0.3591	0.294	0.53	0.06	0.41
29	0.2083	7.0E-4	0.1366	0.1152	0.6	0.0	0.4
30	0.117	0.0029	0.0673	0.0624	0.62	0.02	0.36
31	1.0	0.1019	0.0012	0.3677	0.91	0.09	0.0
32	0.081	0.0011	0.1368	0.073	0.37	0.01	0.63
33	0.0422	0.0052	0.0094	0.019	0.74	0.09	0.17
34	0.0015	0.1094	0.2925	0.1345	0.0	0.27	0.72
35	0.1848	0.2243	0.0157	0.1416	0.43	0.53	0.04
36	0.0461	0.0108	0.0064	0.0211	0.73	0.17	0.1
37	0.0244	0.0263	0.0051	0.0186	0.44	0.47	0.09
38	0.2121	0.0428	0.0168	0.0905	0.78	0.16	0.06
39	0.0555	0.0275	0.0063	0.0298	0.62	0.31	0.07
40	0.0156	6.0E-4	0.0415	0.0192	0.27	0.01	0.72
41	0.0031	0.01	0.0241	0.0124	0.08	0.27	0.65
42	0.0014	0.0081	0.1135	0.041	0.01	0.07	0.92
43	0.0196	0.0033	0.1143	0.0457	0.14	0.02	0.83
44	0.0229	0.0127	0.0171	0.0176	0.44	0.24	0.32
45	0.0485	0.0025	0.0091	0.02	0.81	0.04	0.15
46	0.0062	0.0827	0.1214	0.0701	0.03	0.39	0.58
47	0.0084	0.0267	0.0185	0.0179	0.16	0.5	0.35
48	0.0583	0.1092	0.0627	0.0767	0.25	0.47	0.27
49	0.0491	0.0024	0.0941	0.0485	0.34	0.02	0.65

Table A.4: Using comRAT for query generation – these examples show how the answer (left column) can be used to navigate to the possible query items (right column). A valid RAT query will thus be made of any choice of three words on the right cell, for the answer on the left.

Answer	Candidate query items $w_1, w_2, ..., w_n$
health	care, insurance, problems, services, benefits, professionals, officials, issues, effects, risks, plan, department, system, status, home, food, problem, club, coverage, risk, policy, departments, education, plans, reform, maintenance, programs, conditions, information, outcomes, promotion, experts, workers, agencies, centers, community, state, issue, needs, concerns, clinic, service, clinics, center, hazards, hazard, professional, consequences, program, clubs, costs, reasons, authorities, government, heart, crisis, treatment, practitioners, insurers, threat, bone, providers, questions, child, disparities, condition, research, quality, agency, systems, school, county, impacts, concern, behaviors, organizations, field, facilities, community;
care	health, child, day, reform, system, providers, costs, patient, home, plan, services, unit, bill, workers, center, professionals, centers, facilities, provider, coverage, industry, needs, programs, quality, program, settings, plans, skin, facility, delivery, insurance, physicians, debate, products, organizations, hospital, benefits, hospice, emergency, systems, physician, legislation, units, charity, worker, crisis, companies, issues, spending, policy, doctors, hair;
room	living, dining, temperature, hotel, locker, emergency, waiting, conference, dressing, back, family, operating, control, Table, guest, sitting, hospital, drawing, laundry, service, motel, weight, dorm, engine, floor, door, meeting, jury, chat, storage, war, wiggle, music, delivery, rest, window, reception, breakfast, rec, interrogation, hearing, press, briefing, breathing, screening, training, reading, wall, standing, couch, recovery, examination, break, game, powder, rates, board, throne, computer, exam, number, mail, air, basement, interview;
law	enforcement, school, firm, state, professor, firms, degree, schools, immigration, practice, case, tax, student, students, office, family, labor, canon, practice, rights, election, professors, clerk, partner, copyright, reform, clerks, tort, antitrust, review, offices, books, counsel, competition;
parking	lot, garage, space, area, spaces, spot, valet, tickets, ticket, street, place;
family	members, member, life, values, history, planning, room, business, friend, income, support, man, tree, name, structure, farm, relationships, reunion, doctor, tradition, unit, ties, time, problems, vacation, issues, size, affair, law, therapist, leave, car, photos, farms, background, physician, therapy, practice, dinner, system, court, environment, gatherings, dog, friends, responsibilities, crime, dynamics, systems, involvement, violence, connections, relations, groups, matters, reunification, stories, counselling, businesses, situation, fortune, photo, activities, incomes, medicine, reunions, photographs, drama, farmers, budget, doctors, obligations, vacations, pictures, portrait, home, estate, entertainment, caregivers, trip, group, needs;
ice	cream, water, cubes, vanilla, age, sea, hockey, sheet, cube, crystals, pack, chest, storm, rink, cap, sheets, water, caps, creams, chocolate, ages, bucket;
call	phone, wake-up, conference, telephone, roll, information, center, judgment, wakeup, house; etc.

Fig. A.1: vRAT training and test queries *(continues on next page)*

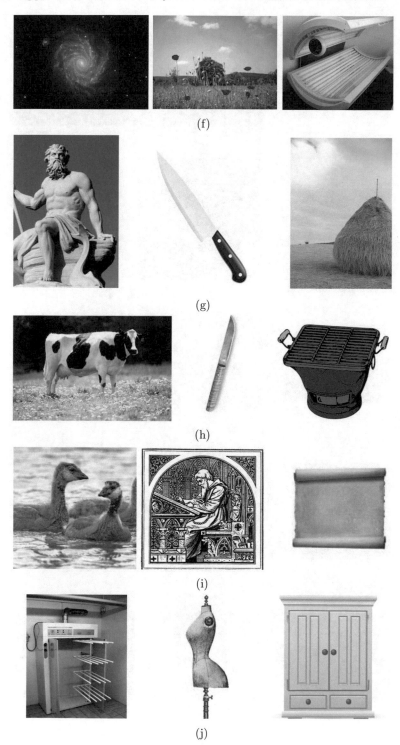

Fig. A.1: vRAT training and test queries *(continues on next page)*

Fig. A.1: vRAT training and test queries *(continues on next page)*

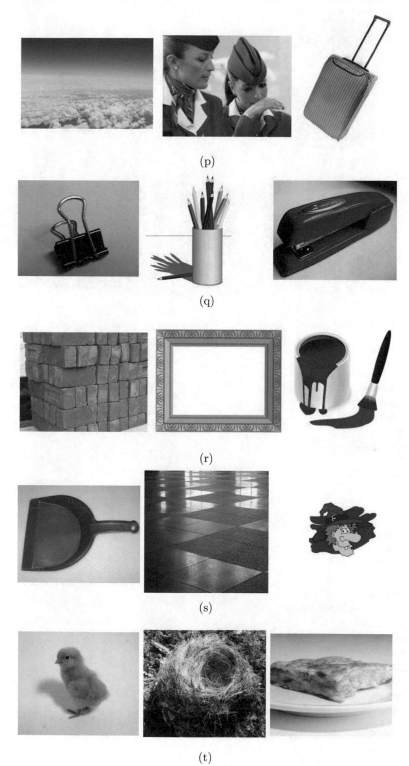

(p)

(q)

(r)

(s)

(t)

Fig. A.1: vRAT training and test queries *(continues on next page)*

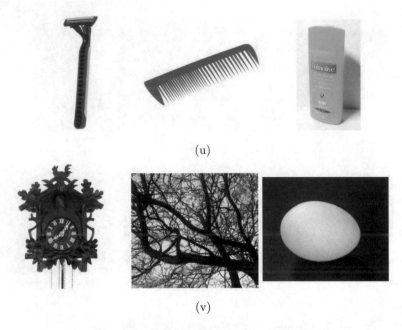

(u)

(v)

Fig. A.1: vRAT training and test queries

Answers:
a) hand
b) water
c) fire
d) electricity
e) foot
f) sun
g) fork
h) steak
i) quill
j) clothes
k) table
l) garlic
m) road
n) needle
o) ATM / cash machine
p) airplane
q) paper
r) wall
s) broom
t) egg
u) hair
v) bird

B

Appendix B – OROC Results

Table B.1: Evaluation of 30 alternative use statements made by the $OROC$ prototype system on Novelty, Likability and Usefulness (mean) by human judges.

No.	Statement	Novelty	Likability	Usefulness
1.	A cup may be used to carry water	1,68	4,53	5,53
2.	A newspaper may be used to wipe kitchen surfaces with	3,03	2,85	3,65
3.	A toothbrush may be used to brush a coat with	4,44	2,91	3,03
4.	A cup may be used to store food in	2,65	3,88	4,47
5.	A newspaper may be used to hang in front of a window in order to shade window with	2,97	3,06	4,56
6.	Dental floss can be used to tie things with	4,65	3,38	4,50
7.	A carpet may be used as wall decoration	2,12	3,71	5,00
8.	A cup may be used to put flowers in	1,88	4,53	5,03
9.	A newspaper may be used to wipe dishes with	4,26	2,00	2,74
10.	A toothbrush may be used to brush shoes with	3,50	3,97	4,41
11.	Dental floss can be used to hang objects on the wall with	5,03	3,53	3,76
12.	A carpet may be used to wrap self with and warm up	4,44	2,88	3,50
13.	A newspaper may be used to wipe your hands with	3,29	2,56	3,50
14.	A toothbrush may be used to sweep the floor	4,44	2,12	1,88
15.	Dental floss may be used for sewing	5,41	3,97	4,29
16.	A carpet can be used to cover and protect the sofa	4,85	2,74	3,62
17.	A cup may be used to hold earth and plants	2,91	4,59	4,85
18.	A newspaper may be used to dry off your body	5,15	1,82	2,59
19.	A toothbrush may be used to clean the toilet with	4,21	2,53	3,03
20.	A cup may be used to keep objects in	2,21	4,79	5,18
21.	A carpet may be used as a bed cover	4,59	2,56	3,32
22.	Dental floss may be used to hang clothes on to dry	6,00	2,68	2,06

Continued on next page.

Table B.1 *Continued from previous page*

No.	Statement	Novelty	Likability	Usefulness
23.	A carpet can be used on the bed as a sheet	5,59	1,79	1,85
24.	A cup may be used to cook in	4,38	3,12	2,94
25.	A newspaper may be used to write on	1,65	3,91	4,32
26.	A toothbrush can be used to paint the wall with	4,85	2,74	2,53
27.	Dental floss can be used to tie shoes with	5,53	2,71	3,03
28.	A carpet can be used to sleep on	2,41	3,47	4,29
29.	A cup may be used to hold a candle	2,53	4,65	5,59
30.	A newspaper may be used to wipe shoes on	3,03	3,71	3,94

Table B.2: More examples of Object Replacement made by *OROC* with a knowledge base that includes items from a household domain.

More object replacement results with *OROC*
Maybe Book can be used as decoration
Maybe Newspaper can be used as decoration
Maybe Newspaper can be used to wipe dishes with
Maybe Newspaper can be used to wipe kitchen surfaces with
Maybe Newspaper can be used to wipe your hands with
Maybe Newspaper can be used to dry off your body
Maybe Newspaper can be used to write on
Maybe Newspaper can be used to wipe shoes on
Maybe Newspaper can be used to hang in front of window in order to shade window with
Maybe Bucket can be used to drink from
Maybe Bucket can be used to put flowers in
Maybe Bucket can be used as food container
Maybe Bucket can be used to hold earth and plants
Maybe Bucket can be used to cook in
Maybe Vase can be used to drink from
Maybe Vase can be used to carry water
Maybe Vase can be used as food container
Maybe Vase can be used to hold earth and plants
Maybe Shelf can be used to surf on
Maybe Surfboard can be used as support
Maybe Bowl can be used to drink from
Maybe Bowl can be used to carry water
Maybe Bowl can be used to put flowers in
Maybe Bowl can be used to hold earth and plants
Maybe Bowl can be used to cook in
Maybe Nail can be used to separate objects
Maybe Nail can be used to pin object in place
Maybe Nail can be used to separate wood
Maybe Nail can be used as a weapon
Maybe Nail can be used to scratch with
Maybe Nail can be used to stop door from closing

Continued on next page

Table B.2 *Continued from previous page*

More object replacement results with *OROC*
Maybe Flowerpot can be used to drink from
Maybe Flowerpot can be used to carry water
Maybe Flowerpot can be used to put flowers in
Maybe Flowerpot can be used as food container
Maybe Flowerpot can be used to cook in
Maybe Flowerpot can be used to keep things in
Maybe Pot can be used to drink from
Maybe Pot can be used to carry water
Maybe Pot can be used to put flowers in
Maybe Pot can be used as food container
Maybe Pot can be used to hold earth and plants
Maybe Pan can be used to defend from rain
Maybe Pan can be used to put on top of a pot so that the warmth stays in
Maybe Rubber band can be used to hold hair with
Maybe Tree stumps can be used to support tabletop
...

Table B.3: Other uses given by human participants for five given objects. How frequently a particular answer was given across participants ("Fr.") is shown in the third column.

Object	Other Uses	Fr.
Cup	to put things in (dessert, pencils/pens/brushes, mix sauce, mix paint, coffee, etc.)	9
	for sound (speaker, headphone, musical instrumental, hear through a wall)	7
	to draw shapes (shapes)	3
	bird feeder	2
	build a tower with other cups (incl sand)	2
	hat	2
	make a mosaic with a broken cup	2
	to cook in	2
	to throw with	2
	to use as a decoration	2
	use as a painting (canvas/)	2
	as a bell	1
	as a shelf separator (for identical one on each corner)	1
	cap for a bottle	1
	clay pigeon (shooting)	1
	device for competitive sport	1
	hammer	1
	mortar to make allioli	1
	paperweight	1
	put publicity in it	1

Continued on next page

Table B.3 *Continued from previous page*

Object	Other Uses	Fr.
	shovel (dig on earth)	1
	to eat from	1
	to measure quantities	1
	use it as a mace to smash a garlic using the basis of the cup	1
	use it as a spoon	1
	use it with a knife	1
Newspaper	to make shapes and origami figures (boat/hat)	10
	to wrap something	8
	clean (glass/brush/toilet)	5
	cover (tablecloth/bed/book)	5
	to cut images/text from and make a collage/word	3
	wall decoration	2
	adjust one of the legs of a table	1
	adjust the window or a pot that does not close hermetically	1
	an umbrella	1
	containers of grains	1
	filling shoes to store for a long period	1
	keep temperature of food	1
	levelling material for tables	1
	make baskets or containers hardening it with strips	1
	preventing bleeding (as a plaster)	1
	protecting against cold weather	1
	protection when painting	1
	rolled around a weak chair-leg or any weak tube to make it stronger	1
	the newspaper can be applied to open a bottle of beer	1
	to burn	1
	to dry the floor	1
	to protect the table when cutting using a cutter	1
	to protect your hands when taking something from the oven or the cooker	1
	twisting it to make a stick to mix paintings	1
	wrapping a mommy for a fancy dress event	1
Toothbrush	clean (small objects, parts, things, copper, corners)	16
	brushing (car, hedgehog, eyebrows, hair)	4
	combing	3
	a toothbrush can be used to hang things	1
	as a nail of a sundial	1
	constructing funny animals	1
	for dying your hair	1
	making sand drawings	1
	rabbets or splines in the windows	1
	stabbing device	1
	sticking holes into things	1
	to exfoliate the skin making circles with the toothbrush	1
	to put grease on it and use it to collect the hair and make a bun	1

Continued on next page

Table B.3 *Continued from previous page*

Object	Other Uses	Fr.
	to put soap and use it to remove something with water to make foam	1
	to put wax and polish shoes	1
	toy for children	1
	tubes	1
	weapon against raptors	1
Dental floss	fishing line	4
	necklace, earring, bracelet like jewelry	4
	crocheting something out of it	2
	as a belt	1
	as a police cordon	1
	caress/massage	1
	crafts	1
	cutting soft materials (e.g. butter)	1
	dental floss can be used as a tripping hazard	1
	dental floss can be used for painting	1
	fire starter (esp. waxed floss)	1
	guitar string	1
	hold a bikini	1
	impregnated with glue can be a 3D printer wire	1
	keyring	1
	macrame	1
	pack	1
	to use as a rope to escape from jail	1
	to cut soft things	1
	to kill a person	1
	to pull a tooth	1
	to stimulate skin	1
	to stop bleeding an injury	1
	to tickle	1
	to tie it to a tissue or handkerchief or scarf and make a bag	1
	to tie it to the handle of a door to close it at a distance	1
	to tie the curtain	1
	to tie the kitchen paper so that it is perfectly folded	1
Carpet	damping noise/vibrations	2
	keeping fire lit	2
	to wrap objects	2
	a carpet can be used as a curtain	1
	as an umbrella to protect from the sun	1
	build a tent for playing with children	1
	carpets can be used to slide a slide	1
	door	1
	easing access to water on stony beach	1
	hiding Cleopatra	1
	hieroglyphic drawings	1
	moving light furniture around with (or objects)	1

Continued on next page

Table B.3 *Continued from previous page*

Object	Other Uses	Fr.
	packing stuff in	1
	posters or drawing sheets by rolling them together	1
	rolled can be a cushion or armrest	1
	separation of spaces	1
	small carpets are a good lying surface for pets	1
	sunbathing on the beach	1
	to add water to and plant seeds to germinate	1
	to cut it and stick it to your shoes to get new soles	1
	to fly	1
	to make spiral drawings by rolling the carpet and put it inside a bucket of paint	1
	to paint it and create a new carpet	1
	to protect a piece of furniture from the dust	1
	to protect against wind	1
	to protect architectural drawings	1
	to stick it to the wall of a bath to transform the bath into a seat	1
	wall	1

References

Adamson, R. E. (1952). Functional fixedness as related to problem solving: A repetition of three experiments. *Journal of Experimental Psychology*, *44*(4), 288.

Aerts, D., & Gabora, L. (2005). A theory of concepts and their combinations II: A Hilbert space representation. *Kybernetes*, *34*(1/2), 192–221.

Ansburg, P. I., & Hill, K. (2003). Creative and analytic thinkers differ in their use of attentional resources. *Personality and Individual Differences*, *34*(7), 1141–1152.

Arnon, R., & Kreitler, S. (1984). Effects of meaning training on overcoming functional fixedness. *Current Psychology*, *3*(4), 11–24.

Bailey, A. M., McDaniel, W. F., & Thomas, R. K. (2007). Approaches to the study of higher cognitive functions related to creativity in nonhuman animals. *Methods*, *42*(1), 3–11.

Barsalou, L. (2003). Abstraction in perceptual symbol systems. In *Philosophical Transactions of the Royal Society of London* (Vol. 358, p. 1177-87).

Barsalou, L., & Wiemer-Hastings, K. (2005). Situating abstract concepts. In D. Pecher & R. Zwaan (Eds.), *Grounding cognition: The role of perception and action in memory, language, and thought* (p. 129-163). New York: Cambridge University Press.

Batchelder, W. H., & Alexander, G. E. (2012, Fall). Insight problem solving: A critical examination of the possibility of formal theory. *The Journal of Problem Solving*, *5*(1), 56-100.

Boden, M. (2003). *The creative mind: Myths and mechanisms*. Routledge.

Bou, F., Schorlemmer, M., Corneli, J., Gomez Ramirez, D., Maclean, E., Smaill, A., & Pease, A. (2015). The role of blending in mathematical invention. In *Proceedings of the Sixth International Conference of Computational Creativity* (pp. 55–62).

Bowden, E. M., & Jung-Beeman, M. (2003). Normative data for 144 compound remote associate problems. *Behavior Research Methods, Instruments, & Computers*, *35*(4), 634–639.

© Springer Nature Switzerland AG 2020

A.-M. Oltețeanu, *Cognition and the Creative Machine*,

https://doi.org/10.1007/978-3-030-30322-8

Brédart, S., Ward, T. B., & Marczewski, P. (1998). Structured imagination of novel creatures' faces. *The American Journal of Psychology*.

Brewer, W. F., & Treyens, J. C. (1981). Role of schemata in memory for places. *Cognitive Psychology*, *13*(2), 207–230.

Cai, D. J., Mednick, S. A., Harrison, E. M., Kanady, J. C., & Mednick, S. C. (2009). REM, not incubation, improves creativity by priming associative networks. *Proceedings of the National Academy of Sciences*, *106*(25), 10130–10134.

Carpenter, J. (2004). Electronic text composition project. *The Slought Foundation*. Retrieved from https://slought.org/media/files/sf_1199.pdf

Chermahini, S. A., Hickendorff, M., & Hommel, B. (2012). Development and validity of a Dutch version of the Remote Associates Task: An item-response theory approach. *Thinking Skills and Creativity*, *7*(3), 177–186.

Chu, Y., & MacGregor, J. N. (2011, Winter). Human performance on insight problem solving: A review. *The Journal of Problem Solving*, *3*(2).

Cohen, H. (1995). The further exploits of AARON, painter. *Stanford Humanities Review*, *4*(2), 141–158.

Colton, S. (2012a). *Automated theory formation in pure mathematics*. Springer Science & Business Media.

Colton, S. (2012b). The painting fool: Stories from building an automated painter. In *Computers and creativity* (pp. 3–38). Springer.

Colton, S., Bundy, A., & Walsh, T. (2000). On the notion of interestingness in automated mathematical discovery. *International Journal of Human-Computer Studies*, *53*(3), 351–375.

Colton, S., Goodwin, J., & Veale, T. (2012). Full-FACE poetry generation. In *Proceedings of the Third International Conference on Computational Creativity* (pp. 95–102).

Colton, S., Pease, A., & Charnley, J. (2011). Computational creativity theory: The FACE and IDEA descriptive models. In *Proceedings of the Second International Conference on Computational Creativity* (pp. 90–95).

Colton, S., & Wiggins, G. (2012). Computational Creativity: The Final Frontier? In *Proceedings of the 20th European conference on artificial intelligence* (pp. 21–26). IOS Press.

Cook, M., & Colton, S. (2014). Ludus ex machina: Building a 3D game designer that competes alongside humans. In *Proceedings of the 5th International Conference on Computational Creativity*.

Craik, K. (1943). *The nature of explanation*. Cambridge:Cambridge University Press.

Csikszentmihalyi, M. (1996). *Creativity: Flow and the psychology of discovery and invention*. New York: HarperCollins.

Cunningham, J. B., MacGregor, J. N., Gibb, J., & Haar, J. (2009). Categories of insight and their correlates: An exploration of relationships among classic-type insight problems, rebus puzzles, remote associates and esoteric analogies. *The Journal of Creative Behavior*, *43*(4), 262–280.

Dale, P. S., Loftus, E. F., & Rathbun, L. (1978). The influence of the form of the question on the eyewitness testimony of preschool children. *Journal of Psycholinguistic Research*, *7*(4), 269–277.

Davidson, J. E., & Sternberg, R. J. (1984). The role of insight in intellectual giftedness. *Gifted Child Quarterly*, *28*(2), 58–64.

Dawkins, R. (1989). The selfish gene. In (2nd ed., p. 192). Oxford University Press.

Dow, G. T., & Mayer, R. E. (2004). Teaching students to solve insight problems: Evidence for domain specificity in creativity training. *Creativity Research Journal*, *16*(4), 389–398.

Dunbar, K. (1993). Concept discovery in a scientific domain. *Cognitive Science*, *17*(3), 397–434.

Dunbar, K. (1995). How scientists really reason: Scientific reasoning in real-world laboratories. In *The nature of insight* (Vol. 18, pp. 365–395). Cambridge, MA: MIT Press.

Duncker, K. (1945). On problem solving. *Psychological Monographs*, *58*(5, Whole No.270).

Eppe, M., Confalonieri, R., Maclean, E., Kaliakatsos, M., Cambouropoulos, E., Schorlemmer, M., & Kühnberger, K.-U. (2015). Computational invention of cadences and chord progressions by conceptual chord-blending.

Ericsson, K., & Simon, H. (1993). Protocol analysis: Verbal reports as data (rev. ed.) MIT press. *Cambridge, MA*.

Evans, T. G. (1964). A heuristic program to solve geometric-analogy problems. In *Proceedings of the april 21-23, 1964, Spring Joint Computer Conference* (pp. 327–338).

Falkenhainer, B., Forbus, K. D., & Gentner, D. (1989). The structure-mapping engine: Algorithm and examples. *Artificial intelligence*, *41*(1), 1–63.

Fauconnier, G., & Turner, M. (1998). Conceptual integration networks. *Cognitive science*, *22*(2), 133–187.

Fikes, R., & Kehler, T. (1985). The role of frame-based representation in reasoning. *Communications of the ACM*, *28*(9), 904–920.

Finke, R. A., Ward, T. B., & Smith, S. M. (1992). *Creative cognition: Theory, research, and applications*. MIT press Cambridge, MA.

Fleck, J. I., & Weisberg, R. W. (2013). Insight versus analysis: Evidence for diverse methods in problem solving. *Journal of Cognitive Psychology*, *25(4)*, 436–463.

Fleuriot, J., Maclean, E., Smaill, A., & Winterstein, D. (2014). Reinventing the complex numbers. In *Proceedings of the 3rd International Workshop on Computational Creativity, Concept Invention, and General Intelligence (C3GI 2014)*.

Floridi, L. (2011). *The philosophy of information*. Oxford University Press.

Forbus, K. D., Gentner, D., & Law, K. (1995). MAC/FAC: A model of similarity-based retrieval. *Cognitive Science*, *19*(2), 141–205.

Freksa, C. (1991). Qualitative spatial reasoning. In D. Mark & A. Frank (Eds.), *Cognitive and linguistic aspects of geographic space* (p. 361-372). Kluwer, Dordrecht, Holland.

Gabora, L. (2005). Creative thought as a non-Darwinian evolutionary process. *The Journal of Creative Behavior*, *39*(4), 262–283.

Gabora, L. (2015). How creative ideas take shape. *arXiv preprint – arXiv:1501.04406*.

Gärdenfors, P. (2004). *Conceptual spaces: The geometry of thought*. Bradford Books.

Gardner, M. (2014). *Mathematics, magic and mystery*. Courier Corporation.

Gattis, M. (2001). Space as a basis for abstract thought. In M. Gattis (Ed.), *Spatial schemas and abstract thought*. MIT Press, Cambridge, MA.

Gentner, D. (1983). Structure-mapping: A theoretical framework for analogy. *Cognitive science*, *7*(2), 155–170.

Gentner, D. (2010). Where hypotheses come from: Learning new relations by structural alignment. *Journal of Cognition and Development*, *11*(3).

German, T. P., & Barrett, H. C. (2005). Functional fixedness in a technologically sparse culture. *Psychological Science*, *16*(1), 1–5.

Gervás, P. (2010). Engineering linguistic creativity: Bird flight and jet planes. In *Proceedings of the NAACL HLT 2010 Second Workshop on Computational Approaches to Linguistic Creativity* (pp. 23–30).

Gibson, E. J., & Pick, A. D. (2000). *An ecological approach to perceptual learning and development*. Oxford University Press, USA.

Gibson, J. J. (1977). The theory of affordance. In R. Shaw & J. Bransford (Eds.), *Perceiving, acting, and knowing*. Hillsdale, NJ: Lawrence Erlbaum Associates.

Gibson, J. J. (1979). *The ecological approach to visual perception: classic edition*. Boston: Houghton-Mifflin.

Gilhooly, K., Fioratou, E., Anthony, S., & Wynn, V. (2007). Divergent thinking: Strategies and executive involvement in generating novel uses for familiar objects. *British Journal of Psychology*, *98*(4), 611–625.

Gillan, D. J., Premack, D., & Woodruff, G. (1981). Reasoning in the chimpanzee: I. Analogical reasoning. *Journal of Experimental Psychology: Animal Behavior Processes*, *7*(1), 1.

Glisky, E. L., & Schacter, D. L. (1988). Long-term retention of computer learning by patients with memory disorders. *Neuropsychologia*, *26*(1), 173–178.

Greene, E., Bodrumlu, T., & Knight, K. (2010). Automatic analysis of rhythmic poetry with applications to generation and translation. In *Proceedings of the 2010 Conference on Empirical Methods in Natural Language Processing* (pp. 524–533).

Guilford, J. P. (1956). The structure of intellect. *Psychological bulletin*, *53*(4), 267.

Guilford, J. P. (1967). *The nature of human intelligence*. New York: McGraw-Hill.

Gust, H., Kühnberger, K.-U., & Schmid, U. (2006). Metaphors and heuristic-driven theory projection (HDTP). *Theoretical Computer Science*, *354*(1), 98–117.

Hadamard, J. (1945). *The mathematician's mind: The psychology of invention in the mathematical field.* Princeton University Press.

Halford, G. S., Wilson, W. H., Guo, J., Gayler, R. W., Wiles, J., & Stewart, J. (1994). Connectionist implications for processing capacity limitations in analogies. *Advances in connectionist and neural computation theory*, *2*, 363–415.

Hamilton, M. A. (1982). "Jamaicanizing" the Mednick Remote Associates Test of creativity. *Perceptual and Motor Skills*, *55*(1), 321–322.

Haven, K. (2006). *100 greatest science inventions of all time.* Libraries Unlimited.

Hebb, D. O. (1949). *The organization of behavior: A neuropsychological approach.* New York: Wiley and Sons.

Hélie, S., & Sun, R. (2010). Incubation, insight, and creative problem solving: A unified theory and a connectionist model. *Psychological review*, *117*(3), 994.

Helmholtz, H. v. (1896). Visual perception: Essential readings. *Physiological optics*(3(26)), 1–36.

Hofstadter, D. R., Mitchell, M., et al. (1994). The Copycat project: A model of mental fluidity and analogy-making. *Advances in connectionist and neural computation theory*, *2*(31-112), 29–30.

Holyoak, K., & Thagard, P. (1996). *Mental leaps: Analogy in creative thought.* Cambridge, MA: MIT Press.

Imai, M., Gentner, D., & Uchida, N. (1994). Children's theories of word meaning: The role of shape similarity in early acquisition. *Cognitive Development*, *9*(1), 45–75.

Indurkhya, B. (1999). An algebraic approach to modeling creativity of metaphor. In *Computation for metaphors, analogy, and agents* (pp. 292–306). Springer.

Jacobs, M. K., & Dominowski, R. L. (1981). Learning to solve insight problems. *Bulletin of the Psychonomic Society*, *17*(4), 171–174.

Johnson, M. (2013). *The body in the mind: The bodily basis of meaning, imagination, and reason.* University of Chicago Press.

Johnson-Laird, P. (1983). *Mental models: Towards a cognitive science of language, inference, and consciousness.* Harvard University Press.

Johnson-Laird, P. (1998). Imagery, visualization, and thinking. In J. Hochberg (Ed.), *Perception and cognition at the century's end* (p. 441-467). San Diego, CA: Academic Press.

Jones, G. (2003). Testing two cognitive theories of insight. *Journal of Experimental Psychology: Learning, Memory, and Cognition*, *29*(5), 1017.

Kaplan, C. A., & Simon, H. A. (1990). In search of insight. *Cognitive psychology*, *22*(3), 374–419.

Kaufman, J. C., & Kaufman, A. B. (2004). Applying a creativity framework to animal cognition. *New Ideas in Psychology*, *22*(2), 143–155.

Kim, K. H. (2006). Can we trust creativity tests? A review of the Torrance Tests of Creative Thinking (TTCT). *Creativity Research Journal*, *18*(1), 3–14.

Klahr, D., & Dunbar, K. (1988). Dual space search during scientific reasoning. *Cognitive science*, *12*(1), 1–48.

Knoblich, G., Ohlsson, S., & Raney, G. E. (2001). An eye movement study of insight problem solving. *Memory & Cognition*, *29*(7), 1000–1009.

Koestler, A. (1964). *The act of creation*. New York: Macmillan.

Köhler, W. (1976). *The mentality of apes*. New York: Liveright. (Originally published in 1925).

Lakoff, G., & Johnson, M. (1980). *Metaphors we live by*. University of Chicago Press, Chicago.

Lakoff, G., & Johnson, M. (1999). *Philosophy in the flesh: The embodied mind and its challenge to western thought*. Basic Books, New York.

Landau, B., Smith, L. B., & Jones, S. S. (1988). The importance of shape in early lexical learning. *Cognitive Development*, *3*(3), 299–321.

Langley, P. (1978). Bacon. 1: A general discovery system. In *Proc. 2nd Biennial Conf. of the Canadian Society for Computational Studies of Intelligence* (pp. 173–180).

Langley, P. (1981). Data-driven discovery of physical laws. *Cognitive Science*, *5*(1), 31–54.

Langley, P. (2000). The computational support of scientific discovery. *International Journal of Human-Computer Studies*, *53*(3), 393 - 410.

Langley, P., Bradshaw, G. L., & Simon, H. A. (1981). Bacon. 5: The discovery of conservation laws. In *IJCAI* (Vol. 81, pp. 121–126).

Lassila, O., & McGuinness, D. (2001). The role of frame-based representation on the semantic web. *Linköping Electronic Articles in Computer and Information Science*, *6*(5), 2001.

Lenat, D. B. (1976). *AM: An artificial intelligence approach to discovery in mathematics as heuristic search* (Tech. Rep.). DTIC Document.

Lenat, D. B., & Brown, J. S. (1984). Why AM and EURISKO appear to work. *Artificial intelligence*, *23*(3), 269–294.

Luo, J., & Niki, K. (2003). Function of hippocampus in "insight" of problem solving. *Hippocampus*, *13*(3), 316–323.

Luo, J., Niki, K., & Phillips, S. (2004a). The function of the anterior cingulate cortex (ACC) in the insightful solving of puzzles: The ACC is activated less when the structure of the puzzle is known. *Journal of Psychology in Chinese Societies*, *5*(2), 195–213.

Luo, J., Niki, K., & Phillips, S. (2004b). Neural correlates of the 'Aha! reaction'. *Neuroreport*, *15*(13), 2013–2017.

MacGregor, J. N., & Cunningham, J. B. (2009, Fall). The effects of number and level of restructuring in insight problem solving. *The Journal of Problem Solving*, *2*(2), 130-141.

Machado, P., & Cardoso, A. (2000). NEvAr–the assessment of an evolutionary art tool. In *Proceedings of the AISB00 Symposium on Creative & Cultural Aspects and Applications of AI & Cognitive Science, Birmingham, UK* (Vol. 456).

Mai, X.-Q., Luo, J., Wu, J.-H., & Luo, Y.-J. (2004). "Aha!" effects in a guessing riddle task: An event-related potential study. *Human brain mapping*, *22*(4), 261–270.

Maier, N. R. (1931). Reasoning in humans. II. The solution of a problem and its appearance in consciousness. *Journal of Comparative Psychology*, *12*(2), 181.

Mandler, J. M. (2010). The spatial foundations of the conceptual system. *Language and Cognition*, *2(1)*, 21-44.

Mandler, J. M. (2012). On the spatial foundations of the conceptual system and its enrichment. *Cognitive Science*, *36*(3), 421–451.

Markson, L., Diesendruck, G., & Bloom, P. (2008). The shape of thought. *Developmental Science*, *11*(2), 204-208.

Marr, D. (1982). *Vision: A computational investigation into the human representation and processing of visual information*. WH San Francisco: Freeman and Company.

McGrenere, J., & Ho, W. (2000). Affordances: Clarifying and evolving a concept. In *Proceedings of Graphics Interface 2000* (pp. 179–186).

Medin, D. L., & Shoben, E. J. (1988). Context and structure in conceptual combination. *Cognitive Psychology*, *20*(2), 158–190.

Mednick, S. (1962). The associative basis of the creative process. *Psychological review*, *69*(3), 220.

Mednick, S., & Mednick, M. (1971). *Remote associates test: Examiner's manual*. Houghton Mifflin.

Metcalfe, J., & Wiebe, D. (1987). Intuition in insight and noninsight problem solving. *Memory & cognition*, *15*(3), 238–246.

Milner, B., Corkin, S., & Teuber, H.-L. (1968). Further analysis of the hippocampal amnesic syndrome: 14-year follow-up study of HM. *Neuropsychologia*, *6*(3), 215–234.

Minsky, M. (1975). A framework for representing knowledge. In P. Winston (Ed.), *The psychology of computer vision* (p. 211-277). New York: McGraw-Hill.

Murphy, G. L., & Medin, D. L. (1985). The role of theories in conceptual coherence. *Psychological review*, *92*(3), 289.

Nersessian, N. (2008). *Creating scientific concepts*. Cambridge, MA: MIT Press.

Nevo, B., & Levin, I. (1978). Remote associates test: assessment of creativity in Hebrew. *Megamot*, *24*, 87–98.

Newell, A. (1969). Heuristic programming: Ill-structured problems. In J. Aronofsky (Ed.), *Progress in operations research, iii.*

Newell, A. (1994). *Unified theories of cognition.* Harvard University Press.

Newell, A., & Simon, A. (1972). *Human problem solving.* Englewood Cliffs, NJ: Prentice Hall.

Norman, D. A. (2013). *The design of everyday things: Revised and expanded edition.* Basic Books.

Ohlsson, S. (1983). Restructuring revisited: I. Summary and critique of the Gestalt theory of problem solving. *Scandinavian Journal of Psychology, 25*, 65-78.

Ohlsson, S. (1984). Restructuring revisited: II. An information processing theory of restructuring and insight. *Scandinavian Journal of Psychology, 25*, 117-129.

Olteţeanu, A.-M. (2014). Proceedings of the workshop computational creativity, concept invention, and general intelligence. In *Proceedings of the international conference on computational creativity* (Vol. 01-2014, chap. Two general classes in creative problem-solving? An account based on the cognitive processes involved in the problem structure - representation structure relationship.). Osnabrück: Institute of Cognitive Science.

Olteţeanu, A.-M. (2015). The Input, Coherence, Generativity (ICG) Factors. Towards a Model of Cognitive Informativity Measures for Productive Cognitive Systems. In *Proceedings of the Computational Creativity, Concept Invention, and General Intelligence workshop* (Vol. 02-2015). Osnabrück: Publications of the Institute of Cognitive Science.

Olteţeanu, A.-M. (2016). Towards an approach for computationally assisted creation of insight problems in the practical object domain. In *Proceedings of the Computational Creativity, Concept Invention, and General Intelligence workshop* (Vol. 1767). Osnabrück: CEUR-Ws.

Olteţeanu, A.-M., & Falomir, Z. (2015). comRAT-C: A computational compound remote associate test solver based on language data and its comparison to human performance. *Pattern Recognition Letters, 67*, 81-90. doi: 10.1016/j.patrec.2015.05.015

Olteţeanu, A.-M., & Falomir, Z. (2016). Object replacement and object composition in a creative cognitive system. towards a computational solver of the Alternative Uses Test. *Cognitive Systems Research, 39*, 15–32.

Olteţeanu, A.-M., Gautam, B., & Falomir, Z. (2015). Towards a visual remote associates test and its computational solver. In *Proceedings of the third international workshop on artificial intelligence and cognition 2015* (Vol. 1510, pp. 19–28). CEUR-Ws.

Olteţeanu, A.-M. (2016). From simple machines to Eureka in four not-so-easy steps. Towards creative visuospatial intelligence. In V. Müller (Ed.), *Fundamental issues of artificial intelligence* (Vol. 376, p. 159-180). Springer. doi: 10.1007/978-3-319-26485-1˙11

Olteţeanu, A.-M., Falomir, Z., & Freksa, C. (2018). Artificial cognitive systems that can answer human creativity tests: An approach and two case studies. *IEEE Transactions on Cognitive and Developmental Systems*, *10*(2), 469–475.

Pachet, F. (2012). Musical virtuosity and creativity. In *Computers and creativity* (pp. 115–146). Springer.

Pearce, M., & Wiggins, G. (2004). Improved methods for statistical modelling of monophonic music. *Journal of New Music Research*, *33*(4), 367–385.

Pease, A., Winterstein, D., & Colton, S. (2001). Evaluating machine creativity. In *Workshop on Creative Systems, 4th International Conference on Case Based Reasoning* (pp. 129–137).

Pereira, F. C., Mendes, M., Gervás, P., & Cardoso, A. (2005). Experiments with assessment of creative systems: an application of Ritchie's criteria. In *Proceedings of the workshop on computational creativity, 19th International Joint Conference on Artificial Intelligence* (Vol. 5, p. 05).

Philbin, T. (2005). *The 100 greatest inventions of all time: A ranking past and present.* Citadel Press.

Qiu, J., Li, H., Yang, D., Luo, Y., Li, Y., Wu, Z., & Zhang, Q. (2008). The neural basis of insight problem solving: An event-related potential study. *Brain and Cognition*, *68*(1), 100–106.

Ritchie, G. (2001). Assessing creativity. In *Proc. of AISB'01 Symposium*.

Rohrer, T. (2005). Image schemata in the brain. In B. Hampe & J. Grady (Eds.), *From perception to meaning: Image schemas in cognitive linguistics* (p. 165-196). Berlin: Mouton de Gruyter.

Rosch, E. (1975). Cognitive representations of semantic categories. *Journal of Experimental Psychology: General*, *104*(3), 192.

Rudy, J. W., & O'Reilly, R. C. (1999). Contextual fear conditioning, conjunctive representations, pattern completion, and the hippocampus. *Behavioral Neuroscience*, *113*(5), 867.

Rumelhart, D. E. (1984). Schemata and the cognitive system. *Handbook of social cognition*, *1*, 161–188.

Schacter, D. L. (2012). Adaptive constructive processes and the future of memory. *American Psychologist*, *67*(8), 603.

Schacter, D. L., Chiu, C.-Y. P., & Ochsner, K. N. (1993). Implicit memory: A selective review. *Annual Review of Neuroscience*, *16*(1), 159–182.

Schacter, D. L., Norman, K. A., & Koutstaal, W. (1998). The cognitive neuroscience of constructive memory. *Annual Review of Psychology*, *49*(1), 289–318.

Schank, R. C., & Abelson, R. P. (1977). *Scripts, plans, goals, and understanding: An inquiry into human knowledge structures.* Hillsdale, NJ: Erlbaum.

Schmidhuber, J. (1991). Curious model-building control systems. In *1991 IEEE International Joint Conference on Neural Networks* (pp. 1458–1463).

Schneider, S., Fischer, J.-R., & König, R. (2011). Rethinking automated layout design: developing a creative evolutionary design method for the layout problems in architecture and urban design. In *Design Computing and Cognition'10* (pp. 367–386). Springer.

Schooler, J. W., & Melcher, J. (1995). The ineffability of insight. In T. Ward & R. Finke (Eds.), *The creative cognition approach* (pp. 249–268). Cambridge, MA: The MIT Press.

Seifert, C. M., Meyer, D. E., Davidson, N., Patalano, A. L., & Yaniv, I. (1995). Demystification of cognitive insight: Opportunistic assimilation and the prepared-mind hypothesis. In *The nature of insight* (pp. 65–124). Cambridge, MA: MIT Press.

Simon, H. A. (1974). The structure of ill structured problems. *Artificial Intelligence, 4*(3), 181–201.

Sloman, A. (1971). Interactions between philosophy and artificial intelligence: The role of intuition and non-logical reasoning in intelligence. *Artificial Intelligence, 2*(3), 209–225.

Smith, B. D., & Garnett, G. E. (2012). Reinforcement learning and the creative, automated music improviser. In *Evolutionary and Biologically Inspired Music, Sound, Art and Design* (pp. 223–234). Springer.

Smith, S. M. (1995). Getting into and out of mental ruts: A theory of fixation, incubation, and insight. In S. R. J. & D. J. E. (Eds.), *The nature of insight* (pp. 229–251). The MIT Press.

Someren, M. W. v., Barnard, Y. F., Sandberg, J. A., et al. (1994). *The think aloud method: A practical guide to modelling cognitive processes.* Academic Press London.

Sowa, J. (1992). Semantic networks. In S. Shapiro (Ed.), *Encyclopedia of artificial intelligence* (second ed. ed., p. 1493-1511). Wiley, New York.

Sternberg, R. J., & Grigorenko, E. L. (2003). *The psychology of abilities, competencies, and expertise.* Cambridge University Press.

Thaler, S. (2013). Creativity machine® paradigm. In *Encyclopedia of creativity, invention, innovation and entrepreneurship* (pp. 447–456). Springer.

Torrance, E. P. (1998a). *Torrance tests of creative thinking: Norms-technical manual: Figural (streamlined) forms a & b.* Princeton, NJ: Personnel Press.

Torrance, E. P. (1998b). *Torrance tests of creative thinking: Norms-technical manual: Figural (streamlined) forms a & b.* Princeton, NJ: Personnel Press.

Torrance, E. P. (1998c). *Torrance tests of creative thinking: Norms-technical manual: Figural (streamlined) forms a & b.* Bensenville, IL: Scholastic Testing Service.

Torrance, E. P. (1998d). *Torrance tests of creative thinking: Norms-technical manual: Figural (streamlined) forms a & b.* Bensenville, IL: Scholastic Testing Service.

Torrance, E. P., & Ball, O. (1998). *Torrance tests of creative thinking: Norms-technical manual: Figural (streamlined) forms a & b.* Bensenville, IL: Scholastic Testing Service.

Tower-Richardi, S. M., Brunye, T. T., Gagnon, S. A., Mahoney, C. R., & Taylor, H. A. (2012). Abstract spatial concept priming dynamically influences real-world action. *Front. Psychology*, *3:361*.

Veale, T. (2006). Tracking the lexical zeitgeist with wordnet and wikipedia. *Frontiers in Artificial Intelligence and Applications*, *141*, 56.

Veale, T., & Hao, Y. (2011). Exploiting readymades in linguistic creativity: A system demonstration of the jigsaw bard. In *Proceedings of the 49th Annual Meeting of the Association for Computational Linguistics: Human Language Technologies: Systems Demonstrations* (pp. 14–19).

Veale, T., & Keane, M. T. (1992). Conceptual scaffolding: A spatially founded meaning representation for metaphor comprehension. *Computational Intelligence*, *8*(3), 494–519.

Ventura, D. (2016). Mere generation: Essential barometer or dated concept? In *Proceedings of the Seventh International Conference on Computational Creativity*.

Vitruvius Pollio, M. (1914). The ten books on architecture. In (p. 253-254). Translation by Morris Hicky Morgan, Harvard University Press, Cambridge.

Wallach, M. A., & Kogan, N. (1965). *Modes of thinking in young children: A study of the creativity-intelligence distinction*. Holt, Rinehart & Winston.

Wallas, G. (1926). *The art of thought*. London: Cape.

Wallenstein, G. V., Hasselmo, M. E., & Eichenbaum, H. (1998). The hippocampus as an associator of discontiguous events. *Trends in Neurosciences*, *21*(8), 317–323.

Ward, Thompson-Lake, D., Ely, R., & Kaminski, F. (2008). Synaesthesia, creativity and art: What is the link? *British Journal of Psychology*, *99*(1), 127–141.

Ward, T. B. (1994). Structured imagination: The role of category structure in exemplar generation. *Cognitive psychology*, *27*(1), 1–40.

Ward, T. B., Patterson, M. J., Sifonis, C. M., Dodds, R. A., & Saunders, K. N. (2002). The role of graded category structure in imaginative thought. *Memory & Cognition*, *30*(2), 199–216.

Watson, P. (2005). *Ideas: A History of Thought and Invention, from Fire to Freud*. HarperCollins.

Watson, P. (2011). *The modern mind: An intellectual history of the 20th century*. HarperCollins.

Wertheimer, M. (1945). *Productive thinking*. New York: Harper and Row.

Whitt, J. K., & Prentice, N. M. (1977). Cognitive processes in the development of children's enjoyment and comprehension of joking riddles. *Developmental Psychology*, *13*(2), 129.

Wiggins, G. A. (2001). Towards a more precise characterisation of creativity in AI. In *Case-based reasoning: Papers from the workshop programme at ICCBR* (Vol. 1, pp. 113–120).

Wiggins, G. A. (2006). A preliminary framework for description, analysis and comparison of creative systems. *Knowledge-Based Systems*, *19*(7), 449–458.

Williams, H., & McOwan, P. W. (2014). Magic in the machine: a computational magician's assistant. *Frontiers in Psychology*, *5*.

Worthen, B. R., & Clark, P. M. (1971). Toward an improved measure of remote associational ability. *Journal of Educational Measurement*, *8*(2), 113–123.

Printed in the United States
by Baker & Taylor Publisher Services